Things I Remember

ERTÉ
Things I Remember

An Autobiography

Quadrangle/The New York Times Book Co.

Originally published in Great Britain by Peter Owen Limited, 20 Holland Park
Avenue, London W 11 3QU.

Copyright © 1975 by Sevenarts Ltd. All rights reserved, including the right to reproduce this book or portions thereof in any form. For information, address: Quad-
rangle/The New York Times Book Co., 10 East 53 Street, New York, New York
10022. Manufactured in the United States of America. Published simultaneously in
Canada by Fitzhenry & Whiteside, Ltd., Toronto.

Library of Congress Cataloging in Publication Data

Erté.
    Things I remember.
    Includes index.
      1. Erté   I. Title
TT505.E78A34   745.4'49'24 [B]   75-8286
ISBN 0-8129-0575-X

To the memory of

my mother

PETER JOSEPH

Contents

St Petersburg 1912

So, there I was on the train bound for Paris. I was nineteen and leaving St Petersburg for a new life. At that moment in January of 1912, the future seemed like a gaily-coloured rainbow, bright with hope, despite the fact that it was twenty-eight degrees below zero. I remember my mother saying that the freezing temperature reminded her of the day I was born. The whole family had assembled on the platform, at least twenty people: my parents, my sister, aunts, cousins – all my closest relatives, male and female. Those final moments had filled me with mixed emotions – joy over the fulfilment of a dream I had cherished since my first visit to Paris at the age of seven, and sadness at leaving my adored parents who had done everything in their power to make me happy. Now, all family squabbling over, my departure was finally at hand. Aunt Ania, a charming old maiden lady who was my father's cousin, cried out as the train started to move, ' L'Aiglon has spread his wings and begun to fly '.

As I entered my carriage, I was thrilled to see that my idol, the soprano Lina Cavalieri, was also Paris-bound. Surely this meant that luck was with me. But I had no sooner arrived at Verjbolovo on the Russo-German frontier than I experienced my first setback. My visa was out of date. Originally, I had planned to leave the previous spring, but I had caught a chill and been ill for several weeks. When I recovered my parents wanted me to stay on for my birthday, 23 November (10 November in the Russian calendar), then my Saint's Day, 1 December, and finally for the Christmas-New Year holidays. Meanwhile none of us noticed that my visa had expired.

I immediately asked to see the Governor of the district of Kovno who knew my father. Although he received me with great kindness, he informed me that since I was still a minor he could not renew my visa without my father's signed permission. So for several days I had to remain in that small provincial town, awaiting my father's signature, while it snowed continuously.

The delay was extremely frustrating but not without its compensations. It gave me a chance to be alone and, for the first time in my life, to enjoy a foretaste of independence from my family. After all the tensions of the past months, I now had an opportunity for some uninterrupted reflections on my past and speculation about my future.

My departure was the culmination of a struggle that had been going on for most of my life. Ever since Peter the Great founded the Imperial Navy, all the male members of my family had been in its ranks. Most of them, including my paternal grandfather, had ended their careers as admirals. Yet it had not been out of a sense of duty that my father had followed the family tradition. He loved the navy. When serious illness forced him to leave it for two years – during which period he became a member of the Czar's Cabinet – he could not wait to get back. He resumed his naval duties the moment his doctors declared him fit.

My father was Piotr Ivanovitch de Tirtoff, my mother Natalia Mikhailovna Nikolenko. The Tirtoff family was of Tartar origin; the Nikolenkos were Ukrainian. Tartars had ruled Russia for more than two hundred years before they were conquered by Czar Ivan III. All the Tartar Khans (chiefs) then surrendered – all but one, my ancestor, Khan Tirt. He held out until the reign of the next Czar, Ivan the Terrible. Since this Ivan had guns and Tirt had none, Tirt was forced to give up the fight. The Khans who had already yielded were compensated by Ivan III with titles. Khan Youssouff became Prince Youssoupoff; Khan Ourouss became Prince Ouroussoff. The resister, Khan Tirt, was downgraded to the status of ' hereditary nobleman '. When his descendants travelled abroad, however, they were entitled to use ' de ' in the Latin countries and ' von ' in the German-speaking countries.

My father's only brother, Uncle Paul, had originally embarked on a naval career but when he married he became a chamberlain at the Imperial Court. My paternal grandmother, Eugenia Tolboukhina, was also from a naval family. One of my great-uncles, Pavel Petrovitch, had been Minister of the Navy. My mother's brother, Nicolas, who was also my godfather, became the youngest general in the Russian Army during the Russo-Japanese War. He ended his career as Military Governor of St Petersburg. Then I came along.

I was born on 10 November, 1892 in St Petersburg, at the Imperial Navy School, and named Romain de Tirtoff. Part of my boyhood was spent within the walls of Cronstadt where my father was Director of the Naval Engineering School. Yet, despite this solid military background, I have always hated everything connected with war and violence.

When I was still a child, I staged my own private peace demonstration. It happened when one of my aunts gave me a present of a set of wooden soldiers. I immediately burst into tears and threw the box out of the window. My aunt was extremely offended and I was severely punished. When other boys of my age were playing with their wooden soldiers, I was busy fabricating characters for imaginary ballets out of my mother's empty perfume bottles. The names on those bottles are still fresh in my memory – ' Peau d'Espagne ', ' Cuir de Russie ', ' Floramie ', ' Tubereuse ', ' Orchidée ' and ' Trèfle Incarnat '. I would fill them with coloured water and make costumes out of bits of transparent lace and chiffon which I got from Maria, the dressmaker who lived in our house and made clothes for my mother and sister.

Maria was a superb seamstress and a clever copyist whose hands were seldom idle and who could recreate Parisian or Viennese models and designs from *Le Moniteur de la Mode* and other French fashion magazines to which my mother subscribed.

I often went window-shopping with my mother on Morskaia Street and the Nevsky Prospekt where all the elegant shops were located. Lamonova, the smartest dressmaker in St Petersburg, imported all her models from Paris. My mother's French milliner, Alphonsine – or was it Alexandrine? – had her establishment on Morskaia Street.

In the early 1900s fashion had decreed that hats must be perched atop huge pompadours reinforced with paddings of false hair. Since my mother and sister were satisfied with nothing short of the height of fashion, they concocted – with the aid of the milliner – an elastic contraption that stretched across the crown of the head to which the hat was attached. As a result, when they walked or when there was a slight breeze, their hats looked as if they were floating in the air. The sight of them gingerly balancing their hats never failed to send me into gales of laughter.

When I was five years old, I designed an evening dress for my mother. She liked it so much that she had Maria make it up. It was a great success. But I must add that my mother was extremely beautiful, with blue-black hair worn in a smooth chignon which contrasted with her white skin. I shall always remember one night when I was quite young; she had come to my room to give me a good-night kiss before going to a ball. She wore a dress of black chantilly lace over pink taffeta; around her *décolletage* was a garland of real roses. I was absolutely enchanted by the perfume and beauty of her image. Perhaps this was the beginning of my love for all things connected with beautiful clothes and elegance.

Until I was twelve years old I had a happy childhood. I was surrounded by loving females – my mother, my sister Natalia, my nurse Euphrosinia, and Euphrosinia's daughter, Aglaé. One of my earliest memories of Euphrosinia was the beauty of her hands with their long, almond-shaped nails. Although she was a simple peasant woman, her hands were those of an aristocrat – the kind I later admired in Bronzini's paintings. I have always been fascinated by beautiful hands. For me, they are an intrinsic part of a beautiful human being. After I had grown out of Euphrosinia's arms, I had an English nanny. As a result, I began speaking English almost simultaneously with Russian. After the English nanny there were French and German governesses. The result was that I nearly forgot my English through lack of practice. Unlike the governesses, who came and went, Euphrosinia stayed on. In those days Russian servants remained in the same house for years, becoming like members of the family. My grandmother, Elena, had her Annouchka, who first came to work in our family as a slave, and remained until the end of her life. It was not until 1861 that Czar Alexander II finally abolished slavery. As I was the youngest member of the family, Annouchka was especially devoted to me. When the time had come for me to go to the Gymnasium, which happened to be directly across the street from my grandmother's house, Annouchka would watch for me from the window. As soon as she saw me approaching, she would rush to my grandmother and announce, ' Your Excellency, Romain Petrovitch is coming. Would you like to see him entering the school? '

Although I was closer to Grandmother Elena, my mother's mother, I loved to visit Grandmother Eugenia's family house, ' Kamenka ', where she spent every summer. She usually invited us with the families of her daughter, Zinaïda, and her son, Paul. I had a wonderful time with Uncle Paul's children, Nicolas and Alia. Our favourite sport was playing with a charming tame bear. The bear loved beer, but whenever he was given it he would get drunk and stagger around in the most ridiculous fashion. He also loved children and would play with us most gently.

For reasons that were always a mystery to me, my two grandmothers never liked one another. I remember one occasion on which they were at our *datcha* in Hungerburg together. Grandmother Eugenia said to Grandmother Elena, ' Darling, you have a mosquito on your face ', as she reached over and gave her a sharp slap on the cheek. Grandmother Elena promptly rose to the challenge with, ' But, dear, you have two on yours ', and retaliated accordingly.

Grandmother Elena was the gayest and youngest-at-heart member of the family. I called her ' Baba Lola ' and loved her very much. When, at the age of eighteen, she became engaged, the doctors discouraged her from marrying with the warning that, because of her weak heart, she could die having her first child. She ignored their advice, married, had eight children and died of pneumonia at the age of one hundred and two. She was elegant and meticulously groomed to the end of her life. Her beauty formula was based on three rules: never to wash her face in anything but rainwater – she had a special tank where this was collected and stored – to eat fresh carrots every morning, and to eat very slowly. She convinced me of the wisdom of this third rule early in my life and I have followed it ever since.

Grandmother Elena rarely missed her Tuesday night opera subscription at the

Mariinsky Theatre where she had a box. I was taken for the first time when I was about seven. The opera was Rimsky-Korsakov's *Sadko,* and it was one of the greatest events of my young life. The music, the orchestra, the singing, the drama and, above all, the visual presentation, made a deep impression on me. That night opened up a whole new world for me; it was my first glimpse of the rich cultural life of St Petersburg during that pre-Revolutionary period. In the ensuing years I took full advantage of everything it had to offer in opera, ballet, theatre and art exhibitions. Later on, when my father became Director of the Naval Engineering School, I would cross the frozen bay separating Cronstadt from St Petersburg by horse-drawn sleigh, bundled up in fur coats and rugs against the freezing air.

In the spring when the ice began to thaw, or in the autumn when it was not hard enough to support a sleigh, I would cross in a ' ledokol ' – a boat equipped with an ice-breaker. After the theatre, I would often spend the night at Uncle Nicolas's house.

Besides the Mariinsky, which was devoted to the opera and ballet, there were two other Imperial theatres in St Petersburg – the Alexandrinsky, which specialized in Russian and foreign classical drama, and the Michailovsky, which offered a repertoire of French plays with a French company. It was at the Michailovsky that I saw Lucien Guitry, father of Sacha Guitry. At the Alexandrinsky I saw some beautiful productions by Meyerhold, in which he was already using modernistic settings. During those years I became familiar with the Mariinsky's large repertoire of French and Italian operas, for many of which I later designed sets and costumes, as well as the operatic works of all the great Russian composers – Tchaikovsky, Mussorgsky, Rimsky-Korsakov and Glinka. I saw modern art on the operatic stage for the first time in a production of Glinka's *Russlan and Ludmilla,* for which Alexander Golovine had designed beautiful costumes and settings. At the Mariinsky I saw most of the visiting celebrities from abroad as well as the stars of Moscow's Bolshoi Theatre – Chaliapin, Sobinoff, Nejdanaova and many others. One of the visiting artists was Nelly Melba. I was about eight or nine at the time and she seemed amazing to me. I could not understand how a voice of such pure, delicate, youthful beauty could emerge from such a mammoth body. She reminded me of an elephant.

Although the permanent opera company of the Mariinsky was first class, the only member who was known outside Russia was Maria Kouznetsoff, who had a brilliant international career. Massenet wrote his opera *Roma,* first performed at the Monte Carlo Opera, especially for her. In 1923-24 I was to design many costumes for her performances in *La Traviata, Tosca* and *Manon.*

I saw the débuts of Russian artists who later became famous, including Tamara Karsavina, Lydia Kyaksht and Nijinsky. And, naturally, I saw the fabulous Anna Pavlova. I later met her in Paris in 1921 when she had her own company, and designed some costumes for her. Also at the Mariinsky I saw the Fokine ballets – *Le Pavillon d'Armide* and *Chopiniana,* known later as *Les Sylphides* – which

revolutionized classical ballet and eventually became part of the repertoire of
Diaghilev's Russian Ballet. The Mariinsky also ushered in a new era in costume
and stage décor. In collaboration with Diaghilev, a group of rising Russian artists
– Leon Bakst, Alexandre Benois and Golovine – were breaking new ground. I was
a passionate collector of the postcards on which Leon Bakst's designs for *The
Fairy Doll* were reproduced. The first of a series of three scandals involving
Nijinsky also took place at the Mariinsky. I was present on the memorable night
of the performance of *Chopiniana* in which Nijinsky neglected to wear a jock strap
and deeply shocked the Empress Mother, Maria Feodorovna. The following day
he was dismissed from the Imperial Ballet. (I was also present later at the opening
nights of Debussy's *L'Après-midi d'un Faune* and Stravinsky's *Le Sacre du Printemps*, productions which scandalized Parisian audiences.)

The interiors of the three Imperial theatres were glamorous as well as beautiful. The Mariinsky was decorated in white and gold with walls of blue brocade.
The Alexandrinsky was white and gold with deep yellow brocade walls. The
Michailovsky was white and gold with red brocade walls. Behind each box was
a small salon – the ' avant-loge ' – where one received friends during the intervals.
Along the velvet ledge of our box there was usually an array of beautiful inlaid
opera glasses and ladies' fans, together with a big box of chocolates and marzipan
which my sister and I would finish off in the course of the performance.

In addition to the three Imperial theatres there was a state opera house,
' Narodny Dom ' (The House of the People). For some mysterious reason, despite
the fact that this theatre had a good repertoire and an excellent company, members of high society never went there. It was not considered ' smart '.

Besides the state theatres, St Petersburg also had many privately managed
houses. One of the most important was the ' Mali ' (Small Theatre) owned by the
famous Russian actress Yavorskaia (Princess Bariatinskaia). Although it was not
ostensibly avant-garde, it occasionally introduced some bold ideas. I remember a
performance of Schiller's *Joan of Arc* in which the title role was played by a male
actor called Glagoline. Although the critics attacked it, it was a big success. It
was at this theatre that I first saw Sarah Bernhardt and Eleanora Duse. Bernhardt
played the Duc de Reichstad in Edmond Rostand's *L'Aiglon*. When she came on
in her tight-fitting white uniform which accentuated her prominent bust and
big hips, I turned to my mother and exclaimed rather loudly, ' What a monster! '
As for ' Sarah's golden voice ', I found it cracked and affected.

What a contrast between Bernhardt and Duse! I later saw both of them as
Marguerite Gauthier in *La Dame aux Camélias*. Bernhardt's inflections and gestures were carefully calculated and they never varied. She worked hard at perfecting
her technique, which was often marvellous in an artificial sort of way. But with
Duse everything was spontaneous. Every time I saw her playing the role it was
a new experience. The difference between Bernhardt and Duse was the difference
between highly polished acting and genius.

Another important private theatre was the Komissarjewsky Theatre, which was truly avant-garde. Komissarjewskaia, a fine actress, opened her theatre to many new authors and ideas.

Then, there was always a brilliant spring season of Italian opera at the Theatre of the Music Conservatory. There I heard some of the most outstanding voices of that period: Tito Ruffo, Mazzini, Adamo Didur, Mattiah Battistini, Tetrazzini, Anselmi, Sigrid Arnoldson, Maria Gai (the first Carmen I ever heard) and my adored Lina Cavalieri.

Until I was twelve my education had been in the hands of a tutor who came regularly to our house. But now my parents decided that the time had come for me to benefit from the more formal curriculum and discipline of a boys' school. My first school, the 'Eighth Gymnasium' (for boys aged eleven to eighteen), was on a street called 'Deviataia Linia' (ninth line). Although the building itself was not drab, the atmosphere of the place filled me with sadness. Everything was painted a dull grey, with the exception of the desks which were black. The school uniform was black all over and no personal variations were permitted. This was particularly traumatic for someone accustomed to Little Lord Fauntleroy velvet suits, a jaunty feather in his beret and, later, dashing black, white or grey Tcherkess costumes with matching fur hats in astrakhan or lamb.

Because I loved solitude so much, I hated school from the very first day. The boisterous noise and violent games of the students were unbearable to me. I could hardly wait until three o'clock when school was over for the day and I could change my clothes and get back to my painting and designing. But despite all this, I made some good friends. My teachers, too, treated me with great kindness. I was, after all, a very quiet child and a good student (my only punishments were for being late for school in the morning). The teacher I liked best was the one who taught Russian literature, since literature – and history – were my favourite subjects. This particular teacher always allowed me to read aloud the poems we were studying. He said my voice had a pleasant sound, like the cooing of doves. As a child I also had a good singing voice and often performed solos with the church choir. Later it was spoilt when the music teacher insisted on making me sing during the time it was breaking. I also started to study the violin but dropped it after a few lessons because I could not stand the horrible sounds I was producing.

As time passed I was overwhelmed by a depressing sense of loss – the loss of my individuality.

Some compensation, however, was to be found in my love for art. When I was a small boy I had found in my father's library a book containing many reproductions in colour of Indian and Persian miniatures. I cannot remember the title of the book but I shall never forget the illustrations. They were my introduction to the kind of exotic feminine eyes with bizarre ascending eye-brows – 'des yeux de biche', as they were called in France – that have always fascinated me. The technical virtuosity and perfection of those miniatures had a tremendous impact on me. Contrary to what many critics later maintained, it was they, rather than the work of Aubrey Beardsley, that profoundly influenced my ultimate style. I did not discover Beardsley until 1913, when I had already been in Paris for a year. Another strong formative influence was the painted Greek vases in the Hermitage Museum. On the days when I did not have to go to school I would spend hours studying the details of these beautiful paintings. When I returned home, I would spend the evening making highly stylized drawings in the manner of those unknown artists.

When my parents began to realize that I had some artistic talent and that I was determined to develop it, my mother arranged to introduce me to Ilya Repine. Repine was considered one of the most important painters in Russia around the turn of the century. He took a great interest in me and gave me several lessons, but the number of private students he could then handle was limited, so he handed me over to one of his favourite pupils, Dmitri Lossevsky, a talented young painter who was studying at the Academy of Fine Arts. Since the approach to painting of both these men was classical and academic, I began by painting models, landscapes and portraits. Fortunately, after a few lessons Lossevsky had the wisdom to allow me to follow my own creative impulses. He gave me the freedom to develop my individuality while he concentrated on grounding me in such fundamentals as perspective, the theory of light and shade, anatomy and art history. I painted portraits of all the members of my family, as well as dogs, birds and other conventional objects. Unfortunately, none of this early work is now in my possession; everything I did in those years disappeared during the Revolution.

As I waited out those long days in Verjbolovo, I thought a great deal about my family. My mother had been highly emotional during our last moments at the station. Yet it seemed to me that whatever lingering opposition my parents had raised during those final weeks was more the result of pressure from all the aunts and uncles than of their own convictions. My relatives were certain that once I got to Paris and was no longer under family supervision, I would become a ' lost child '– a drifter. My sister, Natalia, nine years older and quite unlike me in temperament, was the only one who, from the start, had sympathized with my desire to go to Paris and become an artist. And she had been a decisive ally in winning my parents' consent. Looking back, I wonder if this may have blinded me to the fact that her devotion to me was possessive, domineering and, as we grew older, downright selfish. But in those early years we were close and had a common bond in our love for animals. When our governess took us for walks, we often bought an animal. As a result the house was full of assorted birds, fish, rabbits, white mice, turtles and lizards. One day we brought home a beautiful rooster. The next morning at dawn – it was springtime and the sun rose very early – the rooster woke up my mother with its crowing. After that we were forbidden to buy any more animals. That was a big blow to me because I yearned above all for a cat. Unfortunately I was born into a family of dog-lovers and none of them liked cats. So I remained a frustrated cat-lover until I left St Petersburg and had my own flat.

Since Natalia was closer to me than any of my other relatives or friends, I treated her as a confidante. I told her all about my adolescent adventures, including my first sexual experience when I was thirteen. The King of a Baltic monarchy had sent his two young children to Russia to complete their education. With their tutor they spent a summer on an estate next to our seaside *datcha* in Hungerburg. I became friendly with one of them who was three years older than myself. The attraction was mutual so, despite our sheltered environment, we were able to make a secret rendezvous one night. The next morning the gardeners complained that the vines covering the walls between the two properties had been damaged. As for me – I would not presume to speak for my friend – I did not feel the least bit damaged. I wasted very little emotional energy in trying to fight my own nature, even less in punishing myself with feelings of guilt. Rather, I looked forward to many more delightful adventures. I was not disappointed. Sex has always played an important role in my life, and still does. But my greatest love has been my art. Other desires and relationships have always taken second place to this ruling passion.

Of all the members of my family, it was my father who dominated my thoughts at this time. What a trial I must have been to him! Once I had staged my first rebellion against those wooden soldiers, there was no let-up. I was continually questioning my so-called 'duties' and demanding explanations.

'Why should I become a part of Russia's military establishment?'

'For the sake of patriotism,' my father would say.

His answer was hardly satisfactory, especially since my bible studies at school were teaching me to worship only one God. I knew that those who idolized the Golden Calf would be punished.

'Isn't patriotism like worshipping another God – a sort of Golden Calf?' I would ask.

'You are asking stupid questions. You must accept things as they are.'

For me, this was impossible. To this day, the words 'war' and 'patriotism' still evoke the image of the Golden Calf. I never could reconcile the idea of people who go to church having anything to do with violence and destruction. As for parents who give their children toy guns and other war machinery, I find it unforgivable. Although I have never gone in for public demonstrations, I was in full sympathy with the group of young people in the early 1970s who expressed their anti-war sentiments by upsetting a Christmas display of toy weapons in the Bon Marché department store in Paris.

Despite our periodic clashes and the fact that my tastes and ambitions must have been completely alien and mystifying to him, there was a strong bond of mutual affection between my father and myself. We also shared a deep love for music. My father was a gifted pianist and violinist, while I played the piano. One of the few experiences in my father's background that I had ever envied was his friendship with Rimsky-Korsakov, who had been his classmate at naval cadet school.

When my father had finally reconciled himself to the fact that I would never enter either the navy or the diplomatic service – the two most obvious careers for a boy of my background – he urged me to become an architect. One of my mother's brothers was already well established in this field. Although this meant that I had to stay on at school, which I hated, and was determined to become a painter, I agreed to qualify for a course, passing my baccalauréat examination at the College of Cronstadt with distinction. My father was so pleased that he decided to reward me for my good work.

' What would you like most for a present? '

' A passport,' I replied without a moment's hesitation.

This was hardly what my father had in mind, but by then he had realized that he was fighting a losing battle. So, after much family debate – mine was a large family – I was on my way at last. I had finally won my freedom, to this day one of my most precious possessions.

Paris 1912-1914

When I finally arrived in Paris, at the Gare de l'Est, I went to a small hotel near the Madeleine which Russian friends had recommended as quite comfortable and not too expensive. To my great disappointment, there were no single rooms available, so I had to go out and search for another place. Eventually, in the same area, I found a room that was attractive, clean, comfortable and cheap – an unusual combination of virtues for Paris hotels at the time. I was barely settled in my little room when I became aware of a steady flow of traffic in and out of the hotel, especially by several garishly dressed women. They were all casual, friendly types who would greet me in the lift. Frequently, I would also pass them strolling around in the streets of the quarter, sometimes alone, sometimes with assorted men friends. I was so preoccupied with all the problems of adjusting to my new life that it was several days before I realized that I was living in the midst of a thriving 'maison de passe'. My situation was such a time-worn Parisian stereo-type that it was a source of continuous amusement to me. I kept thinking: What would Aunt Ania say if she could see her 'Aiglon' now? Even though I was obviously an unlikely customer for their services, the ladies soon accepted my presence with good-humoured but detached tolerance. As for the proprietors, they also took me in their stride. Otherwise, those early months in Paris were any-thing but amusing. In fact, my first year there was rather difficult.

In spite of all my efforts, I could find no work. Since I was determined to show my parents that I could support myself, I had firmly rejected all their offers of financial help. As a result, my meagre savings melted away in the most alarming manner. Luckily, my Uncle Nicolas continued to send me a few roubles for pocket money, just as he had always done in Russia. My only other sources of income at that time were some modest fees for drawings which I sent each month to *Damsky Mir* (Woman's World), the Russian fashion magazine. Before I left St Petersburg I had arranged, without my parents' knowledge, to send the editor a series of sketches of current Paris fashions. I had also agreed, reluctantly, to solicit advertising space for the magazine from various French textile companies. Needless to say, I was a dismal failure as a salesman. My drawings, however, were more successful. I used to sign them either ' Romain ' or ' Pitch ', a nickname my sister had given me. Later, as a further declaration of independence and to ensure the privacy of my conventional family, I coined the name ' Erté '. It was made up of the initials of my real name, R for Romain and T for Tirtoff, as pronounced in both French and Russian.

Instead of enrolling at the Ecole des Beaux Arts to begin my training as an architect, as my parents had wished, I started attending the painting class of Jean-Paul Laurens at the Académie Julian. Laurens, who specialized in large canvases on historical subjects, was a well-known teacher. But in spite of my passion for painting, I did not remain very long at the Académie. Being part of a class was simply too distracting for me. I have always required solitude when I work. Even when I was a child, I would close my paintbox and leave if a passer-by stopped to watch me painting a landscape. To this day, I cannot draw a line if someone is looking at me.

During this period, it seemed to me that my daily diet consisted largely of roasted chestnuts which I bought from street vendors. Once a week I would go to the Bouillon Duval for a bowl of boiled beef, *pot-au-feu* – the cheapest dish on the menu. As I explored the city alone – I had no friends – munching chestnuts, I often thought longingly of the lavish dinners and suppers that were served as a matter of course on important holidays and family occasions at home, such as birthdays, Jmianini (Saints' Days) and other anniversaries worthy of celebration.

Family dinner parties lasted for hours and followed an almost ritualistic pattern. Everyone – my grandmothers (both grandfathers had died before I was born), aunts, uncles and cousins – assembled in the salon where they helped themselves, buffet style, to a beautifully arranged spread of about thirty different ' zakouski ' – hot and cold hors-d'oeuvres. The hot ones, on silver platters, were set over spirit burners. With the zakouski there was chilled vodka for the adults and kvass, almond milk, lemonade or orangeade for the children. We then moved into the adjoining dining-room where the remaining courses of the meal were served with everyone seated around a large table. Years later, when I had my house in Sèvres, near Paris, I often invited my French friends for a typical Russian dinner, prepared by my Russian cook. They never failed to react – verbally or otherwise – to the strange Russian custom of serving soup after the zakouski, which they mistook for the main course of the meal. Imagine their surprise when the soup was followed by fish, meat and several other dishes! I was always intrigued by the predictability of their reactions to this unexpected departure from routine.

Christmas and Easter – especially the latter – were the most important holidays in the year of the Russian Orthodox Church. Midnight mass was celebrated at Easter rather than Christmas. Easters at the Naval Engineering School were unforgettable. After midnight mass at the school's own chapel, all the officers serving under my father were invited to supper with their families, along with our relatives. Despite the fact that these parties never broke up until the early hours, my parents always had open house on Easter Sunday, with a steady stream of guests coming and going from noon to midnight, or later. For them the buffet was even more elaborate: a variety of cold fish, whole hams, roast lamb, baby pigs, chicken, turkey and pheasants dressed with their own feathers. In addition there would be the traditional Easter specialities: brilliantly painted hard-boiled eggs, 'paskhas' (pyramids of cottage cheese, cream and almonds decorated with candied fruits and flowers), 'Koulitch' and 'Baba' (large cakes decorated with almonds and icing in floral patterns). With this there were assorted vodkas – 'Riabinovka', 'Zoubrovka', 'Pertsovka' – a vast array of wines, champagnes and liqueurs, and the full gamut of hot and cold non-alcoholic drinks.

As my unemployment dragged on month after month, these gastronomic reminiscences became more obsessive and painful. Finally, in December 1912, I managed to find a job as a draughtsman in an obscure, second-class fashion house called 'Caroline' in the Rue Royale. But at the end of a month 'Caroline' fired me. 'I want to give you a mother's advice,' she said. 'Give up the idea of becoming an artist. You have no talent for it.'

I was somewhat disappointed, but hardly surprised. Fortunately, I had the presence of mind to ask 'Caroline' if I could have some of the drawings I had done for her. She made no objection, so I rescued the lot from the waste-basket and packed them in a neat parcel which I left with the concierge at the great fashion house of Paul Poiret. Since I was much too shy to ask for an appointment, I simply included a card with my name and address. The following day, 3 January, 1913, I was thrilled to receive a *pneumatique* from Poiret saying that he found my drawings extremely interesting, and asking me to come and see him as soon as possible. I rushed over at once.

At that time the greatest couturiers were Worth, Doucet, Redfern and Paquin, all of whom were well established. Poiret had worked for Worth and Doucet before opening his own house. There were also many fashion houses which had more recently become well known: Chéruit, Beshoff-David, Patou, the Callot Sisters and, above all, Jeanne Lanvin. Two of Poiret's sisters, with whom he was not on good terms, also had their own somewhat inferior couture houses – Groult and Bongart.

Poiret himself had recently caused a revolution in the world of fashion and was approaching the pinnacle of his success. In 1911, the year before I left for Paris, he had made a triumphant European tour – the first ever undertaken by a French couturier – which included Vienna, Frankfurt, Budapest and Bucharest. It reached its climax in Moscow and St Petersburg where the Poirets were caught up in a whirl of hospitality, usually laid on only for visiting celebrities. I had not met him then, but I had seen his entire collection and made many sketches. Now he received me most cordially and I was thrilled when he asked me to start work for him the next day.

I was awed by Poiret's appearance. Although he was not a tall man and on the plump side, his full beard, swarthy complexion, bulging eyes and brilliantly-coloured brocade jacket gave him a theatrical air. I felt he was a born showman and that this dramatic flair probably coloured his personal as well as his public life. In fact, the line separating the two was extremely fine. Cocteau had called him 'The Sultan', inspired, no doubt, by the role Poiret had played at one of his most brilliant costume balls, 'The One Thousand and Second Night', a fabulous Persian celebration for three hundred invited guests which was held in his garden. Poiret reminded me more of a sculptured Assyrian bull. Shortly after I started working for him, I was sent to fetch something from his town house and noticed, among many other art treasures, a handsome Assyrian statue, for which he had paid a huge sum.

Poiret's domain was impressive. His fashion business was conducted from a huge house facing on to the Faubourg Saint-Honoré with the main gate on the Avenue d'Antin (now called Avenue du Président Roosevelt). He lived in another house on the Rue du Colisée. Both houses had spacious adjoining gardens which were transformed into enchanted otherworlds whenever he gave one of his celebrated fancy dress balls. Shortly after the end of World War I, he created a night-club in the garden which he called 'The Oasis'. Here he presented a variety of entertainments – recitals by Yvette Guilbert, revivals of plays and assorted fêtes. Although they were mounted with great artistry, Poiret described The Oasis as 'a fiasco that lasted only one season. . . . I left behind in it half a million francs.'

Poiret was an extraordinary animator. He knew how to attract famous artists and how to exploit their talents to the full. Raoul Dufy designed fabrics for him; two of the most outstanding illustrators of the period, Paul Iribe and Georges Lepape, were employed by him. He also had a unique flair for discovering new talent.

Poiret's bad temper was legendary, but I must say that as long as I worked for him he was always very kind to me. He often invited me to accompany him to the theatre, and in this way I saw many splendid performances. I remember best the gala opening of the new Théâtre des Champs-Elysées. I have never seen a more brilliant audience: the women blazed with jewels. That year they were wearing tulle scarfs about their bare shoulders, for dresses were very *décolleté*. They seemed to rise, nude, out of fluffy clouds. Every woman wore a head-dress: dazzling tiaras, embroidered bandeaux, or turbans with aigrettes and birds-of-paradise plumes. All the men wore tails and opera hats and carried evening canes

Dress design for Poiret, 1913.

and white gloves. White silk socks and black, patent-leather opera pumps were worn with tail-coats. Each one, of course, had a flower in his buttonhole.

On that memorable evening, Natasha Trouhanova, the famous dancer, was in Paul Poiret's box. Considered one of the most beautiful women of the day, her jewels were renowned throughout the world. Since at that time nudity in the theatre was unheard of, she wore flesh-coloured tights when she danced ' nude '. A mediocre dancer, she was rich enough to commission Paul Ducas to write the ballet, *La Péri*, for her, in which she danced with considerable success. She married Count Ignatieff, an attaché at the Russian Embassy, and left Paris to return to Russia with him during the Revolution. She always bought her clothes from Paul Poiret, and I had already designed several dresses for her. At that time, special customers never made choices from the couturier's collection. Their dresses were designed personally for them. If two fashionable women met at a party wearing the same dress there was a tremendous scandal.

For several months before my arrival another artist, José de Zamora, had been working in Poiret's atelier. He was a boy of about my own age, very gifted and charming. Some months later, he went back to his native Spain. But after a few years he returned to Paris and was taken on permanently by Henri Varna to design his shows at the Casino de Paris and the Théâtre Mogador.

Zamora and I used to do our work in a large room overlooking the Faubourg Saint-Honoré. One day while I was busy drawing I suddenly heard agonized shouts. I rushed to the window, where a terrible spectacle met my eyes. The pavement opposite was caving in; people were falling, with screams of terror, into a pit that was getting wider every minute. Inadequate precautions in shoring up the roof during excavations for a new Metro line and the station at Saint Phillippe du Roule, had led to this dreadful catastrophe. I shall never forget that sight – to me it was like a scene from Dante's Inferno.

In late January 1913, a few weeks after I started work with Poiret, he asked me to sign a contract with him. Since I was still a minor, my father had to sign it for me. This he did with considerable reluctance, remarking that he was angry and humiliated that his only son, the descendant of a long line of admirals of the Imperial Russian Fleet, should be employed by a dressmaker. I myself had no such qualms, especially when, some months after the contract was signed, Poiret began to give me a percentage on each of my designs that was sold.

When I began working for Poiret, I designed only dresses, coats, head-dresses and hats. Then he was commissioned to design the décor and costumes for a play by Jacques Richepin, entitled *The Minaret*, to be put on at the Théâtre de la Renaissance. The décor was executed by Ronsin, under Poiret's supervision, but I designed most of the costumes. The remainder were by Zamora, who had not yet left Poiret's atelier.

Poiret began by establishing the range of colours to be used during each act of the play: green, black and silver for the first act; red, black and gold for the second; white, silver and orange for the third. No one had ever done this before, but after *The Minaret,* the innovation became a convention in the theatre, especially in the music-hall.

Several famous actors played in *The Minaret,* including Cora Laparcerie who was Richepin's wife and the director of the Théâtre de la Renaissance, Harry Baur, Marcelle Yrven and Jean Worms. To promote the play's fiftieth performance Madame Laparcerie decided to introduce a special attraction. At the suggestion of Gabriel Astruc, one of the most astute impresarios in Paris (it was Astruc who sponsored the first appearances in the western world of Diaghilev's Russian Ballet), she engaged one of his clients, an oriental dancer who had been attracting considerable attention in Paris and other European capitals. She performed under the name of Mata Hari. So, one of my very first theatrical assignments – designing an oriental costume for the third-act Nuptial Festival – was for this legendary creature. She was not really beautiful. She had a sensuous body, but she lacked personality and there was even something a little vulgar about her, although she would come to fittings wearing smart, classically tailored suits. She was always even-tempered and easy to get on with. When the French later arrested her on charges of spying for the Germans, I was amazed. Despite her shrewd sense of publicity in matters concerning her career, I was never convinced that she had the intelligence to be an effective spy. Her exotic image was the product of her own vivid imagination. She claimed to have been a Hindu Temple dancer but her origins were Dutch bourgeois and provincial.

Mata Hari acted out her romantic fantasies right up to the moment when she met her tragic end with stony courage. Her countryman, Sam Waagenaar, whose biography, *The Murder of Mata Hari,* was published in 1964, confirmed my youthful doubts about Mata Hari's talents for espionage. As his title implies, Waagenaar, on the basis of extensive research which included access to Mata Hari's private and hitherto unrevealed scrap books, maintained that she did not deserve such extreme punishment and that she was really the unfortunate victim of the ' virulent temper that pervaded France in July 1917 '.

Throughout 1913, fashion was influenced by the costumes of *The Minaret.* Skirts were draped tightly around the legs, rather like the trousers of Eastern dancing-girls, and belts were wide like oriental sashes. But the main feature of this style was the little tunic-crinoline shaped like a lamp-shade, inspired by the transparent veil skirts of the Hindu miniatures, and by the pleated kilts (or ' fustanelles ') of Greek folk costumes.* Romantic fantasies of the East, influenced by Diaghilev's Paris production of *Schéhérazade,* were popular. Poiret's fashions reflected them in both style and choice of colours. He himself always wore brilliantly coloured, Chinese-style brocade jackets at his fashion house. Even his wife, the dazzlingly beautiful Madame Poiret, looked like a tiny Chinese porcelain

---

* In 1969 I was in Chicago for the opening of the exhibition of my ' Formes Picturales '

figure, with her smooth black hair drawn tightly back. Poiret's Oriental period, with his famous 'jupes-culottes', which caused a scandal, was the second phase of his fashion revolution. The first had been the 'Directoire' style, when he did away with corsets, thereby completely changing the female silhouette and carriage. During this period, all the salons in his fashion house were decorated in Directoire style.

The Poiret silhouette was glorified in the person of Jacqueline Forzane, a demi-monde actress of light comedy and one of the most 'chic' women I have ever met. In 1913 she was the 'Parisienne' incarnate. The first time I saw her she was wearing a tailored dress designed in the manner of a man's evening tail-coat. With the dress, which had a tall Robespierre collar, she wore a pleated jabot, a hat turned up on one side with a long feather and a thick umbrella under her arm. Her carriage was typical of that period: head held high, torso tilted backwards and stomach thrust forward as in the paintings of many medieval ladies. None of this would have been possible had not Poiret liberated women from the corset – the most revolutionary achievement of his fabulous career.

Walking slinkily ' à la léopard ' was also the vogue in 1913-14. It was inspired by Ida Rubinstein who, in Gabriel d'Annunzio's play *La Pisanelle ou la Mort Parfumée*, walked a leopard on a long chain. Such is the power of fashion, which dictates not only the colour of hair and complexion but also the shape of the body. The feminine body is, to the designer, essentially a malleable entity which fashion moulds in its own way.

After *The Minaret*, I designed costumes for another play by Jacques Richepin, called *Le Tango*, starring two celebrated actresses of the day – Spinelly and Eve Lavallière.

The two main roles in *Le Tango* were a young married couple. The wife was played by Spinelly, and the husband (much to the astonishment of the audience) by Eve Lavallière dressed as a man. In fact, Lavallière had such a deep voice that every time she called me on the telephone without identifying herself I invariably answered with a ' Hallo, monsieur '. She was a brilliant actress and one of the stars of the famous company of the Théâtre des Variétés. I never saw Offenbach's *La Vie Parisienne* more dazzlingly performed than it was at the Variétés. But Eve Lavallière's career was soon over. She became blind and entered a convent.

(paintings in three dimensions). During the first of several luncheons in my honour, I met the Director of the Chicago Historical Society, who showed me a photograph of one of Poiret's dresses and asked me for details about it. The dress was in the Society's beautiful museum which houses a splendid collection of twentieth-century costumes. Imagine my surprise when I recognized a dress called ' Sorbet ' that I had designed when I was with Poiret. It was an evening gown of satin crêpe, of which one half was black, the other white; it had the wide pink belt and tiny lampshade-like crinoline of the *Minaret* style. Copies of my original design had been sold over and over again. It was, in fact, one of the best-sellers of 1913.

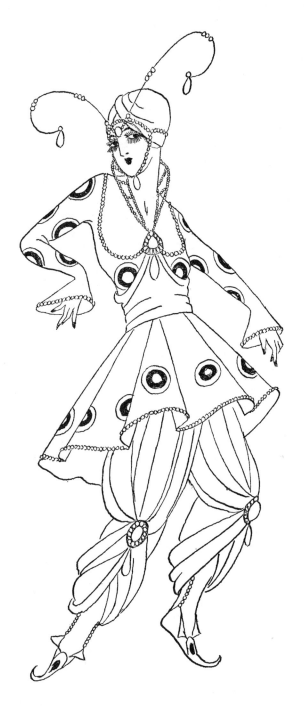

Costume design for *The Minaret*, 1913.

Spinelly epitomized the fashion of the period. She even built a large house near the Champs-de-Mars and had it entirely decorated by Poiret. I still remember the silver-lamé dress I designed for Spinelly in *Le Tango*. No one had ever made a dress entirely out of lamé before. I also designed several dresses in orange, a colour which came to be known as 'Tango'. Poiret loved using it – before him no couturier had ever dared. Another of his favourite colours was a striking oriental pink, which he called 'Rose Ignoble'. Many years afterwards, the late Elsa Schiaparelli revived it as 'Shocking Pink'.

Poiret's use of bright colours for clothes, outside as well as inside the theatre, was another aspect of his fashion revolution. As he said:

> The taste for the refinements of the eighteenth century had led all the women into a sort of deliquescence and on the pretext that it was 'distinguished', all vitality had been suppressed. Nuances of nymphs' thighs, lilacs, swooning mauves, tender blue, hortensias, niles, maizes, straws, all that was soft, washed-out and insipid was held in honour. I threw into this sheepcote a few rough wolves – reds, greens, violets, royal blues that made the rest sing aloud. I had to wake up the good people of Lyons, whose stomach is a bit heavy, and put a little gaiety, a little freshness, into their colour schemes.

Many people accused Poiret of bad taste. But what is good taste? It is a very personal question. Proverbs tell us 'Chacun a son goût' (Every one to his own taste) and 'On ne discute pas des goûts' (One doesn't argue matters of taste).

In addition to his couture house, Poiret had an interior decorating business. He called it 'Martine' after one of his daughters. Martine launched the 'Munich' style, as it was called at the time. Guy-Pierre Fauconnet and Paul Iribe were the moving spirits behind the company. I designed a number of cushions for them, and I suspect that my love for interior decoration began at that point.

Poiret's third business, which manufactured perfume, was named Rosine, after another of his daughters. He was the first couturier to enter this field. The scents were most unusual: I particularly loved 'Toute la Forêt' and 'Le Fruit Défendu', but especially the latter which smelled deliciously of peaches.

In 1914, while I was still working for Poiret, I designed the costumes for two other shows: a revue by Rip, and *Aphrodite*. The latter, based on a novel by Pierre Louys, was produced, like *The Minaret*, at the Théâtre de la Renaissance, with Cora Laparcerie in the main role. This time I did all the designs myself, as Zamora had by now left. My costumes introduced something entirely new – draperies falling from the arms which became part of the dress.

Poiret was the only couturier to have a workshop specializing in theatrical costume design. It was directed by a charming old lady, Madame Régiane, who had formerly been 'Première' (head seamstress) with the greatest theatrical costume designer of the day, Landolff.

At that time, people were mad about fancy-dress balls and Poiret had endless orders for fancy-dress costumes. Most of these balls had a specific theme, frequently oriental. Some were lavish affairs. The first for which I designed a large number of elaborate costumes was the Ball of Precious Stones.

For the ' Grand Prix Ball ' at the Opéra, I designed an oriental-style costume for myself, in silver-lamé. Closely moulded to the body, it had hundreds of strings of pearls linking the legs to the arms and forming pearly wings. A pearl and silver helmet crested with black plumes, and a black silk chiffon cape with a long, pearl-embroidered train completed the ensemble. My arrival created a sensation. A Russian artist, Princess Eristoff-Kazak, asked me to pose for her in this costume. She was just finishing a portrait of Arlette Dorgère, an actress famous for her elegance and beauty. I was present at the final sittings. When I met Dorgère again, thirty years later, she was still startlingly youthful and a charming woman. Some years before sitting for Kazak, she had been painted by Jacques Emile Blanche, the most fashionable portrait painter of the time.

Among the painters and portraits of the period, I recall particularly Besnard with his wonderful use of colour, Seroff's stylized portrait of Ida Rubinstein, and the dry-point etching of Helleu, who captured exactly the elegant woman of the 1900s. But above all I preferred Boldini, who alone of his contemporaries did not treat his subjects with conventional realism. I shall not forget his fantastic portrait of the Marquise Cazatti. At the huge annual exhibitions of the Salon, held at the Grand Palais, realistic paintings were the rule. I myself much preferred the Salon des Indépendants, where the group known as the Fauves showed their works. I was also struck by the boldness and daring of Matisse, Picasso and Braque.

During one of my sittings at Princess Eristoff-Kazak's atelier, I met Prince Nicolas Ouroussoff, a distant cousin of mine. Oddly enough, we had never met in Russia because he was thirteen years older than myself, and had already been living abroad for several years when I left home, mostly in London. His brother, Prince Serge Ouroussoff, had introduced him to a rich American woman to whom he had become engaged. But the time they had spent together convinced Prince Nicolas that the marriage would never work, and shortly after we met the engagement was broken. Following our first meeting – we dined that evening at Le Doyen, a fine restaurant on the Champs-Elysées – we saw a great deal of each other and became close friends. Nicolas was a handsome man with fine features, light blue eyes and extremely beautiful hands. When he returned to London we exchanged letters frequently. Apart from our mutual affection, I found myself relying more and more on Nicolas's advice and guidance in my career. Later on, when we came to share our lives, he took over all my business affairs and handled them brilliantly. Every year on 2 July, the anniversary of our first meeting, we celebrated the occasion at Le Doyen.

Nicolas's brother Prince Serge, with whom he lived, was married to Sheref, a niece of Abdul Hamid, the ' Red Sultan ' of Turkey. The heroine of Pierre Loti's

novel, *Les Désenchantées*, was based on Sheref. During this same period I met
Loti at one of Princess Eristoff-Kazak's receptions. What a bizarre figure he was
with his theatrical make-up – vivid red lips, rouged cheeks, eye-shadow – and full
beard. His conversation was equally arresting. At that point in my life, I never
dreamed that sixty years later, in 1972, I should be illustrating a new edition of
his book *Azyade*.

As soon as I had signed my contract with Poiret, I took an apartment in Auteuil
at 9 rue de Civry. I decorated and furnished it in my own style, with low divans
and lots of cushions, each one more fantastic than the last.

By the summer of 1913, I was at last able to afford a holiday, and I left for
Biarritz with my sister who had been staying with me in Paris. That season in
Biarritz was particularly brilliant. Everyone was very smart, but one woman whom
I met seemed the incarnation of elegance and ' chic'. She was tall and slender
and when the breeze blew along the beach she swayed like a reed in the wind.
Her Borzoi dog went everywhere with her. The dog was as thin as its mistress, and
its collar and leash always matched her ensembles. She was called Dolly Canada,
and she was a high-class ' demi-mondaine', one of the last of the famous
courtesans such as Marie Duplessis (' La Dame aux Camélias '), Coral Pearl and
the great La Paiva, who had their heyday during the nineteenth century.

I once saw Paiva's bed sold at an auction. It was a fantastic piece of furniture
made of solid ebony inlaid with intricate motifs in malachite and ivory. The
décor of her house in the Avenue des Champs-Elysées – the quintessence of a style
known as Napoleon III – was as extraordinary as her life-story. One day, when she
was poverty-stricken and unknown, she was walking in the Champs-Elysées. Completely exhaused and weak with hunger, she collapsed on to a nearby bench. When
she had revived, she resolved that ' On this very spot I shall build my own special
house '. Shortly afterwards, her dream became a reality.

The apartment where Marie Duplessis lived (and eventually died), on the
Boulevard des Capucines, was considerably less ostentatious. I saw it after it had
passed into the hands of a firm with which I did business. The interior decoration,
which must have been lavish in the extreme, had of course disappeared.

What names they had, these light ladies of the nineteenth century: ' Lionnes '
and ' Biches ' during the Romantic era, ' Cocottes ' and ' Cocodettes ' (chickens)
at the time of the Second Empire and until the end of the century.

Many courtesans of the eighteenth and nineteenth century were also stage
actresses. Fashion was influenced by the clothes of these women and new styles
were often launched in the theatre, since all the great couture houses designed
special models for the well-known actresses. However, the race-tracks at Long-
champ and Auteuil later became the most important fashion show-cases. It was

at the races that Poiret's famous ' jupe-culotte ' made its first appearance. It created an uproar when a gifted and elegant actress, Jeanne Provost, wore it on the stage at the Comédie française.

When I first arrived in Paris I could not afford to see many plays. Sometimes I did without food so that I could buy theatre tickets. One show that greatly impressed me was *Sumurun*, a pantomime adapted from the Tales of the Arabian Nights and produced by Max Reinhardt. The exquisite costumes and décor, and the magnificent production, took my breath away. I always had unbounded admiration for Max Reinhardt's work and saw nearly everything he produced. Perhaps his most impressive production, for me, was *Die Fledermaus*, by Johann Strauss, at the Théâtre Pigalle. He used the splendid stage machinery in this theatre brilliantly to create the most astonishing effects during the scene of Prince Orloff's ball. It is tragic that such a fine theatre as the Théâtre Pigalle and many other theatres and music-halls – the Apollo, the Alhambra, the Tabarin – have been torn down.

After I started working with Poiret, I was able to go to the theatre and opera as often as I wished. Naturally, I went to every new work created by Diaghilev's Russian Ballet, at either the Théâtre du Châtelet, the Théâtre des Champs-Elysées or the Opéra. At the opening of the ballet *The Legend of Joseph,* when Massine made his début, I was seized with a great ambition to design sets and costumes for the superb stage of the Paris Opéra. Many years later my wish was fulfilled when, in 1951, I designed the décor and costumes for *La Traviata,* for the fiftieth anniversary of Verdi's death.

One of the most extraordinary shows of 1913 was Gabriel d'Annunzio's *La Pisanelle ou la Mort Parfumée,* an historical drama set in medieval Cyprus, with marvellous décor and costumes by Leon Bakst, and starring Ida Rubinstein. I have always been a passionate admirer of Ida Rubinstein. The first time I saw her dance was in *Schéhérazade* with the Russian Ballet. After that I saw everything she either danced or acted, except *The Martyrdom of Saint Sebastian.* I imagine that when she appeared in the first performance of this work, it had none of the silliness which distressed me when I saw it a few years ago at the Opéra with Ludmilla Tcherina in the same role. I like Ludmilla Tcherina and admire her looks and talent, but I can only say that it shocked me to see a Saint Sebastian-cum-Hermaphrodite in a pink body stocking, which only served to accentuate the ridiculous aspects of d'Annunzio's script.

Ida Rubinstein must have created an entirely different effect. With her strange and completely asexual type of beauty she was like a medieval carved ivory figure. I loved her in all her roles – even the Lady of the Camellias, which was unfavourably reviewed. She failed for me only in the realm of classical ballet. I intensely disliked her version of ' The Dying Swan ', perhaps particularly because I had seen Pavlova dance it a few months earlier.

An evening I shall always remember was the opening of Gabriel Fauré's

Penelope at the Théâtre des Champs-Elysées, with Lucienne Brévol in the title role. The premiere of this opera had taken place in Monte Carlo two months earlier, in March 1913. René Fauchois's three-act libretto is based on the classical story of Ulysses and Penelope. After its Paris production there were, as far as I know, no further performances until its American premiere at Harvard University on 29 November, 1945. The occasion for this revival was a festival celebrating the centenary of Fauré's birth. The work is, I think, still unjustly neglected.

The most popular entertainment of the time was known as Boulevard theatre. These were frivolous comedies, sometimes wittily written, like those of the talented Tristan Bernard, De Flers and Caillavet. *The Green Suit* and, especially, *The King*, brilliantly acted by Eve Lavallière, Marcelle Lender and Brasseur, stay in my memory. The two most famous playwrights of the time were Henri Bernstein and Henri Bataille.

With four friends I had taken a box for the dress rehearsal of one of Bataille's plays at the Théâtre du Vaudeville. *La Phalène* was based on the life of the Russian artist, Marie Bachkirtseff, who died young of consumption. As was the custom then, dress rehearsals were always attended by high society. I decided to add a touch of spice to the occasion.

I invited one of Poiret's models to accompany us. His models were allowed to borrow dresses from his collection if they were going to a party which was a particularly smart affair. The girl I invited managed to get hold of the most extravagant dress in the whole collection together with a fantastic ermine and red velvet coat, which I believe was called 'Eminence'. I wore the dress and coat, with a red velvet turban (no wig), long red gloves and huge ear-rings. My four friends were in tails with red camellias in their buttonholes.

As soon as we entered our box, the whole audience turned to stare at us. Next morning one of the biggest newspapers published a report on the event:

> In that brilliant audience all eyes were fixed on one of the boxes where two of Paul Poiret's models were sitting, accompanied by four gentlemen in impeccable evening dress. One model was an attractive blonde, but the other, with her scarlet turban, was irresistible, wearing her remarkable ensemble with an air and a sense of style that few models are lucky enough to possess.

Poiret read the article and, after checking some further details, summoned me to his office. Expecting the worst, I was extremely surprised when, instead, he made me an offer to design a variety of dresses especially for me, which I would then model at his next collection. I found the idea vastly entertaining, but begged off with the excuse that I felt I was born to be an artist and designer, not a model!

At that period of my life I was rather fond of the social whirl. It intrigued me because it was still a novelty. As a boy in St Petersburg, with the exception of

1 *Fedora.* Costume, 1920

2 ' L'Orage '. Cover, 1917

family dinners and celebrations, I had gone to very few parties. Since my sister and most of my cousins were several years older than myself, my childhood had been unusually solitary. But my 'social-butterfly' phase in Paris was soon over, and the parties began to seem boring and monotonous. Above all, they interfered with hard, conscientious work for which I always had a consuming passion. As I achieved some degree of success, I began to feel more and more strongly that I had a responsibility to develop, to the highest possible point, the talent God had given me. This feeling of responsibility became a motivating force in shaping the future course of my life. It is still one of the cornerstones of my artistic and personal credo.

One dinner party of this period, however, is still fresh in my memory. It was given by some friends in honour of Countess Anna de Noailles, the well-known writer who later became France's official poet. About twenty guests had been invited for nine o'clock. By ten o'clock the conversation began to languish. Anna de Noailles had still not appeared and everyone was beginning to be hungry. The hostess decided to telephone the Countess. The Countess's secretary replied, saying that the Countess was lying down with a bad migraine but that she would make a superhuman effort to pull herself together, and start dressing at once. Another hour went by. No sign of the Countess. The atmosphere was now chilly in the extreme. The hostess telephoned again and the secretary replied that the Countess was quite incapable of making the effort to come. This news was received with consternation by the guests. As for the hostess, she had just given orders for dinner to be served when the telephone rang. It was the Countess herself. She was now perfectly restored and would be coming immediately. A quarter of an hour later she arrived, fresh as a rose, completely oblivious of all the trouble she had caused.

Everyone's spirits revived at once, for she began to talk – and her conversation was sparkling. She talked for the rest of the evening; no one else had a chance to say anything.

There is a word that has almost disappeared from our present-day vocabulary: it is 'tact'. Tact has nothing to do with class or education; a peasant, without realizing it, can be highly endowed with this rare quality. Tact is something you are born with, like elegance: it is, in fact, a certain elegance in the way you feel about things. A high-born, educated lady like the Countess de Noailles can be tactless, as was indeed the case on this occasion.

A great many society evenings took the form of dances. Many people today believe that the craze for dancing arose after the end of the 1914 war. This is not so. Paris had already been conquered by the tango several years before 1914. One could say that the craze was crazier after the war, encouraged by a frantic urge to live life to the full.

The fashion for 'Tango Teas', which began about 1910, spawned a special type of young man, the professional dancing-partner with brilliantined hair shining like a mirror. The partners of these youths – mostly middle-aged ladies – tipped them for their services.

The craze for dancing led to another development – the rise of the amateur dancer, especially the amateur female dancer. It all began with Isadora Duncan and her 'free dance' which was influenced by Greece and Greek art as opposed to the rigid disciplines of classical ballet. Isadora Duncan introduced a new era. As Gordon Craig wrote at the time, 'She was speaking in her own language, not echoing any ballet master, and so she came to move as no one had ever seen anyone move before.' With her sound musical intuition and taste she projected a visual interpretation of the spirit of the music to which she danced. She deserved all the adulation she received. During her lifetime, as well as after her death, she was a source of inspiration not only for dancers but for many other artists. Unfortunately, she was followed by a host of artistically sterile imitators with a dilettante attitude to dancing. Since the classical disciplines had been abandoned, many young people were convinced that they could become dancers without any previous training. Formerly, the hard work and harsh discipline of the ballet schools would have frightened them away.

I met Isadora Duncan through Poiret; she had been one of his early champions. According to the legend, she was very beautiful. In real life she was not beautiful, but her vibrant personality created its own legend. It was said that she once asked Georgette Leblanc, then married to Maurice Maeterlinck, if she could 'borrow' her husband for a few days. The child conceived in this temporary union, she explained, would be the most perfect human being imaginable. It would inherit her own beauty and Maeterlinck's genius. Madame Leblanc's reply, if any, is unrecorded.

One of the favourite roles of the female amateur dancer was that of Salome. In fact, Salome was the most fashionable figure of the period. She was dished up in every possible way. This preoccupation began with Oscar Wilde's play and Beardsley's superb illustrations. As soon as Richard Strauss had made Wilde's play into an opera, other composers followed. We had *Salome* by Mariotte, *The Tragedy of Salome* by Florent Schmidt and *Herodias* by Massenet. An American journalist published an article maintaining that Salome was not really the daughter of Herodias at all but her son, an uncommonly beautiful boy named Salomon. This immediately encouraged several male dancers to take up the role.

When I was twenty-one years old, I was stricken with scarlet fever. For children this is not a serious illness, but it can be fatal in adults. (My father nearly died of it when he was thirty-five.) My condition became so critical that my parents were called to Paris. Nicolas had already come over from London to be with me. Meanwhile, war was imminent. My mother and father had barely arrived when World War I broke out. My father immediately left for Russia but he never completed the journey. The official Declaration of War was proclaimed a few minutes before his train cleared the frontier between Germany and Russia. He was taken prisoner, and we had no further news of him for the next few months.

Since my sister, who had been living with me in Paris, had gone to join her fiancé in London, my mother and Nicolas were left to look after me. When I finally recovered, my doctor advised me to convalesce in the more temperate climate of the Côte d'Azur. In view of the fact that when war was declared, Poiret had shut down his fashion house, leaving me without a job, we decided to head for Monte Carlo.

Monte Carlo 1914-1922

Travelling in France at that time was extremely difficult. The authorities had urged people to leave Paris for their own safety. As a result, all out-going trains were packed. By sheer luck we managed to find three seats, but once in the compartment we were trapped, for the corridors were clogged with people sitting on suitcases. As for a dining car, that was out of the question. With luck we might be able to lean out of the window and buy a sandwich or a glass of water from a vendor on a station platform while passing through. Since military convoys had priority, the journey to Monte Carlo took two exhausting days. When we finally arrived we settled into a hotel which Nicolas knew from previous visits.

In addition to the disruptions of war, our family was also upset by the machinations of my sister. She was jealous of my friendship with Nicolas and tried to turn my mother against him. However, my mother remained on good terms with Nicolas for the rest of his life. My relationship with him, which continued until his death, was one of the most important of my entire life.

As for my sister, she had become so difficult and irrational about everything that concerned me that I finally had to face up to the fact that the only way to prevent further unpleasant complications was simply to avoid seeing her. This situation prevailed for several years, despite the fact that I later contributed, through my mother, to her support.

Although the physical aspects of the war seemed remote, our early days in Monte Carlo were filled with anxiety, especially for my mother. There had been no news of my father since his capture at the border three months earlier. One day my mother asked me to go to the monastery of Laghet where there was a reputedly miraculous statue of the Madonna. It is in the hills above Monaco, beyond La Turbie. I went up to the monastery and prayed. Two weeks later my mother received a letter from my father, dated the very day of my pilgrimage. I often went back to Laghet after that.

As I grew older, I became a firm believer in the power of prayer. Throughout my adult life it has been a source of great comfort and strength. But, since I feel that religion is a private matter, I am likely to do my praying in empty cathedrals, or in none at all, rather than at formal church services.

My father's letter told us that he had been a prisoner in Strahlsund, a small island in the Baltic. After a short time, he had been transferred to Heidelberg. Since she was now able to write to him, my mother decided to go back to Russia. My sister met her in Norway and together they returned. So, once more my mother and I were separated. We could not know that in a few years' time the Revolution would again render my family's future uncertain and ominous.

Meanwhile, the problem of earning my living became more and more urgent. Since I was still recovering from the after-effects of my illness, I was unfit for military service. Also, according to pre-Revolutionary Russian law, the eldest son of a family was not required to serve in the armed forces. At that time I was still a Russian citizen. Shortly after my arrival in Monte Carlo I decided to try placing a cover design and some drawings of several original dress designs with an American magazine. My first choices were *Vogue* and *Harper's Bazaar*. I tossed a coin and chance decided that I should try *Harper's Bazaar*. On 23 November, my twenty-second birthday, I received a cheque from *Harper's Bazaar*, together with a letter asking me to send them a set of drawings every month. I was relieved and excited.

My first cover design and what I believed to be my first American fashion drawings were published in the January 1915 issue. It was not until I had been working on *Harper's Bazaar* for some time that I made a startling discovery. In going through some back numbers I came across some black and white drawings of dresses I had designed while I was with Poiret. They were signed by Poiret. People who live and work in the world of fashion may consider me naive for mentioning this. I am sure that many young designers, working behind the scenes, have created designs anonymously for which the great couturiers have taken public credit. It has long been a fairly standard practice – all in the day's work in the fashion business and, I gather, business in general. Yet, there was something profoundly upsetting about seeing, in a magazine of international stature, a drawing of mine signed with the name of Poiret. Even so, I shall always be grateful to Poiret. He was a catalyst. Although his motives may often have been more self-serving than altruistic, his talent for making things happen was extraordinary. It was Poiret who, while I was still in his employ, called my work to the attention of Lucien Vogel, editor of *La Gazette du Bon Ton*, France's most prestigious fashion magazine at the time. As a result, in 1913 Vogel published my first signed fashion drawings.

Towards the end of 1914, despite the war, I managed to make a short trip to Paris – I still had my apartment in the rue de Civry. I looked up Adrienne Ridou, a charming young woman who had been one of Poiret's best seamstresses. When his house closed down she, too, had lost her job. I worked out an arrangement with her whereby she would make dresses to my designs for American buyers, who normally came to Paris to acquire haute couture dresses. Due to my business naivety and legal ignorance, I rashly ordered printed cards which I sent to buyers, announcing that my designs were made up by Adrienne Ridou, a former 'first hand' at Paul Poiret. Then, for the first time, I experienced the full impact of the unpleasant side of Poiret's character. He promptly sued me for using his name. Since I was in the wrong according to French law, of which I knew nothing, I lost the case. I was forced to pay what then seemed to me to be a very large sum in damages. After that, an icy wall sprang up between us. Poiret omitted my name from his memoirs, and I did not mention him in an article I wrote on the evolution of twentieth-century fashion for the 1929 edition of the *Encyclopaedia Britannica*.

The memory of this painful incident came sharply alive for me in the late 1920s. By then, Poiret's financial affairs were in such a bad way that he sold his fashion house to a syndicate. He made the classic error of staying on as an executive of the company. Poiret as an organization man surely constituted the height of bad casting. He was soon forced out and in the summer of 1929 the House of Poiret finally closed its doors. Poiret attempted a come-back in 1931 when a group of silk manufacturers backed him in a small fashion house. Since the syndicate still controlled the name of Poiret, and he was himself unable to use it, he christened his new venture with its telephone number, 'Passy 10-17'. However, what with Poiret's chronic addiction to luxury and the deepening economic Depression, 'Passy 10-17' quietly gave up after its second collection.

Despite my unfortunate initial experience with Poiret, the idea of exporting my own designs to America turned out to be a good one. I promptly secured an order for thirty-five dresses and coats from Henri Bendel, one of the best-known high-fashion shops in New York. B. Altman and Company, the Fifth Avenue department store, also gave me large orders. For the next three years I designed two collections of dresses and coats each year.*

In 1916, *Vogue* asked me to do a set of designs each month. I was delighted to accept since I did not have an exclusive contract with *Harper's Bazaar*. Also, I needed the money. But William Randolph Hearst, who owned *Harper's Bazaar*, soon offered me an exclusive ten-year contract on excellent terms. So my association with *Vogue* was terminated after only six months. Under the new

---

* In 1967, the Director of the Victoria and Albert Museum in London asked me for some information about a set of my fashion drawings which had just been acquired by the Museum. To my surprise, they turned out to be designs I had left with Adrienne Ridou. The Ridou family had presented them to the museum after her death.

arrangement, each issue of *Harper's Bazaar* carried my cover design, a feature which turned out to be a great boost to news-stand sales. The magazine also included many of my drawings and original designs for interior decoration; fashion accessories such as hats, jewellery, bags, shoes, gloves, parasols, muffs and fans; hair styles and head-dresses. As a result of my various contributions, *Harper's Bazaar* developed a distinctive and characteristic style.

The magazine's editorial comments, coming on the heels of my humiliating experience with Poiret, were especially gratifying to me. The following typical excerpts spell out why my future began to look up considerably:

> In the January 1915 issue of *Harper's Bazaar,* Monsieur Erté began to contribute his extraordinary designs to the *Bazaar.* At first his eccentric drawings were not fully understood by the general public, and his ideas were criticized as impracticable.
>
> But to those who are able to interpret his charming originality and develop in fabric and garniture his clever ideas, Erté has been an inspiration. (October 1915)

> To glance at an Erté design is amusing. To look at one is interesting. To study one is absorbing. That any human being can conceive – and execute – such exquisite detail is positively miraculous, and we become even more impressed when we consider his combinations of colours and materials. (October 1917)

> The designer for one of the best known New York houses told us the other day that he has obtained more ideas from Erté's drawings in the *Bazaar* than from any other source of fashion. Many others, to whom originality, in good taste, means everything, have told us the same thing. From Erté they take a touch here, a touch there, and adapt them to their own needs. (January 1918)

Shortly after I started doing cover designs, I added a written commentary on the theme of the design. This appeared on the first inside page of the magazine along with my black and white illustrations. Later on, when I decided to settle permanently in Monte Carlo, the editor asked me to write a monthly letter reporting my observations and impressions of life in what had become the most fashionable resort in the world.

Normally, fashion artists simply reproduce the couturier's models for the fashion journals. Apparently I was the only one who designed for the sheer pleasure of creation. For many many years couturiers all over the world have been inspired by my designs. Thus, when in 1967 I was preparing a retrospective show of my drawings in New York and had dug out a design for a dress I made in 1927 for the musical comedy *Manhattan Mary* (produced by George White at the Majestic Theatre in New York), I realized that a few days before I had seen the same model in the collection of one of the greatest Paris fashion houses.

Fashion is all too often a routine affair. I am an individualist as far as my creations for women's clothes are concerned, and have never followed ephemeral crazes. Among the styles I have created, each woman can find something that suits her type of beauty without becoming a slave to current trends. How dull it would be if, each season, all women had the same figure, said the same things and thought the same thoughts. That is how I feel when I see women dressed more or less alike and why I am against the tyranny of fashion. While trying to create a paradise of female beauty, it often has just the opposite effect.

When we first moved to Monte Carlo, Nicolas and I lived in furnished houses. Two years later I found a delightful place – one floor, with a large terrace full of flowers and fine palm trees, in the Villa Excelsior. The view from the terrace was magnificent. When the weather was good, we used to lunch and dine under an awning on the terrace. I have always kept up the practice of eating out of doors. Even now, I have lunch on the little terrace of my apartment in Boulogne-sur-Seine when the weather is mild.

I decorated the place in my own style and filled it with antique furniture that I found in shops all along the Côte d'Azur. The first thing I did was to have a comfortable and practical worktable made. It was a simple oak table, the top of which could be tipped up to serve as an easel, with a flat arm-rest on one side. It contained a variety of drawers for my tools; my tubes of paint were arranged by colours. In this way everything could be kept tidy.

I love order. To me disorder is ugly – unless, of course, it is organized disorder, which can be picturesque. But then it is no longer the disorder that is due to carelessness.

I still have the same worktable; it has been my best friend for more than half a century. I have spent the happiest years of my life at it.

I have always loved working at night. No one interrupts me. No telephone calls disturb my train of thought. I feel I have unlimited time. One bright lamp (its bluish light helps me to see the true colours) lights the drawing on which I am working. The rest of the house is plunged in darkness except for a few dimly-lit shells which afford enough light for me to leave my worktable if I have to. Everything is focussed on the brightly-lit square of my table – a perfect aid to concentration. Even my cats pretend to be sleeping: they know that I am working. I had one cat called Micmac who used to lie in one corner of the worktable without moving a muscle all the time I was drawing. One night I had finished a design for a stage set that was urgently required for next day and had just stood up to go to bed. Micmac, glad to be able to move at last, stretched herself luxuriously and knocked over the glass of water I used for cleaning my paint brushes. The dirty water ran all over the drawing and completely ruined it. When I telephoned the director of the theatre next day and explained what had happened, he would not believe me.

Being alone is vitally important for me and my work. I am a solitary person, and this may explain why I have such a great love of cats. Cats and I are very much alike. The cat is a solitary animal, very independent, very quiet by nature. Like cats who hide themselves away when they are ill, I cannot stand people visiting me when I am indisposed. I want to be left alone.

I love listening to music when I work. Throughout the long night, while I am at my table, I always have soft music playing in the background – on the radio, on records or tapes. My taste in music is eclectic.

Since I always go to bed late, I get up late in the morning. When I wake up I exercise for fifteen minutes before breakfast. Sometimes I supplement my morning work-out with an additional five minutes before dinner. I have never deviated from this routine even when I am travelling. The habit of morning exercises goes back to my father's early training. I have always been grateful to him for this.

After the outbreak of the Russian Revolution, I had no more news of my parents. Then one day my cousin Kolia turned up. He was the son of Uncle Paul, my father's brother. My hopes soared when I saw him, but not for long. He was unable to tell me anything about either my parents or my sister. His parents, as well as his sister Alia and her husband, had been shot during the first days of the uprising. Alia's two children, a girl and a boy, were being cared for by a woman relative of her husband. Although Kolia and I were about the same age and had been boyhood playmates when we met at our Grandmother Eugenia's summer house, we were never very close. Except for those summer holidays we seldom saw each other. Nevertheless, I was touched by the plight of Alia's children and wanted to adopt the little boy. (I would have found it difficult to bring up a girl.) Kolia assured me that he could have the boy brought to France. He would, however, need quite a lot of money to arrange it. I immediately gave him the amount required. A few days later I was shocked to learn that he had left for America, taking my money with him. I never heard from him again. And that was the last I ever heard of the children.

During my first year in Monte Carlo, I was commissioned to design the costumes for the 'Revue de Saint-Cyr' by Rip, the best-known stage satirist of his day. This show, an annual event at the famous military academy, was a brilliant social occasion attended by France's top military-political brass and the diplomatic colony. Saint-Cyr productions were always highly professional. The cast for this one included such stars as Edouard de Max, whom I had admired in d'Annunzio's *La Pisanelle ou la Mort Perfumée*, and Marguerite Deval, hilarious in the role of Madame de Maintenon; the delectable Yvonne Printemps played Cupid. Twenty years later Printemps confessed to me that the delicately pleated chiffon wings attached to her shoulders were always catching in her hair and impeding her movements, but the costume was so attractive that she willingly put up with the inconvenience.

My costumes for the ' Revue de Saint-Cyr ' were so successful that they brought me two new offers – one from Rip and the other from Madame Rasimi. Rip had a charming young lady friend who wanted to make a name for herself in the fashion world. He asked me to go into partnership with her but I refused, because I cherished my independence. Rip was deeply offended and never asked me to design costumes for him again.

I was, on the other hand, delighted to accept Mme Rasimi's proposal. Amazingly versatile, she directed several theatres, produced shows and made the costumes. She carried out her costumes brilliantly in rich materials and never permitted false economies. The first costumes I designed for her were for the revue *Panachot the Dictator*. Mme Rasimi produced this at the Ba-ta-Clan Theatre, which she owned.

The following year, 1917, I designed a variety of costumes for her revue *Gobette of Paris* and its two stars, Mistinguett and Maurice Chevalier. This was my first meeting with Mistinguett. I designed lavish costumes for her, with long trains and huge feather head-dresses, which she had never worn before. After this, enormous plumes and yards of material for her dresses became part of her image. Some time later she asked me to design the costumes for her next show. I said that I would be delighted and asked when my agent could conveniently come to discuss terms. ' What terms? ' said she, ' I never pay for anything.' I answered that I was perfectly willing to contribute costume designs to new performers or to those who were down on their luck, but not to stars who could well afford to pay. She never forgave me.

Two years later I designed a series of dresses for another music-hall star, Gaby Deslys. She had star quality for the French: she was beautiful, she had ' chic ', she danced superbly and had a fine revue voice. She was also the mistress of King Manuel of Portugal. She came over from her native Marseilles, where she was on holiday, to see me in Monte Carlo, accompanied by her partner, Harry Pilcer. We discussed all her costumes, including one I particularly liked. The skirt was made of ermine, with two enormous trains, one on each side.

When this talented and lovable star died young, Harry Pilcer never got over it. He dedicated a corner of his apartment to her memory; there he had a kind of altar with her portrait surrounded by candles that were always kept burning. After her death, he danced alone. His most famous act was an elegant drunk staggering down the grand staircase of the Casino de Paris. To the end of his days he looked astonishingly youthful. He would apply an astringent lotion to his face in the morning and this kept the skin tightly-stretched until the evening.

I did several other shows for Mme Rasimi at the Théâtre Fémina and the Apollo. Her daughter, who lived in nearby Cannes, often came to see me. We went to fancy-dress balls together, at the Sporting Club in Monte Carlo or the Cannes Casino. Mme Rasimi made the costumes I designed and wore on these occasions.

My work during those first years in Monte Carlo was divided between *Harper's Bazaar* and designing for Mme Rasimi's theatres. But in 1919 I first met the costumier Max Weldy. He wrote from Paris asking if I would design several scenes for the Folies Bergère, for which he made all the costumes. Our first conference took place in Paul Derval's office. He was the owner of the Folies Bergère and also director of the Olympia Theatre where his office was located. Present at the first meeting were Paul Derval, Louis Lemarchand (producer of all the Folies shows), Max Weldy, Nicolas and myself.

Lemarchand was really the soul of the Folies Bergère. During his ' reign ' the shows reached their zenith. When he left the Folies at the beginning of the 1930s, they gradually became dreary and banal.

We agreed that I should design two scenes: ' At the Bottom of the Sea ' and ' Venice in the Eighteenth Century ' – a period that was becoming fashionable at the time. Both of these scenes were highly successful. And so began my long and fruitful association with the Folies Bergère and Max Weldy.

Except for three or four short trips to Paris each year, Nicolas and I lived in Monte Carlo for eight years. I was considered rather odd because at that time most people went to the Côte d'Azur only in the winter. Regular visitors were known as ' winter migrants '. Since I have always loved solitude, I particularly enjoyed the long, hot summer months. I sunbathed long before it was considered ' chic ' to be tanned. I think I was probably making up for all those childhood years in a cold and gloomy climate.

All the winter population of Monte Carlo looked pale. Little by little, my skin, which used to be so white when I lived in Russia, became naturally brown and retained its colour, even when I later moved back to Paris. Around 1925 a very fashionable American make-up was called ' Erté's Skin ' – a fairly dark ' coquille d'oeuf ' shade, resembling the tan of the local fishermen.

Lying in the sun gives me acute pleasure. I slide half-asleep into another world where dreams and reality intermingle in a curious and wonderful way: fantastic images come and go. Pure line mutates to make solid forms that continually shift and change. At the same time, the sounds of the world outside blend into each other to form the beat of strange, bewitching music.

My life in Monte Carlo followed a well-organized pattern. I found nearly all the inspiration I needed for my drawings during long, solitary walks. In summer I spent the morning on the beach, which was rather far away from the Villa Excelsior. Since Monte Carlo Beach did not exist at that time, I used to bathe at a little sandy bay where the Beach is now. This shore, with its bathing huts and restaurant, was called Mondo's Beach after the owner, an amusing and talkative Italian.

Among the people who used to bathe there was the well-known opera singer Mary Garden, who had a summer apartment in Monte Carlo. Like me, Mary Garden loved Monte Carlo during the quiet summer months. She usually combined her between-season holiday with work on the roles in which she was scheduled to appear. Since the windows of her apartment overlooking the Casino gardens were always wide open, we enjoyed many glorious free concerts.

She had her own swimming-instructor, who carried her into the water so that she should not bruise her feet on the stones of the beach. He was a magnificently-built local lad. He would follow her as she swam in case she needed help.

After Nicolas and I came to know Mary Garden, she asked me to design her costumes for Montemezzi's *L'Amore dei Tre Re*, which she was rehearsing for the coming season, with the Chicago Opera Company. It was 1920 and my first professional contact with the opera.

In winter, when it was too cold to bathe, I went for long walks along the seashore to Cap-Martin, into the mountains towards La Turbie and on the Moyenne Corniche. The latter was one of my favourite walks. The view was magnificent and there were very few motor-cars. I often met a solitary, bearded gentleman on the Moyenne Corniche. He walked briskly, stripped to the waist, with his jacket and shirt on his arm. He looked vaguely familiar but since I was usually deep in my own thoughts I attached no great significance to this. After several passing encounters, we began to greet one another. Eventually we would stop to exchange the usual banalities about the weather, which was invariably fine. One day I happened to mention our meetings to Nicolas. When I went on to describe the gentleman's appearance, Nicolas, who paid closer attention to the activities of visiting celebrities than I did, informed me that I had been making small talk with none other than George Bernard Shaw.

Nicolas hardly ever came with me on my walks. He knew I needed to be alone to create new ideas and work them out in my mind. My morning bath was also a productive time. Many of my best ideas came to me then. All my ideas are worked out in my head, right down to the smallest detail. I find it impossible to sit down in front of a blank sheet of paper and begin drawing without a previously thought-out plan. But when I start to draw, my designs come in a flash. I rarely make any preparatory sketches. Sometimes I make a tracing of a drawing if the paper is soiled with too many pencil strokes.

Since 1915, I have kept as many of my original drawings as possible. Originals sent to *Harper's Bazaar* were always returned after reproduction in accordance with one of the clauses in my contract. As for my theatre designs, I nearly always kept the originals and gave copies to the costumiers.

I trained several copy-artists who were remarkably accurate – so much so that many people have taken their copies for my originals. I have frequently spotted these at auction sales and exhibitions. Normally I would stamp every original drawing on the back with the words 'Composition Originale'; copies were stamped ' Reproduction par Erté de son oeuvre originale '. Unfortunately, due to the fact that I often had to supply designs at short notice, some of my drawings were not properly stamped. For this reason I am now kept busy verifying my original drawings from among studio copies. Occasionally, when I had time, I would design some compositions for future exhibitions, using the idea of my original with a suitable setting.

In Monte Carlo I trained two young men as copy-artists. They were excellent pupils but, since they both married, they could not follow me when I left Monte Carlo for Paris. My best copy-artists were Emile Gallois, who has now been dead some years, Jacques Pellerin, who has retired, and Madame Diselyn who is still working with me.

On our short trips to Paris, Nicolas and I usually travelled by car. We had a chauffeur, since neither of us could drive. I had tried to learn but, since my mind was usually wandering, I never managed to pass the driving test, although I took it five times. Over the years, the toll of my chronic absentmindedness has run into countless numbers of lost wallets, tickets, pairs of glasses, scarfs, sweaters and gloves, but it wasn't until I had turned eighty that I decided that something had to be done about my wallets. I was about to leave Paris for a holiday in Greece and had stopped at a drug-store for some sun-tan cream. When I reached for my wallet it wasn't there. I suddenly realized that I had probably lost it in the taxi that had just dropped me. Since the wallet contained my identity card and a large amount of money I was, naturally, upset. The chemist assured me that I would probably find the taxi at either of two nearby stands. Instead of pursuing the taxi I entered the cathedral of Saint Augustine, which was close to the shop, and prayed. Then, as I arrived at one of the stands a taxi pulled up. By the time I reached the car the driver was looking through my wallet for some clue to my identity. It was a happy moment. And, finally, the lesson sank in. My wallet is now equipped with a sturdy gold chain which can be firmly attached to my trouser belt.

My cat Mischa always accompanied us to Paris. We took a different route on each occasion, so that in time I became acquainted with a considerable area of France, which had been largely unknown territory to me. My favourite road went through the Cevennes. The first time I took it was in springtime. When we were high up in the mountains I noticed great sheets of white above us and thought they were patches of snow that had not yet melted. But as we got closer I realized that they were fields of narcissi whose scent hung heavy in the air.

Our journeys were always leisurely. We used to stop at many different kinds of restaurant. I have always been a gourmet although I actually eat very little. We found wonderful local wines that can only be drunk on the spot, as they lose all their bouquet if one attempts to transport them. I shall never forget one I drank near Valence: it was a very dry white wine, the colour of burnt umber, with a faint honey bouquet: it was called dry Saint-Perret.

On one of my trips to Paris I met the mysterious Sir Basil Zaharoff. He had started his career as a sleeping-car attendant and made his fortune selling munitions on an international scale. Although he had played an important part in World War I and could be considered a super-criminal, on the personal level he was a philanthropist, and totally sympathetic to individual need. He had an over-ruling passion for flowers. His homes in every capital city throughout the world were always filled with them in case he might suddenly arrive.

In Monte Carlo one of my main pastimes during winter and spring was going to the opera and the theatre. The exquisite Monte Carlo theatre was built by Garnier (the architect who designed the Paris Opera House) and is actually inside the Casino. It is quite small, with no balcony and odd acoustics. There are two stalls right in the centre from which you can hear absolutely nothing; no one has ever fathomed the reason.

The operas were always brilliantly produced. Many new works were launched there, including Puccini's *La Rondin*, *Il Tabarro*, *Suor Angelica* and *Gianni Schicchi*. The world's greatest singers performed upon this stage. It was one of the major opera centres of the world.

Raoul Gainsbourg, director of the Monte Carlo Theatre, had a great nose for scenting new talent – literally and figuratively speaking. He had once been the director of The Aquarium, a big music-hall in St Petersburg and, according to rumour, was the father of the opera singer, Gigli. It was in the Monte Carlo Theatre that I first heard Tito Schipa in *Rigoletto*; he was then a young singer just beginning his career. Gainsbourg also helped build the career of my idol, Lina Cavalieri. Over the years, hundreds of journalists have asked me whom I regarded as the most beautiful woman in the world. Invariably I replied: 'Lina Cavalieri'. Why? She was tall and extremely slender – a rarity among turn-of-the-century prima donnas. Her classically pure features were enhanced by dark hair and eyes, and a long, swan-like neck. Yet her beauty was not cold. Her expression was full of animation and she moved with grace and authority. Cavalieri's most dominant quality, however, was her extraordinary charm. What is charm? I would define it as a quality of mind and soul which finds expression in a person's physical appearance and behaviour. Cavalieri possessed it to a superb degree. Although her voice had its limitations, she worked so diligently on its development and handled it so deftly that she emerged from her debut in Milan's La Scala – a theatre which attracted the most sophisticated, discriminating and critical opera audiences in the world – as a fully-fledged star.

I had first seen Cavalieri at the Conservatorium Theatre in St Petersburg when I was about fourteen. During the next few years I heard her sing every role in her repertoire. One day I made a portrait of her from memory – a pastel – and sent it to her. I was thrilled when it was presented to her on stage, along with a great number of baskets and bouquets of flowers. The next day I received a charming letter from her, together with a beautiful autographed photograph. But it was not until 1929 that I finally met her. It was at the opening of a new production of Edmond Rostand's *La Princesse Lointaine* at the Sarah Bernhardt Theatre, for which I had designed the costumes and settings. Cavalieri congratulated me on my success and I told her the story of our one-sided romance, which amused her. Although she was then over fifty, she was still as beautiful as when I first saw her.

When the opera season ended, it was followed by a season of Diaghilev's Russian Ballet. The opulent *ambience* of Monte Carlo at that time gave these performances extraordinary éclat. I came to know many members of the company through Michel Pavloff, a dancer I had met several years before at Princess Eristoff's house, when she was painting my portrait. Pavloff, a delightful and entertaining boy, introduced me to another young dancer who had just joined the company, Constantin Tscherkas.

Tscherkas looked like a fledgling that had fallen from the nest. Descended from an old aristocratic Ukrainian family, he had studied at the ' Pages' School ', the most exclusive military school in St Petersburg. He had escaped from Russia alone at the time of the Revolution and, after a hard year in Constantinople, had managed to find work with a ballet company in Sofia. He was extremely gifted and worked tremendously hard with Cechetti, the greatest classical ballet master of the time. Tscherkas later became an excellent classical dancer in the Diaghilev company, but although he performed Nijinsky's roles in *L'Oiseau Bleu*, *The Sleeping Beauty* and *Spectre de la Rose*, his self-effacing personality prevented him from becoming an internationally famous star. After Diaghilev's death, he became *danseur-étoile* (leading dancer) and then choreographer at the Opéra-Comique in Paris.

It was perhaps because he was so shy and lonely that Nicolas and I soon came to regard Tscherkas as a member of the family and, indeed, he remained a life-long friend of mine.

I remember two ballerinas whose beauty struck me particularly – Tamara Gevergeeva (who later became the actress Tamara Geva) and, even more so, Kaschouba. Although the latter only danced supporting roles, I found her beauty hypnotic while she was on stage. But despite her dazzling looks, she had a very unhappy life. She was the mistress of Lord Carnarvon, the man who discovered Tutankhamun's tomb. He had given her a marvellous emerald that had been one of the tomb's treasures. As soon as this fabulous jewel came into her possession, she was dogged by ill-luck. Since she believed in the curse of Tutankhamun, she decided to get rid of it, but instead of throwing it in the Seine she sold it to Cartier. According to her, the money she acquired from the sale continued to bring her bad luck. When I saw her twenty years later – she had come to Paris from South America where she was living – she told me she had never managed to find happiness again.

I also recall the delightful and charming Tamara Karsavina, whom I met at the home of Princess Tenicheff, an amazing woman who, back in Russia, had

established a centre for Folk Art on her estate ' Selo Talachkino '. There were
workshops for furniture, all kinds of wooden objects and knick-knacks, and looms
for weaving materials. Everything was made in the Russian style and designed
by great artists of the period, such as Roerich and Bilibine, who were associated
with the enterprise. Among the exhibits were marvellous balalaikas decorated
with paintings by Wroubel. When the Revolution broke out, the Princess left
Russia and came to live in Monte Carlo.

It was through the Princess that I met Diaghilev. I had recently been commissioned to design the décor and costumes for a spectacular scene in an American
film, *Restless Sex*, to be produced by Cosmopolitan Productions, one of William
Randolph Hearst's many enterprises. The film was to star Hearst's mistress,
Marion Davies. When the Princess showed some of these designs to Diaghilev,
he was impressed by them and wanted to meet me.

My first impression of Diaghilev was certainly at odds with his legendary
reputation as one of the most dynamic innovators in the history of the ballet.
He was slow-moving and his eyes were unusually heavy-lidded. In fact, his whole
manner struck me as sleepy. When we shook hands after being introduced, I felt
as though I had clasped a ball of cotton wool. Needless to say, such false impressions were soon forgotten once our discussions got under way. He asked if I
would like to design décors and costumes for *The Sleeping Beauty*. All Bakst's
splendid sets for the ballet had recently been confiscated by Sir Oswald Stoll,
director of the London Coliseum, with whom Diaghilev was involved in a financial
dispute. I was, of course, overjoyed to accept this commission. Since the designs
were wanted urgently, I started work at once.

I had barely completed the designs for the first two costumes when I received
a telegram from Max Weldy asking me to design, as quickly as possible, some
sets and costumes for a lavish new edition of John Murray Anderson's *Greenwich
Village Follies*. Since I was quite broke at the time and the terms of the offer were
excellent, I could not afford to refuse, although this meant disappointing Diaghilev.
When I explained the situation to him, he was very understanding; in fact, he
said that he would have done exactly the same in my position. But I have always
regretted *The Sleeping Beauty*. In the end, he staged an abridged version of the
ballet, partly with old Benois costumes from Fokine's *Le Pavillon d'Armide*, and
partly with new ones by Gontcharova.

I hardly ever went to the gaming rooms of the Monte Carlo Casino, as I found
gambling boring and seldom won. On the rare occasions when I did go, I would
carry very little money. I just wanted to lose what I had as quickly as possible so
that I could leave with a clear conscience. But it was entertaining to watch the
other gamblers.

Inveterate gamblers are a strange breed. One's best friends become unrecogniz-
able under the hypnotic spell of the game. The change is, alas, rarely for the better.

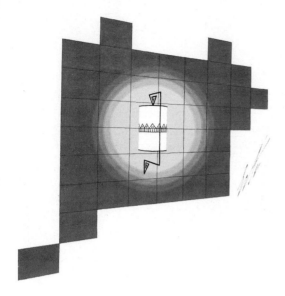

3   Lamp, 1918

4   Umbrella cover, 1922

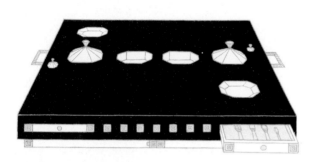

5a   Table, 1926

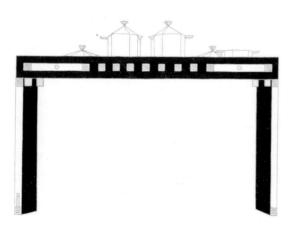

5b   Table, 1926

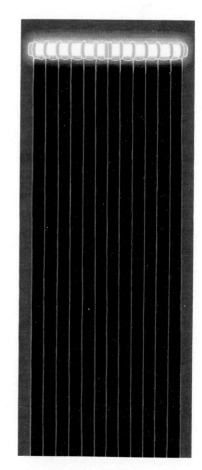

6   Curtain rail, 1926

7 ' Les Esclaves de Salome '. Costume, 1926

They seemed stunned rather than inspired, and certainly bereft of the most elementary common sense. There appeared to be two distinct types: born gamblers and system players. Most of the system players in Monte Carlo were old ladies. Every morning they would wait outside for the Casino doors to open so that they could be sure of a seat at a table. They would play all day and most of the evening. By the time they left, they had usually made a small profit, probably enough to cover their modest day-to-day needs. Most of the systems were based on two factors: runs, and the way the numbers seem to even out at the end of the day. Oddly enough, by closing time all the numbers will have come up roughly the same number of times.

I well remember Madame Euphrussy, a member of the Rothschild family. She would scatter her chips all over the table. Then, while the wheel was turning, she would remove a small chip from a low-paying number like ' Red ' or ' Evens ' as if she did not want to waste it. But she never won, for she had more chips on the table than any win could possibly pay off.

The Grand Duchess Anastasia of Russia was a very special type of gambler. She had ' her ' croupier – a handsome, well-bred man of about thirty – and only played when he was officiating. She was extremely tall and thin and her clothes were slightly old-fashioned. I remember a dinner given in her honour at the Café de Paris in Monte Carlo, to which I was invited. The *maître d'hôtel* went through the ritual of quietly identifying the various wines as he filled each guest's glass, but when he poured the Grand Duchess's champagne, he announced in a loud, clear voice: ' Imperial Brut! '

The old ladies of the Casino were an eccentric-looking lot. There was a Danish poetess who always wore black. Her enormous hat was garnished with a long veil of black lace which trailed on the ground for nearly five feet. She was in mourning for humanity which, she said, was morally dead.

Another Casino *habituée* was the celebrated courtesan and Spanish dancer, La Belle Otero. According to legend, she had celebrated her thirtieth birthday at the Café de Paris with an intimate little supper party given for her by a group of admirers. This included King Leopold II of Belgium, Prince Nicolas I of Montenegro, Prince Albert of Monaco, Grand Duke Nikolai Nikolaevitch of Russia and Albert Edward, Prince of Wales, soon to be crowned Edward VII of Great Britain.

La Belle Otero gambled compulsively – and non-systematically – for years. It was estimated that she had lost twenty million dollars at Monte Carlo alone. Every time I saw her at the Casino she was wearing a fortune in jewels. Individually they might have been beautiful, but Otero piled them on with such abandon that the final impact was utterly tasteless – in keeping with the vulgarity of her manners. I once saw her whistle through her fingers like a ruffian to attract the attention of a friend who had just entered the Casino.

La Belle Otero was in her ninety-seventh year when she died in 1965. Death came while she was cooking a rabbit stew in her modest, furnished room in a third-rate Nice hotel. Among her meagre possessions was a packet of Czarist bonds with a pre-Revolutionary value of around a million dollars, the gift of a Russian nobleman. Otero had not set foot in the Monte Carlo Casino since the late 1920s, but she was a gambler to the end.

The day the World War I armistice was signed, an English lady appeared in the Casino wearing a huge hat studded with long hat-pins flying the flags of all the Allied Nations. The same day another woman topped her hat with a large red, white and blue cock. The following day there were most spectacular fireworks.

I have never seen more beautiful displays of fireworks than those put on in Monte Carlo. Every year, on the birthday of Prince Louis of Monaco, there was a magnificent extravaganza. But the most brilliant of all was given on the occasion of the wedding of Princess Charlotte of Monaco (mother of the present Prince Rainier) to the Prince of Polignac. Most of the crowned heads of Europe were there in full panoply. It was the most dazzling wedding I have ever attended.

I am always surprised that fireworks, which I adore, change so little from one decade to another. Every year, on 14 July, I watch about twenty different displays from my apartment in Boulogne-sur-Seine, where I have lived since 1935. My apartment has windows on two sides overlooking the south-east suburbs, the Bois de Boulogne and Paris. The fireworks are much the same as they were when I moved in. (Apropos of fireworks, I am reminded of the comment someone I very much liked made after making love: ' What a shame – it was as short as the finale of a good firework display '!)

Immediately after the armistice, it became the fashion to dance during one's meal. It was a strange custom. Between each course one would dance either the one-step, the foxtrot, the tango, the pasodoble or the shimmy. Sometimes one even let one's dinner get cold. Professional dancing partners held sway – the same kind who had appeared at the ' thé-dansants ' before the war. Some of these young men made extremely successful marriages with very rich ladies whom they partnered on the dance-floor.

Once there was a series of performances of *Parsifal* at the Monte Carlo Opera House. Since it is a very long opera, there was a lengthy interval to allow the audience time to dine. During dinner, which was served at the Café de Paris, people were dancing the foxtrot and the tango between courses. Afterwards they went calmly back to the theatre to listen again to Wagner.

I do not think I have ever seen so many outrageous characters as I saw at Monte Carlo and all along the Côte d'Azur at that time. It was like a zoo. I remember an old Russian lady of the pre-Revolution aristocracy, Madame Bachkirtseff, who was the mother of Marie Bachkirtseff, the well-known artist. Madame Bachkirtseff had a splendid villa on the Promenade des Anglais in Nice, where she lived with her sister. Those two women hardly ever washed. Once or twice a week, they dipped a bit of cotton wool in eau-de-cologne and wiped it over their faces. They dressed in old clothes that were faded and completely shapeless. One day, near the end of World War I, Madame Bachkirtseff was sitting on a bench on the Promenade des Anglais, right in front of her own garden. There were a lot of American soldiers in town at the time. One of them took her for an old beggar-woman and tried to press a few coins into her hand. She rose, full of indignation and, pointing to her splendid house, cried, ' That, sir, is my house.'

Nicolas and I often used to visit one of his distant aunts, Princess Pauline Ouroussoff, another remarkable character. She was the wife of the Russian ex-ambassador in Paris, Prince Leon Ouroussoff. Although she had not lived with him for years, she had never agreed to a divorce. He also lived in Monte Carlo, with his friend, Madame de R., whom he had long wanted to marry and whom his wife disparagingly called ' My husband's girl '. We also saw him from time to time, but not often, since neither he nor Madame R. was particularly entertaining.

On the other hand, Princess Pauline, although she was getting on in years (she was about seventy-five) was witty and full of vitality. She was Greek by birth, and had been a great beauty. Her lovely eyes looked strikingly youthful until the end of her life. Once the cold weather set in, she never left her house. She called this ' Doing my tortoise act '. She spent several months indoors, being read to all day long by her housekeeper-companion, or having sessions with her dress-maker. She possessed innumerable dresses which she had altered every season.

During World War I she engaged a new companion – a young Polish refugee. A short time later one of her rings, a superb sapphire, disappeared. She accused the girl of stealing it and lodged an official complaint. But when she saw the Police Commissioner, he informed her that the companion had also made a state-ment about the Princess, accusing her of having asked the girl to ' bed her '. This was the picturesque way the Commissioner described it. The Princess retorted indignantly, ' In the first place, I do not know what that means – and anyway, she is so ugly, it would never enter my mind.'

During this period, members of royal families stayed on the Côte d'Azur, especially at Monte Carlo. King Gustav of Sweden, who was a famous tennis player, came to Cannes every year for the tournaments. He loved to do em-broidery. Each year, at the end of his stay, he would give several of the cushions he had made to the Mayor of Cannes. Unfortunately, they were so ugly that the Mayor hid them away until the King came back the following year.

Every winter the ex-Empress Eugénie, widow of Napoleon III, came to stay at her villa in Cap-Martin. I was presented to Her Royal Highness by one of Nicolas's friends, the Count of Saint-Hilaire. She left me with a feeling of infinite sadness. There was something tragic about that black silhouette. It seemed as though there was in her no hope, no desire; she was living only in the past.

The Count of Saint-Hilaire was engaged at that time to an English woman, a Mrs Mackenzie. She was very tall and thin and one could not say she was pretty, but she had style and, above all, charm. She was the daughter of King Edward

VIII's private secretary and a godchild of Queen Alexandra, who had given her an odd Christian name – Louvima. It was made up of the first letters of the names of the three princesses, Louisa, Victoria and Mary. She had been brought up in the royal family circle. When she was sixteen, her father wanted to give her a practical birthday present so he opened a bank account in her name, with a limited sum of money. Some months later the Bank sent her a letter, asking her to stop writing any more cheques. In reply she telephoned the Bank Manager, saying that she could not understand this request since she still had plenty of cheques left.

One day I was visited by Madame Baldina-Kozloff. She had been a ballerina at the Mariinsky Theatre and had married the dancer, Theodore Kozloff. He lived in Hollywood where he had a large ballet school. He had also made many films. Madame Baldina-Kozloff, who was visiting her sister in Monte Carlo, made me a very interesting offer: Cecil B. de Mille, with whom Kozloff often worked, was planning an epic film on the theme of ' The Prodigal Son ' with Paramount. De Mille wanted me to create the décors and costumes. Naturally, I was delighted. But when William Randolph Hearst heard about the negotiations he promptly offered me a three-year contract with his own film company, Cosmopolitan Productions. I signed this contract for two reasons: I did not wish to break with Hearst; and the financial inducements were irresistible. I was compelled to refuse Cecil B. de Mille's offer, but Nicolas and I remained good friends with Mr and Mrs Kozloff. I designed a poster for his ballet school and, later on, costumes for a film he made with MGM called *Time the Comedian*, in which he played a symbolic personification of Time.

The scene I was working on for the Marion Davies film, *Restless Sex*, was a fancy-dress Arts Ball. People were to be dressed as gods from different countries of the world. There were the Greek gods, Zeus, Hera, Aphrodite, Pallas Athene, Dionysus, Artemis and Apollo; Egyptian gods such as Osiris, Isis and Horus; the Aztec gods Tlalec and Chalchiutlikue; Hindu gods and Chinese gods. Each god was accompanied by his retinue; worshippers laid embroidered carpets at his feet wherever he went. My designs for these costumes were published in the April 1920 number of *Harper's Bazaar*.

The décor, which was gigantic, was in neo-Assyrian style. The production was a great success, but I soon realized that my contract with Cosmopolitan Productions had been made largely to stop me doing *The Prodigal Son* for Cecil B. de Mille. Obviously, Mr Hearst did not wish my name to be associated with any company that he did not control. So, although I drew a good monthly salary during the three years of my contract, *Restless Sex* was the only film on which I worked.

In that time I never saw Marion Davies. I met her only very much later, in 1925, when I went to America to work at Metro-Goldwyn-Mayer and was the guest of honour at a dinner she gave in her New York house on Riverside Drive. She was very beautiful and sumptuously gowned. I saw her again a few months later at a fancy-dress party given at Hearst's fantastic ranch in San Simeon, in California.

Several years before, I had met Mrs William Randolph Hearst in Paris. She invited me to lunch at the Hotel Crillon, where she was staying, and asked me to design an evening dress and coat for her. This I did with pleasure. I sent the drawings to her in a box lined with quilted satin, and placed them on a layer of freshly picked orange roses. She was thrilled with the designs as well as with their presentation.

In 1920 I received a letter from a Polish singer named Ganna Walska, announcing that she would soon be coming to Europe from New York to make the acquaintance of ' the most imaginative man in the world '. She asked me to design her costumes for Massenet's *Thaïs* and Giordano's *Fedora*, which she was preparing to sing with the Chicago Opera Company. Her photograph was enclosed: she was really very beautiful. Nicolas remembered having seen her some years before in a ' Café-chantant ' in Russia, where she was singing popular songs.

I prepared the designs and sent them off. Two weeks later I received a letter and a cheque. Walska said she was delighted with the designs and would be coming to see me in Monte Carlo. Soon after that, and without any further notice, she turned up. Her face with its flashing, panther-like, green eyes was even more beautiful than her photograph. Unfortunately, she was beginning to put on weight. Shortly after she arrived at my villa she said, ' I know you were not expecting me today. How is it then that you are so well-dressed, with your house in beautiful order, as if you were giving a party? ' I did not appreciate the significance of the question until later when I got to know her well. If she was not expecting visitors, she would spend the day in a grubby old bath-robe, although she always wore her famous pearls.

At that first meeting she asked me to design costumes for all the roles she was planning to sing at the Chicago Opera. Her repertoire was staggering: *Thaïs, Fedora, Manon, Rigoletto, I Pagliacci, Tosca, Madame Butterfly, Faust, Martha, Zaza, Aphrodite, Monna Vanna, Louise* and *La Bohème.* This elaborate wardrobe was later made up by Redfern. My drawings subsequently covered the walls of a large room in her Paris house. Occasionally, after a luncheon or dinner party, she would model the costumes for her guests, but she very rarely performed the parts for which they were designed.

When I first met Walska she was still married to Alexander Smith Cochran, heir to the Smith Carpet Mills in Yonkers, N.Y. He had been known as the ' richest bachelor in America '. They had a splendid house in Paris on the rue de Lubeck. Cochran had originally bought it from James Gordon Bennett, celebrated *bon vivant* and publisher of the *Paris Herald.* But the marriage had quickly foundered in stormy domestic-operatic seas and Walska was barred from the premises. The

Paris property later figured in prolonged litigation in which Walska was represented by the famous American attorney, Dudley Field Malone. Walska ultimately
recovered the house but not as part of her divorce settlement. Cochran eventually
sold it to his old friend and fellow millionaire, Harold (International Harvester)
McCormack of Chicago, who later gave it to Walska.

While the honeymoon was still on, however, Cochran had used all the influence
at his command, which was considerable, to manoeuvre his bride into the principal role of *Zaza* with the Chicago Opera Company. At the first rehearsal
Walska's voice – mediocre at best – was so paralyzed with stage fright that her
co-star, Tito Ruffo, stalked off the stage in a temper and Gino Marinuzzi, the
conductor, dismissed the company for the day. Marinuzzi's verdict on Walska's
future with the Chicago Opera Company was quickly delivered to the management. Several days later the Cochrans sailed back to France wrapped in a veil of
silence. But Walska, never one to give up easily when she really wanted something, now devised a master-plan: she would first divorce Cochran; then she
would get McCormack, one of the principal sponsors of the Chicago Opera
Company, to divorce his wife and marry her. Once she was McCormack's wife
she could have her way with the Chicago Opera.*

On one of my later visits to Paris I had supper one evening with Prince Felix
Youssoupoff. An elated Ganna Walska was seated next to me. She told me that
her dearest wish had come true. McCormack's divorce had just come through and
he had asked her to marry him. Meanwhile, she had herself achieved a divorce.
Cochran's life with Walska had become such a misery that he had made her the
beneficiary of a sizeable trust fund in order to be rid of her. Walska also announced
that she would soon sing the role of Gilda in *Rigoletto* at the Paris Opéra, in my
costumes. It was to be a one-night charity gala before a smart, wealthy audience.
I promised to come up from Monte Carlo for the occasion.

I kept my promise. Walska asked me to have supper with her after the performance, provided it was a success. If on the other hand it was a failure, she
would be so upset that she would not want to see anyone. The first act went
off splendidly, with the famous Russian tenor Smirnoff in excellent voice. As soon
as Walska appeared in the second act things began to go wrong. When the
moment came for her to begin her famous aria, ' Caro Nome ', standing at the
top of a staircase with a lighted candle in her hand, her mouth opened wide but
no sound came out. The orchestra went on playing but Walska, completely panic-

---

* The Chicago fiasco reminds me of another incident in Walska's stormy theatrical
career. When she first arrived in New York from Europe, Lee Shubert, the American
producer, dazzled by her beauty and sex appeal, had cast her in the operetta, *Mlle
Nitouche*. By the time the show was in rehearsal Walska was firmly ensconced as his
mistress. When the conductor once complained to Shubert that Walska was not
following the music, Shubert replied: ' Never mind the music. You follow her.'

stricken, started to run from one side of the stage to the other, hitching up the enormous skirts of her white dress as she ran. Finally she managed to produce a sound but it was more like the screech a cat makes when you tread on its tail than a human voice. The audience did not boo or whistle – it simply burst into uncontrolled laughter. It was obvious that I would not be going out to supper.

I was astonished when Walska called the next day to ask why I had not shown up after the performance. I explained that I had only gone along with her wishes, which put her in a furious temper. 'Ah, so you thought it was a failure?' she shouted. 'Of course you must have noticed how the audience was against me. It was all organized by Prince Youssoupoff. He's furious because I wouldn't buy his wife's black pearl necklace. He paid people to laugh as soon as I started to sing.'

After that she was very cool towards me. But not for long. As a wedding present McCormack had given her the Théâtre des Champs-Elysées, where she could sing whatever she liked. I suspect he did it to avoid any further complications between Walska and the Chicago Opera Company. He was dazzled by her beauty but not by her voice.

She now needed new costumes for all the new roles she planned to sing at the Théâtre des Champs-Elysées. These included Mélisande in *Pelléas et Mélisande*, which she performed before an invited audience only, the Countess in *The Marriage of Figaro* and Donna Elvira in *Don Giovanni*. She also sang the soprano solo in Beethoven's Ninth Symphony. For this concert I designed a special costume which symbolized the theme of the symphony.

On stage, Walska never knew what to do with her hands. Since I was well aware of this, I always gave her small objects to hold. As part of one of her costumes for Donna Elvira, I had designed an accessory that ladies used to wear on their wrists during the Renaissance – a mink bracelet. The mink's head was made of jewels (the jewels warded off fleas that were attracted by the fur). On the opening night of *Don Giovanni*, during one of the most important scenes which was played downstage, she compulsively plucked the fur to bits.

When she became the owner of the Théâtre des Champs-Elysées, however, she began to study under the famous conductor Walter Staram and her singing improved somewhat. It was he, in fact, who became the power behind the Théâtre des Champs-Elysées. He managed the theatre, and eventually went into partnership with Walska. His influence over her was amazing: she who had ruled her husbands with a rod of iron blindly carried out his smallest whim.

Ganna Walska's jewels became more and more fabulous after she married McCormack. He once gave her a clock made of diamonds from Cartier. The most fantastic emeralds I ever saw in my life were in her *parure*, which was also made by Cartier. There was a diadem-comb, a pair of ear-rings and a long necklace, made entirely of rectangular-cut or tube-shaped diamonds, embellished with great carved emeralds. She wore this *parure* with a simply cut black velvet dress that I had designed especially to set it off; the effect was dramatic and imposing. She had two more extremely beautiful sets of jewels; one of rubies, the other of diamonds. Her pearls, too, were wonderful. Once, when she was about to sail for America, she insisted that I have lunch with her because she wished to discuss her future plans. People were always streaming in and out of her house, with tradesmen waiting to be paid and others to take orders. Walska apologized for the fact that lunch would be half an hour late and asked me to wait in the drawing-room with a glass of port. She then handed me three small bundles tied up with old table-napkins and asked me to guard them carefully. When lunch was finally ready, she came back for the bundles and explained that one contained the emerald *parure*, the other the ruby *parure* and the third the diamond *parure*!

She had bought many splendid gems from Russian refugees who had managed to bring them out of Russia at the time of the Revolution. Since she was extremely mean with her money, she always concealed her identity in these negotiations. Posing as a poor Polish refugee she would pretend to be representing (for a tiny commission) some rich patron. On these occasions she would dress for the part. Instead of driving up in her enormous Rolls Royce, she went on foot. The car had a collapsible hood which was always down, winter and summer, because Walska preferred extremes in everything – freezing cold wind in winter, and burning sun in summer. In view of her buying tactics, there was naturally no question of her ultimately acquiring the famous necklace of black pearls which belonged to Princess Irene of Russia, wife of Prince Felix Youssoupoff.

Over the years, Walska's artistic aspirations gradually subsided and our paths crossed less frequently. Once so newsworthy, she finally dropped out of the headlines and retired to Santa Barbara, California, where she lives in seclusion. In 1971, however, she cropped up again in an unobtrusive news story when some of her jewels were auctioned at the Parke Bernet Gallery in New York for $916,185. As for all the costumes I designed for her, they are now in the Los Angeles County Museum.

I first met the Youssoupoffs around 1921 at Ganna Walska's house in Paris. What a handsome couple they were! The Prince had been regarded as one of the best-looking men in Russia. Even in old age his finely structured face, though wrinkled, was still striking. He had a wry sense of humour. In reminiscing about his life in Russia, he once said to me, ' I married my wife out of snobbery. My wife married me for money ' – a not-so-subtle reminder of the fact that the Youssoupoffs had once been the richest family in Russia, much richer than his wife's family, the Romanoffs. Princess Irene used to wear turbans and ear-rings: one ear-ring was a large pink pearl and the other a black pearl of matching proportions.

After the Prince had master-minded Rasputin's assassination – ' to save the Czar and Russia ' – he was exiled to central Russia where he lived on one of the various family estates. When the Youssoupoffs finally left Russia in April 1919

8 My father

9 My mother

10 Grandmother Eugenia

11 Uncle Nicolas

12 With my parents, 1923

13 My sister Natalia

14 Myself in 1911

15   With Prince Nicolas Ourousoff, Hollywood

16   With Nicolas, Monte Carlo

17   At the Colonial Exhibition, Paris, 1931

18   In costume, Monte Carlo, 1919

19   In costume, Monte Carlo, 1919

20   In costume, Paris, c.1924

21 Costume from *Dance Madness*, 1925

22 Costume from ' The Seas ', 1922

23 Carmel Myers in *Ben Hur*, 1925

24 Aileen Pringle in *The Mystic*, 1925

aboard the British dreadnought *Marlborough*, they were able to bring out many of their valuable possessions – jewels, paintings, furniture and assorted *objets d'art*. Proceeds from the sale of these treasures supported them for years, if not in the opulent style to which they were accustomed, at least in comparative, non-imperial luxury. In addition to an estate in Corsica, they had a house with a large garden near the Parc des Princes in Boulogne-sur-Seine, not far from my apartment building. The Prince had added a wing which contained a charming little theatre. Its walls were decorated with frescoes by Yakevleff, the great Russian painter. It was pulled down a few years ago to make way for a block of flats. I was heart-broken when I saw the ground littered with those beautiful frescoes. How can such vandalism be permitted?

The Paris house was always full of friends and there were many fascinating parties. After an exquisite meal guests were often served a variety of luscious fruits from the Youssoupoffs' Corsican estate.

One of the many guest rooms in the house was permanently occupied by Youssoupoff's cousin, Volodia Lazareff. Lazareff's sister and my cousin Alia had gone to college together and had been good friends. Volodia, who was in the Youssoupoffs' St Petersburg palace the night Rasputin was murdered, gave me a dramatic account of this fateful event: he told how Rasputin was still alive more than two hours after he had eaten several poisoned cakes – he loved sweets – and drunk some wine well laced with cyanide: how, after having been shot, he staggered up a flight of stairs and into the courtyard where he was shot again: how the body, which had been wrapped in a piece of heavy linen, was thrown into the Neva River that night: how, when he was later dredged out of the river, Rasputin was found to have died neither from poison nor from bullet shots but from drowning.

Volodia was also the source of an unrecorded footnote to Rasputin's assassination. Since Rasputin's sexual prowess with the ladies of the Imperial Court was legendary, Youssoupoff was naturally curious about his physical proportions. When he lifted the cover which had been thrown over the body he said, with some degree of disenchantment, ' I thought it would be much bigger than that '.

I came across Volodia Lazareff several years later in Hollywood where he was trying to build a career in the movies. Despite his good looks and theatrical flair, he never managed to progress beyond bit parts, mostly in crowd scenes.

Unlike Lazareff, Youssoupoff would never talk about the Rasputin affair. He wrote a book about it only when he needed money. Having lived and entertained on a lavish scale, year after year, he finally exhausted all his resources and was forced to sell his house. During their early years in Paris, Youssoupoff and his wife had opened a couture and perfume house. It was called ' Irfé ', a word made up of the first two letters of their names, Irene and Félix, after the manner of ' Erté '. Since they had no experience of running such a business – or, for that matter, any business – they soon failed and lost their investment. Later, after he won his prolonged suit against Metro-Goldwyn-Mayer, involving its film based on the Rasputin murder, the Prince bought a flat in the glass structure designed by Le Corbusier and built over the Jean Bouin Stadium.

Meanwhile, my career with the Hearst magazine *Harper's Bazaar* flourished. I was on the very best terms with the editorial staff. My memories of the Editor, Henry Blackman Sell, are particularly happy. Working with him was a constant pleasure. (Apart from work, we had another bond in common – our love of cats.) During the 1920s he was responsible for the artistry and sophistication which made the magazine famous. Celebrated writers and glamorous personalities in the society world wrote articles, short stories and serials.

Sell put me in touch with the magazine *International Cosmopolitan,* for which I did many illustrations, especially for the stories of John Erskine and Lord Dunsany. He also introduced me to the *Ladies' Home Journal,* which published many of my dress designs. He was an extraordinary man, extremely good-looking with his prematurely grey hair. When I last saw him in New York he was still remarkably youthful and active. He was then editing *Town and Country Magazine.* Unfortunately I have seen him rarely in recent years.

Besides my work for *Harper's Bazaar,* I began taking on more and more theatrical commissions, which came to me through Max Weldy. In addition to featured scenes for each new production of the Folies Bergère and shows at the Alcazar in Marseilles, I designed for many shows in other countries.

In 1922 George White, on a visit to Paris, saw my setting for ' The Seas ' at the Théâtre des Ambassadeurs. This was his introduction to my ' Costume Collectif ' (Group Costume) which I had invented a few years before. In this concept, extensions of the costume worn by the main character linked a whole group of secondary characters. I had developed the idea for several ensembles in Madame Rasimi's shows, as well as in ' Rivers ' and ' The Hindu Tale ' at the Folies Bergère. Many colleagues imitated the idea of the Group Costume. This kind of plagiarism has often occurred during my career as a designer, but I have never sued my plagiarists, since I have always pitied them for their lack of imagination. Besides, all the legal hair-splitting would consume too much time and energy. So, I simply look the other way – to my inner resources of creative inspiration and my drawing board. George White was so excited by the décor and costumes for ' The Seas ' that he bought it at once for his current show, George White's *Scandals* and also asked me to design the next edition. Thus began a long association.

In New York, from 1922 to 1929, my costumes and sets were featured in seven productions of George White's *Scandals,* as well as two productions of Irving Berlin's *Music Box Review;* also at the *Greenwich Village Follies* and the *Ziegfeld Follies.* However, since all the work was done under my supervision in Weldy's Paris workshop (specially built for the *Scandals* décors) at 18 rue Siulnier, I did not attend the openings of any of these.

For 'Gold', one of my sets for the *Ziegfeld Follies*, they used six and a half miles of gold-lamé made in Lyons. The scene took place against a background of show girls wearing enormous coats and lined up on a flight of stairs. 'Gold' was later reproduced at the Folies Bergère in Paris. Weldy had worked out a splendid scheme by which all the sets I created for Paris or New York were subsequently reproduced and sold to other countries. I gave the copyright to only one city at a time. Sometimes there were as many as ten reproductions of one set. They appeared on stages all over the world: London, Berlin, Buenos Aires, Madrid, Barcelona, Brussels, Rio de Janeiro, Amsterdam and others.

Since I was now doing so much theatrical work in Paris, I decided with great reluctance that I would have to leave Monte Carlo. The eight years I had spent there would have been the happiest of my life had they not been overshadowed by a nagging worry – the fate of my parents.

Then some friends told me about a wonderful organization, the American Relief Administration, which had been responsible for saving the lives of many people. Through it I discovered that my parents and sister were living in a small town named Valiky Oustioug in the north of Russia. Although they were having a very hard time, my father managed to support them by teaching mathematics at the local school. I also learned that when the Revolution broke out, my father had been on duty at Cronstadt. He had managed to leave, with my mother, for Vologoda, where all the allied ambassadors had been given accommodation. My sister joined them there. It was not until many years later that I heard from my sister the harrowing details of his escape from Cronstadt. On two different occasions he had been singled out for execution and each time he had been saved by his devoted students. They formed a human wall before him and gave the firing squad the ultimatum: 'You'll have to shoot all of us to get to him.'

Thanks to the American Relief Administration, I was now able to correspond with my parents. Then some friends at the Geneva Red Cross helped me to obtain a medical certificate stating that my mother must come to a French spa for her health. Since she was too delicate to travel alone, my father would have to accompany her. Fortunately there were no complications at the border. Thus, in 1923 I was overjoyed to be reunited with my parents at last. They had lost everything, but in the false bottom of her trunk, my mother had managed to hide the last relics of their vanished world – our beautiful sixteenth-century family icon, a few pieces of jewellery, my father's decorations and an exquisite Fabergé cigarette case. This had been presented to my father as a parting souvenir by the members of His Majesty's Cabinet when he left to return to the navy. The case was covered with the engraved signatures of all his colleagues. Since my father arrived in France around the time of my birthday, he gave it to me as a gift, and I carry it with me to this day.

Years later, one lovely summer evening, I dined with some friends at the

Pavillon d'Armenonville in the Bois de Boulogne. After dinner we strolled over to the Pavillon Dauphine for a drink. My friends then drove me home. As I started to undress I discovered that the case was gone. I immediately telephoned my friends and the two restaurants, but none of them had found it. After a sleepless night, I telephoned the restaurants again, since I had spoken only to the night porter the previous evening. I also checked the Lost Property Office. My hopes of ever seeing the case again were quickly fading. Later that day, on my way to an important business appointment, I impulsively stopped the cab, telephoned from a café to say that I would be slightly delayed and went back to the Pavillon Dauphine. The moment I entered the restaurant, a waiter came up and handed me the case. He had found it on the floor under our table but had decided to look after it himself rather than leave it with the night porter. It was a happy moment for me – and typical of many small personal miracles I have experienced throughout my life.

After leaving Monte Carlo I managed to find a charming, well-designed country house with a fine garden in Sèvres, near Paris. I did not give up my place in Monte Carlo, hoping that I could use it from time to time. Since my parents preferred to live in a mild climate, far from the noise and bustle of Paris, I settled them comfortably in the Villa Excelsior.

My sister, who was still in Russia, managed to leave some months later. By arranging a marriage in name only, she was able to obtain a Greek passport. She then went to Scandinavia and later to Germany. In Germany her legitimate husband, who had escaped from Russia shortly before, joined her. So, at long last, the curtain finally came down on that phase in the life of my immediate family.

I soon discovered that my parents were reluctant to talk about their last years in Russia. Whenever I questioned them, they put me off, saying ' The nightmare is over. We want to forget all about it and enjoy a happy life at last.' But through my sister and my parents' occasional references, I was able to piece together the bare facts of what had happened to some of our other relatives.

For a while my mother had corresponded with her sister, Aunt Liocha, the wife of Uncle Petia, a professor at St Petersburg University. Petia was, I gather, considered left-wing by his royalist in-laws. I myself could recall one family gathering during the anxious days of 1905 when my father had all of us sleeping in our outdoor clothes, ready to flee in case of emergency. My father and Petia got into a political discussion which became so heated that my mother ordered me from the room. As the Revolution intensified, Aunt Liocha's letters to my mother became more and more sporadic. The final one ended with these ominous words, ' Do not write any more. It is harmful for us.' That was the last we ever heard of them.

My mother's brother, Uncle Nicolas, who became the Commander of the Peter and Paul Fortress, had his share of tragedy even before the Revolution. It started with his son, Youra. When I was living at Cronstadt, I often spent the night at

Uncle Nicolas's home in St Petersburg after going to the theatre. Once, when I was already asleep, there was a knock on my door. Youra entered the room and delivered a long, incoherent monologue. Luckily for me he left as suddenly as he had appeared, but it was an upsetting experience. In the morning I reported the incident to Uncle Nicolas and urged him to arrange for Youra to have some medical help. The following day, during dinner, Youra attacked his mother with a knife. His father immediately committed him to a hospital for the insane.

Uncle Nicolas also had a daughter, cousin Lucia. Although Lucia had married a man of whom her parents disapproved, they loved Lucia's child – a lovely little girl. But this too ended unhappily and Lucia went off with another man. The marriage was terminated by a divorce. Finally, Uncle Nicolas's wife, Aunt Ellen, was stricken with cancer and died after much suffering. By the time the Revolution broke out, my Uncle's spirit was already broken. In his despair he drowned himself in the River Neva.

I soon came to indulge my parents' desire to turn their backs on those terrible years. For now, the important thing was that they enjoyed living in Monte Carlo, where they remained for several years. The fact that I was finally in a position to give them this second chance of a happy life was a source of deep and lasting satisfaction to me.

The Twenties

I was soon settled in Sèvres. Fortunately, the house did not require any major alterations. On the ground floor I had four large rooms – drawing-room, dining-room, studio and smoking-room, which I used as a picture gallery for my drawings.

Two walls of the smoking-room were hung with black curtains, ornamented with grey cords and tassels. The two facing walls had pale grey curtains with black cords and tassels. When a tassel was pulled the curtains parted, revealing a whole wall covered with my framed drawings. I have always masked my drawings with curtains, because I do not wish to be influenced by previous designs when I am working. The carpet consisted of four triangles – two black triangles which continued the colour of the black walls, and two pale grey in front of the pale grey walls. The ceiling was formed by a black net; alabaster wall-lamps shed a soft light. The room was furnished solely with grey and black cushions, and low tables. The rest of the house contained antique furniture, especially Directoire and Empire pieces.

Another room on the second floor was also used as a gallery. Here the walls were covered with panels hung with framed drawings; the panels opened like cupboard doors. The exteriors of the panels were decorated with black and white cubist patterns. To get to my studio, one went through the smoking-room and down a few steps. The studio was very large, with a glass roof. I had also designed a leaded window for it, using only opaque white glass cut in various shapes. My studio walls were covered with curtains horizontally striped in shades of white deepening to grey. When the curtains were drawn apart, they uncovered more paintings. The carpet was the same shade of grey as the curtains.

The door at the end of the studio opened directly on to the garden, whose path was bordered with white lilies. It was a gorgeous sight in May, when the lilies were in full flower.

My working clothes were usually chosen to match the colour-scheme of my studio. They were thus mainly grey and white, or black and white. My studios and working overalls have always been neutral in colour: this is a great help in appreciating the real values of the colours I use in my paintings. The walls and ceiling of my present studio are entirely covered in straw, which gives a neutral yet warm effect. Straw is wonderfully receptive to sunlight. In this neutral atmosphere I like to have a few touches of red here and there – a vase of flowers, or a few candles – since I find red a stimulating colour.

The drawing-room and dining-room walls at Sèvres were covered with dark bronze-lamé. A see-through mirror separated the two rooms; when the lights were extinguished in the dining-room, the wall of the drawing-room appeared to be one enormous mirror.

My first floor bedroom was done in violet and gold, Nicolas's bedroom in various shades of blue. There were two bathrooms, and a room for my daily exercises. The second floor contained a library, the picture gallery I mentioned earlier, and two guest-rooms.

It was in this house, in 1923, that I first met George White. He had already commissioned my work the previous year and now came over to see me in connection with a new edition of his *Scandals*. He arrived for dinner with Max Weldy at about nine and, after we had spent the rest of the night discussing the various scenes, they left around seven in the morning. This went on for three successive nights. By the end of the third session the entire show had been blocked out. White then sailed back to New York and I went to work filling in the picture. One of the great pleasures of working with him was that once he had projected a rough outline of his basic idea, he would often say, ' Elaborate on this as much as you like.'

He was a raffish, dynamic man, then in his early thirties and extremely handsome, with dark hair and vivacious brown eyes. He still looked like a dancer, though he performed less frequently as his career as a producer flourished. He was always elegantly dressed, but invariably wore dark blue double-breasted suits, black ties and black shoes. I never knew the reason for this. White, Weldy and I were about the same age, height and weight. We were quite an act.

White was an incorrigible gambler. He once boasted of having bet $40,000 on a horse that was left at the post. His passion for horses and racing was full-blown before he reached his teens: he was only eleven years old when he ran away from home and became a race-track exercise boy. But that form of jockeying must have been too restrictive for someone of White's talents. Besides, he had already tasted the heady excitements of show business. As a young boy he had danced for small change in the saloons and music-halls of New York's Bowery. By the time he was fourteen, he was a song and dance man in burlesque. He then worked in vaudeville as a hoofer (a soft shoe and tap dancer) and eventually graduated to the *Ziegfeld Follies* as a featured dancer. With his showman's flair and gambler's drive, it was inevitable that he would wind up as a Broadway producer. White's shows reached their pinnacle of success during the 1920s. There were times when he earned as much as $20,000 a week.

Those years were also very good for me. My costumes and décors for the *Scandals* were received enthusiastically by the press as well as by audiences.

My design for the 'Congo' curtain featured in the *Scandals* of 1924 is now in the Museum of Modern Art in New York. The décor and costume drawings for 'Mah Jong' in the same production are in New York's Metropolitan Museum of Art along with a large collection of other *Scandals* décors and costume designs.

As well as seven editions of *Scandals*, I did the costumes and décors for *Manhattan Mary*, which White produced in 1927 at the Majestic Theatre. This was his first venture into musical comedy and it, too, was a hit despite endless script troubles during rehearsals. Song and lyrics were written by the highly successful team of De Sylva, Brown and Henderson; comedians Ed Wynn and Lou Holtz and *ingénue* Ona Munson headed the cast.

The last time White and I worked together was in 1939 when he staged a show for the Universal Exhibition in San Francisco. As he moved into the next few decades, his misfortunes mounted. He lost vast sums through a Las Vegas night-club fire on the opening night of a new show. An automobile accident in which a newly-married couple was killed sent him to jail on a hit-and-run conviction. He went into bankruptcy: his liabilities amounted to $500,000, his assets were $500 and a Rolls Royce. Yet White survived into the late 1960s. He was seventy-eight when he died in Hollywood, where he had finally settled. In an interview during his lean years White said, 'I've had money. More than once I've had a million dollars. I believe money is there to be spent. I don't believe you can take it with you.'

He didn't.

I had many guests at Sèvres, since I preferred entertaining at home to visiting other people's houses. Moreover I had an excellent Russian cook. I always invited small groups of people, perhaps six or ten guests; in this way a pleasant atmosphere was created between people who had things in common. Nicolas was an excellent social organizer. He would often bring in some *tziganes* (gypsies) to play and sing during the meal. Or he would vary the evening's background music with three or four balalaika musicians. I, on the other hand, would sometimes intrigue our guests by modelling my collection of beautiful old Chinese robes. I once wore five of them, one on top of the other, removing one with each course.

I recall one dinner-party at which Francesca Bertini, the famous Italian star of silent films, was a guest with her husband, M. Cartier. I considered her the most beautiful cinema star of her time. The other guests were the well-known

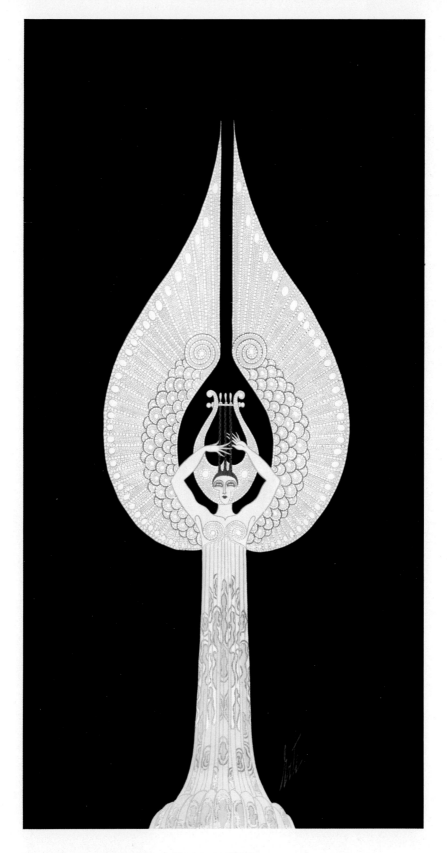

25 'Blue Angel Musician'. Costume, 1926

26   Coat, 1924

27   Dress, 1924

writer Claude Farrère, and his wife, Henriette Rogers, *sociétaire** at the Comédie française. I often saw the Farrères, who were charming people. Claude Farrère's appearance was extraordinarily powerful – he gave the impression of almost animal-like physical strength. He once told me that he owed his energy to the use of opium, to which he had become addicted during many visits to the Far East, while he was in the Navy. He tried to persuade me to take it up, but I firmly refused. I have never used drugs. I am so easily transported into a dream world that I have never needed them to expand or intensify my consciousness. Sometimes when I am working and the telephone suddenly rings, it takes me several moments to realize who and where I am.

I often gave evening parties for young people, especially those connected with the theatre; among them was Jean Weber, who was one of the youngest *sociétaires* of the Comédie française. I got to know him when he was studying at the Conservatoire. While he was still a student he was already acting Cherubino in *The Marriage of Figaro* at the Comédie française. He played a small part in Jean Cocteau's *Romeo and Juliet*, which was produced by Count Etienne de Beaumont during a season Weber had organized at the Trianon Lyrique. He was one of the first male actors to play parts that had formerly been given to women dressed as men, such as Cherubino or the Duke of Reichstadt in Rostand's *L'Aiglon*. His performance in this role was the greatest of his career. He was known as ' L'Aiglon national '.

I met Madame Edmond Rostand (she was a poetess under the name of Rosemonde Gérard) and her son Maurice Rostand in about 1924. Maurice Rostand asked me to design costumes for his next play, *Le Secret du Sphinx*, which was to be produced at the Théâtre Sarah Bernhardt. The main role was to be played by a very beautiful actress, Gilda Darthy. I agreed with pleasure.

I sometimes went to theatrical and literary parties given by Madame Rostand and Maurice in their apartment at La Muette. They were a remarkable pair. One was never seen without the other; we called them ' The Inseparables '. No dress-rehearsal in Paris ever took place without both of them in the audience. (When Madame Rostand died, Maurice became a recluse.) They were delighted when, later on, the Isola brothers, who directed the Théâtre Sarah Bernhardt among many other Parisian theatres, asked me to do the décors and costumes for a new production of Edmond Rostand's play, *La Princesse Lointaine*.

I often saw another pair of inseparables, Madame de Sciemkewitch and her son, Alex. Alex was a designer with Doucet. (His beautiful sister, who, unfortunately, died very young, had been the first wife of André Maurois.) I dined many times at the Sciemkewitchs' house in his company: he was a delightful person and his conversation was scintillatingly witty.

---

* A *sociétaire* was a senior member of the strictly-ranked company of the Comédie française.

Another frequent dinner guest at the Sciemkewitchs' was Count Boni de Castellane, one of the most elegant personalities of his time. The Count was a Proustian character. His ancestry was impeccably Almanach de Gotha, but the family fortunes had dwindled drastically. In order to restore them he married an American heiress, Miss Anna Gould, the plain but strong-willed daughter of Jay Gould, one of the richest of the American industrial-financial ' Robber Barons '. With her railroad millions, Boni built the famous ' Palais Rose ' which was a copy of the Palais du Trianon on the Avenue Foch. Whenever the Count showed friends around the palace, he would open the door to the bedroom he shared with his wife and say, ' And this is " La Chapelle Expiatoire ".'

Eventually, the combination of Boni's legendary extravagance and his flagrant extra-marital dalliance led Anna to divorce him. She later married Boni's cousin, Duke Hélie de Sagan de Talleyrand Périgord. With money once again in short supply, Boni's friends would sometimes invite him to dine at Maxim's, which he could no longer afford to frequent. On one of these occasions, Hélie appeared. Boni's friends, anxious to avoid an awkward confrontation, called the Duke's arrival to Boni's attention. He merely shrugged and said, ' Ah, yes, the Duke. We both did service in the same corps.'

I often met Boni at parties and occasionally he dined at my house in Sèvres. Despite his straitened circumstances he always conducted himself like a Grand Seigneur. In her memoirs entitled *Misia and the Muses,* Misia Sert pin-pointed the essence of Boni de Castellane's quixotic character when she said, ' He is the only man I know who moved from an income of ten million francs a year to the platform of a bus with perfect indifference.'

When the Palais Rose was torn down in 1972 I felt as if a page of history had disappeared.

There was another famous Palais Rose, the house of the poet Robert de Montesquiou at Le Vesinet. I saw it only after the Marchioness Luisa Cazatti had bought it. She had added wonderful marble floors, bought from her Venetian *palazzo,* and fine, late eighteenth- and early nineteenth-century Italian furniture. Everything was white, black and gold, with numerous tiger and panther skins.

The first time I lunched there with her I was much impressed by these surroundings. After a very pleasant and lively meal, we went into the huge drawing-room for coffee. It was lit by a row of French windows on each side, overlooking the garden. The room was divided into two parts by an enormous sheet of glass. Behind the glass crawled a hundred snakes of all shapes and sizes. I stopped in my tracks, absolutely terrified. I love all animals except snakes and crocodiles. Since it would have been impossible for me to drink even a cup of coffee in that room, I invented an important appointment for which I was already late and almost ran out of the room.

One of the Marchioness's great friends, the opera singer Lucrezia Bori, told me an extraordinary story many years later, when I was designing her costumes for the Metropolitan Opera. According to Bori, after the Marchioness Cazatti had spent all her money on extravagant living, she decided to marry again, setting her sights on one of the richest men in the United States. She wrote to Lucrezia Bori in New York, saying that she was coming over to visit her by the next boat, and asking her to arrange lunch with the man she had chosen as her future husband, for the day after her arrival. Lucrezia Bori cabled back saying this was impossible, for the gentleman in question was already married. The Marchioness cabled by return, 'No matter. He will divorce. I am coming.' Lucrezia Bori arranged the luncheon-party, and La Cazatti arrived. She had barely unpacked, when she exclaimed, 'I've forgotten my snake'. Over Lucrezia Bori's vigorous protests, she telephoned the zoo and asked them to lend her one. After much discussion, the directors of the zoo agreed to do so, for a very high price. The snake was delivered and, next day, when her intended fiancé had arrived for lunch, the Marchioness made a regal entrance with the snake twined round her arm. The gentleman was so terrified that he fled without saying either 'how do you do' or 'goodbye'.

La Cazatti also had a passion for felines. One evening she made her entrance to a fancy-dress ball in Venice in a chariot dragged by a lion. It caused a sensation: the crowd was panic-stricken. This particular obsession had violent repercussions even after her death. When the Palais Rose at Le Vesinet was sold, the new owners had some alterations made. Near the staircase in the hall, where two painters were working, there was a stuffed panther, but nobody realized that it was an automaton. One of the painters was on top of a very high ladder when the other, who was painting the stairs, accidentally pressed a button. The panther began to roar, move its limbs and roll its glowing eyes. The workman on the high ladder was so shocked that he lost his balance and fell to his death.

Around 1924, I joined the Marchioness Cazatti in making an 'entrance' at the last 'Bal du Grand Prix' at the Paris Opéra for which I also designed all the costumes. It was a Spanish Ball. Our 'entrance' depicted La Castiglione, the famous beauty and mistress of Napoleon III, coming to the Ball at the Opéra. No one has ever been able to explain the origin of this weird idea. The Marchioness, of course, was La Castiglione; Don Luis of Spain, son of the Infanta Eulalia, played the part of her son, and Nicolas played Cavour. La Castiglione was preceded by two pages who scattered rose petals in her path. One of the two pages was portrayed by Don Luis's friend, Vasconcelos, a very handsome boy, and the other by myself. The 'entrance' was staged by the Ballet Master from the Opéra, Leo Staats. We rehearsed it for nearly a month.

Whenever we came out after rehearsals, there was always a crowd waiting at the stage door. One day someone, spying the Marchioness, shouted, 'Look – Sarah Bernhardt's come back to life.' La Cazatti did, in fact, look exactly like a ghost. Her face was painted white like a plaster mask, and her eyes were ringed with black which she painted on in Indian ink. She was very tall and thin, and usually dressed either in white or black with immense hats from which fell veils of black lace.

For La Cazatti I designed a huge crinoline of tulle and black lace, spangled with diamonds. Don Luis was dressed as a young boy, in grey and silver brocade; he played with a little monkey who sported a tiny plumed hat. Vasconcelos's costume was all silver: he carried a great silver swan filled with white roses. Mine was in different shades of gold-lamé, set with diamonds. It had an enormous golden cape, lined throughout with freshly picked red roses (a whole car-load had been delivered to me from Les Halles that morning). The cape scented the air deliciously.

Our 'entrance' was planned so that we would come in at the back of the stage (the depth of the stage at the Opéra is vast) and proceed down into the auditorium across the orchestra pit by means of a specially-built staircase. We would then cross the auditorium and walk down the main staircase of the hall. Everything went well at the beginning, but when we started to go down into the auditorium the Marchioness suddenly got stage-fright and refused to go any further. I pleaded that it would be heart-breaking to have put in all those weeks of work for nothing, and went down first, taking Vasconcelos and Don Luis with me. The Marchioness was obliged to follow. Loud applause from the audience drowned the orchestra during our entire act.

The Marchioness was, in fact, a shy person. Her eccentric behaviour was a cover for her shyness. I think this is true of many eccentric people. She was certainly the most extravagantly odd woman I have ever met. I was reminded of her when, a few years ago, I saw the play La Contessa. The main role, brilliantly acted by Elvire Popesco, was inspired by La Cazatti, and by another famous woman, Countess Morosini, the mistress of Kaiser Wilhelm II.

One day I had a telephone call from Baroness de Mayer, wife of the well-known Harper's Bazaar photographer, inviting me to lunch with Cécile Sorel, who wanted to meet me. (It was at a dinner party at the de Mayers' home that I had first met La Cazatti.) Baroness de Mayer was Italian, and rumour had it that she was the illegitimate daughter of King Edward VII. She was both lovely and 'chic'. She once showed me a photograph taken about 1910 or 1911, in which she was wearing a large hat decorated with an immense trailing feather that reached the ground.

We had a pleasant lunch, and I became quite friendly with Cécile Sorel. She was delightful when chatting with three or four friends. As soon as there were more, she became less agreeable, putting on airs and behaving with incredible conceit. I believe that she really did not know how to be herself and was always playing a part. She was never a very great stage actress but she did have one personal advantage: she had style and panache to a high degree. Her stage presence was astounding. I never saw another actress with a more regal manner. People criticized her when she was at the Comédie française for acting as though she were in a music-hall. Then when she dropped the state theatre for the music-hall, they said she was acting as if she were still at the Comédie française.

Before appearing at the Casino de Paris, she had undergone her first face-lift, but the result was most unfortunate. Since her neck had not been treated, she now had a smooth, unlined face on a neck that was wrinkled like a tortoise. To make matters worse, the surgeon had drawn the skin too tight on one eyelid. Consequently, she could never shut that eye, even when she was asleep.

Some women can persuade people that they are beautiful. Isadora Duncan had this talent and so did Cécile Sorel. Sorel talked so much about her beauty that most people finally believed her. Despite her reputation, however, she was not at all beautiful: she had a large nose and bulging, lobster-like eyes. Her pale-pink, dyed hair accentuated the hardness of her features. She was extremely sensitive about her face. At one of the exhibitions of the 'Salon des Humoristes', the famous cartoonist Sem showed a caricature of her. It was perfect. Sorel came to the *vernissage*. When she saw the drawing, she flew into a rage and smashed the glass with her ring, damaging the drawing.

She became less aggressive as she grew older. At the height of her career, however, there had been many scathing articles about her in the press. When one of her friends asked if these upset her, she replied, ' What does the Arc de Triomphe care if a dog pisses on it? '

She adored sensational publicity. In this area she wanted to equal Sarah Bernhardt, whom she idolized and who had such a flair for publicity that she rivalled the Hollywood superstars.

I often went to lunch or dine with Sorel in her splendid apartment in an eighteenth-century house on the Quai Voltaire. All the walls were covered with panelling of the period. She had a fine collection of paintings, including some very beautiful Longhis and Canalettos. The eighteenth-century furniture would not have seemed out of place in a museum. Her bedroom was planned around a gilded bed which she said had belonged to Countes Dubarry: the bedspread was made of sumptuous ermine. This bed was the one piece of furniture which she never wanted to sell during her lifetime. After her death, however, experts discovered that it was not a genuine antique but had been made for her by an obscure cabinet-maker.

Sorel sold her apartment on the Quai Voltaire, together with most of her furniture, painting and *objets d'art*, to save her husband, the Count of Ségur, when he was fined a huge sum for having caused a fatal accident while driving his car. She then moved into a fine apartment on the Rond-Point des Champs-Elysées, which she decorated in a more modern style. She always had plenty of taste, both in her clothes and in her surroundings.

I visited the apartment on the Quai Voltaire after the new owner, Raymond Lazare of the banking family, had moved in. It had become as cold and inhuman as a museum: hardly any of the chairs could be sat on, lest they should be

Design for evening dress, 1924.

Design for coat, 1924.

damaged; all the bibelots which used to be scattered round the rooms were in locked, glass-fronted cupboards. It was dismal. I hate small objects and valuable plates displayed under glass. I feel that beautiful things should be in daily use, not locked up in order to impress visitors.

I designed many costumes for Cécile Sorel: for *The Taming of the Shrew* at the Comédie française; for *Sappho* by Alphonse Daudet at the Théâtre Sarah Bernhardt; also décors and costumes for the sketches she acted at the ABC and the Alhambra. The last play for which I designed her décors and costumes was *Cécile and the Dictator* by Paul Nivoix. Everything was ready, when Paris was occupied by the Germans. There was, of course, no question of putting on this play; it was a satire on Hitler.

After the war, Cécile Sorel gave up acting. After giving a few series of lectures she became a nun and entered the Order of *Soeurs Tertiaires* as had Ida Rubinstein – but with a difference. Ida Rubinstein gave her enormous riches to the poor; Sorel unfortunately had nothing to give. From then on, she wore a highly fanciful nun's habit, with silk chiffon veils. She used to wear it to all sorts of society parties until the Pope, in a letter, criticized her behaviour as being out of keeping with her station.

She lived to an advanced age – over ninety – and was full of energy right up to the end.

Towards the end of 1924 I received a letter from Metro-Goldwyn-Mayer's Paris representative, asking me for an appointment. As a result of this he offered me a six-month contract to design décors and costumes for two films: *Paris* and *Monte Carlo*. The work was to be done in Hollywood and the financial arrangements proposed were highly satisfactory. I could bring with me my manager, Nicolas, my secretary/copy-artist, M. Gallois, and my valet. We were to leave on 25 February, 1925, after I had finished work on George White's next revue. I was full of enthusiasm at the prospect; my head was bursting with new ideas for the film world.

On the night of our departure, after we had packed, we spent the rest of the evening with a group of friends at *Le Boeuf sur le Toit* (The Ox on the Roof), the most fashionable night-club at the time.

I still remember our luggage. One New York newspaper commented that no one had arrived from France with so much luggage since Cécile Sorel had embarked on her American tour. I have always travelled with too much luggage. This does not matter when you go by boat or rail, but now that I travel mostly by air I spend a fortune on excess weight.

I recall with amusement the things one of my great-aunts used to carry on a journey. Her toilet articles in tortoise-shell, which now decorate my dressing-table, were packed in a leather trunk built like a wardrobe. The top formed a dressing-table; underneath there were three drawers for clothes. It was a veritable piece of furniture.

We had an excellent crossing on the *France*, the steamship of the Compagnie Transatlantique. A sea-voyage is really wonderful. I have only been seasick once, coming back from New York on the *Paris*. This was due to the fact that I was suffering from overwork and had had only one hour's sleep the night before I left. As soon as I began to feel ill, Nicholas took me to the bar. After three dry martinis we sat down to dinner. Since then I have never felt any discomfort: apparently one should never have an empty stomach if one wants to avoid being seasick. My poor secretary, M. Gallois, who was terrified of seasickness, had a dreadful cross-ing, lying in a deck-chair on the deck and sipping cups of clear soup – his only form of nourishment.

As I was going through customs in New York the Officer pointed to one of the cases and asked me what was inside. I replied, very naively, that I had no idea since my valet had done all the packing. The Customs Officer smiled and waved me through without opening a single suitcase. In a similar situation, asked ' Have you anything to declare? ', Oscar Wilde replied, ' Yes – my genius.'

I had planned to spend some time in New York on my arrival because Henry Sell, as a gesture of friendship to me, had arranged for a large exhibition of my work in one of the public rooms at the Madison Hotel. The exhibition was a huge success and was glowingly reviewed by the critics.

A suite had been reserved for us at the New York Ritz which, alas, no longer exists. Prohibition was then in full force, and I remember how I laughed when, during dinner, the champagne bottle was hidden under the table and our wine was served in cups from a teapot.

But prohibition also had more drastic consequences. People used to drink inferior mixtures without knowing what they were. Many cases of poisoning and even blindness were caused by drinking gin made from wood alcohol. In Holly-wood, we had a ' bootlegger ' who used to deliver wine at night. He hid the bottles in spare tyres and among the tools in his car. One evening he brought me a case of ' Veuve Cliquot ' champagne. When we uncorked the first bottle, it turned out to be tinted water.

During our stay in New York, an MGM representative took me to all the MGM movie-houses. The first evening, as I entered my box, the orchestra began to play the Czarist National Anthem despite the fact that it was now 1925, eight years after the Russian Revolution, and I had been living in France since 1912. Many New York newspapers reported the incident but the humour of the situation eluded all of them. American journalism has certainly come a long way since those innocent years.

For the first time I had an opportunity to see my work on a New York stage. The 1925 edition of George White's *Scandals* featured my costumes and curtains.

The 1924 edition of the *Ziegfeld Follies*, which was still running, also included some of my costumes.

I thoroughly enjoyed my New York visit. I met some interesting people and made a number of friends, including Ralph Barton, the highly successful and talented caricaturist, and his beautiful actress wife, Carlotta Monterey. Carlotta, who originally came from California, was a great champion of the beauties of her native state. Barton, on the other hand, was convinced that I would find the film capital very frustrating. He did a marvellous cartoon showing me in Hollywood which was published in *Harper's Bazaar*. I suspect that his cynicism was a reflection of his personal bitterness and despair. In 1928 Carlotta Monterey, whom Barton later described as 'the only woman I ever loved', divorced him and three years later married the playwright, Eugene O'Neill. After years of commuting between France and America, Barton finally returned in 1929, saying, 'New York is a crazy city and America is a madhouse. . . . I feel I belong here. Americans are crazy . . . and I find that I'm crazy too.' He finally killed himself in New York two years later. He was only forty years old. I was greatly saddened by the news of his death.

Another 'transplanted Californian' whom I adored was Anita Loos. Her famous, best-selling novel of the 1920s, *Gentlemen Prefer Blondes*, had been illustrated by Ralph Barton. Anita was a small, doll-like figure with black hair cut in bangs. She once said to me, 'All the clever people in America come from California, but none of them stay there.'

At a dinner-party I met an interesting old lady called Mrs Cochran. She was a famous astrologer and offered to cast my horoscope. I was delighted. The day I left New York for Los Angeles, her secretary appeared at the station and presented me with a sealed envelope. Since there was rather a large crowd of friends and reporters seeing me off, I slipped the envelope into the pocket of my travelling-bag and forgot all about it.

At that time, it was chic to make the journey from New York to Los Angeles by a fast train, the 'Twentieth Century Limited'. The trip took four and a half days, but it was wonderful. The carriages were very comfortable and at the end of the train there was a special, glass-enclosed coach called the 'Observation Car'. I spent my days there, looking at the magnificent and awe-inspiring scenery. As we made our way through the vastness between the Atlantic coast and the Pacific ocean, I was overwhelmed by the natural grandeur of the country. Many months later, when we returned to France and were travelling from Le Havre to Paris on the boat-train, I remember how surprised I was by the cosy look of the Normandy countryside. The landscapes, framed by the compartment windows, seemed like miniatures.

We stopped for a day in Chicago and again at the Grand Canyon in Colorado, where we spent the night so that we could watch the sun rise. It was the most beautiful sight I had ever seen in my life. As the sun came up, the enormous cliffs seemed like precious stones melting into each other. It was magical.

When we arrived in Hollywood I unpacked in a great hurry and was at once swept into a whirlwind of interviews and parties. The horoscope in the pocket of my travelling-case lay completely forgotten.

An apartment had been booked for us at the Beverly Hills Hotel until we could find a house. The next day there was a big press-conference luncheon at the hotel. Because I had said in one of my New York interviews that my favourite colours at the moment were orange and green, a huge table had been decorated with oranges, tangerines and green roses. As the final touch, they had seated on my right the authoress Elinor Glyn (sister of Lady Duff Gordon who ran an important dress house under the name of Lucille) because she had green eyes. Elinor was a fascinating woman with a peculiar fixation: she believed that in a previous incarnation she had been Catherine the Great of Russia.

The lunch went off in a pleasant, friendly atmosphere. When it was over, the journalists wanted me to make a speech but I preferred to answer their questions.

As, by a strange coincidence, reporters always asked me the same questions, Nicolas decided to collect some statistics on the subject. According to his figures, during the year I spent in America I was interviewed 197 times: on the boat from Le Havre to New York, and on the return journey; in New York, Chicago and Hollywood.

152 journalists asked me which I preferred – blondes or brunettes.

Answer: brunettes.

182 asked me if I liked women with short hair.

Answer: yes.

I was asked 89 times ' Who is the smartest woman in the world? '

I never replied. This was an impossible question since there were so many elegant women about.

And 138 times: ' Who is the most beautiful woman you have ever met? '

Answer: Lina Cavalieri.

Harper's Bazaar, foreseeing that my life in Movieland might not be all roses, wrote, in February 1925:

> Welcome to Erté in America! At last Erté has consented to come to America to observe and to work, Erté has left the seclusion of his monastic little villa in Sèvres for the rough and tumble of a trip to Movieland. What will be the effect of the clatter on our precise and gracious friend who always draws curtains across closed windows before he begins a drawing because he fears the intrusion of ideas from without? It is hard to imagine what will happen to cloistered Erté, whose servants never make a sound and whose gorgeous orange cat, Mischa, sleeps all day on a black cushion. What will become of Erté in the city of backless houses in the wilderness, on the lot?
>
> Something important, you may be sure of that. Erté is austere, precise, gracious, with the graciousness of courtly old Russia, but

Erté is also much alive to new impressions and new influences. A true
modern. We can look for splendid new things coming from his contact
with the sharp new world. It will be a breathless experience for Erté,
those few months in Movieland, but it will make a new Erté. Not
everything will please him. He is as ready to cut back the cheap and
vulgar as he is willing to concede the clear sharp vision of the
modern artist.

My own comments about fashion and styles of dressing were widely quoted in
the American press including, among others, the following:

How many women could be beautiful if they only studied themselves
a little! If they would impartially analyse their defects as well as their
advantages. Unfortunately, most of them cannot be bothered. If they
need a new outfit, what do they do? They go to one of the couture
houses, or into a shop, and ask for a dress in the latest fashion.

The Latest Fashion! What a cruel tyrant! It forces fat women and
thin women to wear the same style; an older woman must dress like a
young girl. Really, to accept blindly the dictates of a fleeting whim
is nothing but laziness of mind. There should be a fashion which could
be adapted for each different person. As it is, the American woman
goes into a shop and sees a dress which will be bought by twenty
million other women; she tries it on and the salesgirl, anxious to make
a sale, tells her how well she looks; alas, this is not always the case.

The majority of women are always tempted to wear something they
see on another woman. It does not occur to them that women differ
enormously, and that what suits one woman to perfection will look
quite dreadful on another. . . .

No woman is irredeemably ' ordinary '. Introduce some sort of
harmony into the line of her clothes, her hairstyle, her make-up, all
the little details of her toilette and her grooming, and the woman who
for years you have thought of as ' ordinary ' will become a revelation
to you. . . .

It is necessary to accentuate all one's physical qualities; as for the
defects, there are two possibilities: they can be disguised as well as
possible, or, on the contrary, they can be exaggerated in such a way
as to create a very personal style.

In order to be ' chic ' everything must hang together perfectly. The
woman whose looks, whose clothes, whose mannerisms are all of a
piece – that woman has ' chic '. . . . The uniformity of present-day
fashions (I refer to the Chanel style which paralyzed fashion for nearly
five years, enveloping women in decorated sacks) shows a terrible lack
of imagination. Monotony will finally kill off this uniform style.

What caused most excitement in the American press, however, was my desire
to develop more colourful and imaginative designs in men's clothes. Here are a
few press reactions to my ideas:

Erté sees rainbow hues for men. Paris designer predicts bright colors for evening clothes beginning with violet. A conspiracy against the peace of mankind is being hatched out. The evening clothes, purchased when leaving college and worn until the bottoms burst, are about to be taken away. They are not to be replaced by similar suits cut along ampler lines. Men have got to begin by wearing brownish-violet evening suits and continue on the same path until they have formed the habit of consulting the fashion pages as feverishly as women.

Mr R. de Tirtoff-Erté . . . just arrived from Paris, has brought us this message. [At his suite in the Ritz-Carlton] Mr Erté told a representative of *The Sun* that men are a blot on the social scene. 'Their clothes are never harmonious,' continued the designer, 'they ruin the ensemble.'

Mr Erté himself was an extremely harmonious picture at the moment. He was wearing a boudoir costume of grey crepe de chine trousers and blouse with narrow rose-coloured borders, over which was a dressing-gown of grey and fuchsia printed crepe. (*The Sun,* New York, 26 February, 1925)

Clothes need reformation, but the reformation should begin with the man, not the woman, according to Romain de Tirtoff-Erté.
'Women,' he says, 'may make many mistakes in dress, they may be exploited and imposed upon by unscrupulous dealers, but at least they make an attempt to express beauty in their clothes and to emerge from the commonplace and the deadly dull. Men don't even attempt to escape from the ugliness of line and material that characterizes the garments they have adopted as their uniform. Apparently they are satisfied.'

Nothing, he believes, could be uglier than men's evening clothes. 'Entirely out of keeping with everything beautiful,' he asserts. 'Picture the modern homes, clubs and restaurants, with artistic decorations, subdued colors, shaded lights and flowers. A woman enters in shimmering cloth of gold or silver or delicate chiffon. With her is a man in a stiff black uniform that is an entirely discordant note and ruins the picture.'

Erté does not entirely subscribe to the dull customs he deplores. He has one evening suit of violet and another of brown. He admits he would like to go forth clad in silks and satins, but believes the time is not yet ripe for such radical departures. . . . Erté wore a small bracelet of pearls and a diamond ring on the little finger. His suit was of the faultless cut we associate with the finest English tailors. (Hortense Saunders, Newspaper Enterprise Association [NEA], 11 March, 1925)

Naturally, the papers made much of my own suits, coats, shirts, shoes, robes, jewellery and hair-style. All my life I have always spent a great deal of money on clothes and accessories. This was true even after the 1929 crash when I was in financial difficulties. The only time I ever exchanged any of my drawings, it was for furs. Women dress for other women; I dress for myself. As for my hair, at that time I wore it very smooth (this was not easy since it was naturally wavy). I would sometimes divide it into two partings so as to form a V-shape, and at other times would fashion a zigzag parting like a lightning bolt. Here are a few press comments:

> Erté, who is 32 years old, sat in his rose damask suite, wearing a gorgeous crimson and black brocaded coat over his pajamas of pongee. The coat, sumptuous and silken enough for an eastern potentate, was lined with cloth of gold and sashed with the same; his pumps were inlaid with crimson leather. (*Brooklyn Daily Eagle*, 28 February, 1925)

> Erté, who is a youngish man, was attired in a quiet suit of some color which the reporter from *The World* could not definitely ascertain. The presence of a watch was indicated by a golden chain of large links, woven carelessly yet carefully through the buttons of his waistcoat of which there were many. One waistcoat, that is, but many buttonholes. The waistcoat was double-breasted, after the latest mode. The shirt was striped alternately with white and what seemed to be a sort of dark gray, restful for the eye. (Frank Sullivan, *The New York World*, 28 February, 1925)

> Erté's own appearance might be taken for an illustration of his theory; physically small and slight with sensitive features, he looks, as a prominent motion picture figure remarked, ' like a nice kid '. He had chosen gray and red as color notes and carried them through his entire costume. His suit, tailored by Larsen of Paris, was gray with double stripes of dull red. With neither pocket flaps nor vent, his jacket was slightly shaped to follow the lines of his body, and was cut out in a single-breasted, two button model with wide peaked lapels. He expressed himself as also extremely partial to double-breasted models as suiting his slim figure. His attached silk collar, which he wore plain, with basket-weave tie in a gray and red zigzag pattern, was pale gray with a darker quarter-inch stripe around the middle, with fine dull red stripes on either side. His trousers were cut medium width and did not hide pale gray socks. Here Erté declared his fondness for distinctive footwear (he admits to over twenty pairs of shoes) in an unusual modification of the Deauville sandal. These oxfords had wing-tips and heels of soft calf which met low on the sides and extended up the eyelets. The remainder of the shoe was made of closely woven thin leather stripes of grayish glint. (*Daily News Record*, 23 March, 1925)

Helena Rubinstein, owner of a vast cosmetics empire, inspired by all this publicity, wanted to start a beauty salon for men, something which did not exist at that time. She asked me to lend my name to the products she was about to manufacture. Although the proposition was an interesting one financially, I declined because I did not want my name to become commercialized. What a strange woman she was! Although not beautiful herself, she created beauty around her. I shall never forget her marvellous sequinned portrait by Pavel Tchelicheff, one of the first modern surrealists, and the more recent portrait by Graham Sutherland. Both evoked so much of the strong character and taste of this tiny, remarkable woman.

I received a warm welcome from Louis B. Mayer. He introduced me to his wife and two charming daughters, Evie and Irene, and often invited me to lunch, dinner or family outings. On the basis of my own relationship with him I could never understand how the legend of his quick temper and difficult character had developed. In all my dealings with him I never saw any sign of either.

The entire Mayer family came to the house-warming party at my studio. Since he wanted me to feel at home, and as part of his red-carpet treatment, Mayer had previously arranged for my studio in Sèvres to be photographed. With these photographs as a guide, a crew of his superb workmen had built a new studio especially for me. Like my Sèvres workshop, it was done in neutral colours – cream and black – and contained many cushions. Naturally, my antique furniture could not be duplicated, but the modern pieces it contained were copied from my own designs which had appeared in various magazines. So, although the studio was not a faithful reproduction of the original, it did capture much of the spirit of my interior designs. I used this studio primarily as an office because I preferred to work quietly at home where I would not be disturbed. I soon found a charming house at the top of a hill in a very quiet area. As this was the last house on Beechwood Drive, I was able to walk from my garden straight out into the mountains. Thus my love of solitude was satisfied.

While searching for a suitable place, I had been particularly struck both by the interiors of some of the Hollywood houses and by their exterior architecture. There were a great many white-painted Spanish-style bungalows that were very pretty and harmonized well with the magnificent landscape and luxuriant Californian vegetation. On the other hand, I saw many monstrously ugly houses, like the pseudo-medieval castle with numerous turrets which once stood near Hollywood Boulevard.

The interiors were for the most part terrifyingly banal, betraying a total lack of imagination. I was astonished to find so few modern interiors in such a new country. However, I did love the ' sleeping porches ', a common feature of Californian bungalows. I hardly ever slept in my bedroom.

Once I was settled in my new house I bought a dog, a likeable black and white collie which I called Chéri. The following day at the studio I found a stray cat, a white one, and took it home. Thinking it was a female, I called it She, only to discover one morning, as She was washing herself, that She was in fact He. But the name stayed; he was after all used to it. The two animals became friends. Unfortunately, She did not live long. He was suffering from TB and died soon after. The vet who tended him, and who ran a clinic and a hotel for animals where actors could leave their pets while they were away, persuaded me to take a poor cat which had been abandoned by its owner and had, therefore, spent quite a long time living in a cage. He was completely black, very beautiful and very gentle. He too got on very well with Chéri.

My secretary-copyist, M. Gallois, lived with Nicolas and me. Each morning he went to my studio and kept me informed, by telephone, of what was going on there. From time to time I would spend the day at MGM observing all the activity so that I could learn as much as possible about the cinema. My dream was to make a film fantasy. After all, hadn't the cinema evolved from that series of bizarre pictures which had originated in the fertile imagination of Georges Méliès, pioneer film-maker, inventor and magician? But it was *The Cabinet of Dr Caligari*, produced by Erich Pommer in Germany in 1919, that had first fired my enthusiasm for the possibilities of the film medium, especially in the realm of fantasy. In retrospect, I realize that *Dr Caligari* contained the seeds of *The Blood of a Poet* and all the subsequent Cocteau films of the 1930s and 1940s. (When they were revived by a Paris cinema club in the early 1970s, I was astonished at their freshness. Not a wrinkle.)

As for the Hollywood studios of the mid-1920s, it seemed to me that they were a world of fantasy in themselves. There were royal facades without palaces; sumptuous interiors without walls; kings and queens in full regalia eating sandwiches in the cafeteria with beggars in rags.

In order to familiarize myself with all aspects of the cinema, I watched many films from a projection room. I was particularly struck by *The Phantom of the Opera*, starring that marvellous actor Lon Chaney, and by *The Merry Widow*, starring Mae Murray and directed by Erich von Stroheim, which had just been released.

My six-month contract with MGM stated that I was to design the costumes and décor for two films: *Paris* and *Monte Carlo*. When I arrived in Hollywood, however, neither script was finished. Nonetheless, I was asked to begin sketching the décors for *Paris* immediately. When I asked how I could possibly be expected to do designs without having read the script, the reply was simple: ' Never mind. We'll adapt the script to your décor.'

All the information I could extract was that I was to design the interior of a nightclub. There was also to be an ultra-modern, rather extravagant house with a large garden and an open-air theatre. An oriental ballet would be staged in this theatre. It was decided to use the costumes I had designed the previous year for the ' Ballet de Perles ' at the Folies Bergère. Copies were ordered from Max Weldy. (I learned subsequently that these costumes were eventually used in 1929 for the film, *Hollywood Revue*.)

I set to work enthusiastically. My night-club was triangular, and decorated entirely in red and gold. Although *Paris* was to be shot basically in black and

28 Evening dress, 1924   29 Evening coat, 1925

30 *Manhattan Mary.* Costume, 1927

white, the more important scenes were to be in colour, which was still rare in those days. Technicolor was then in its infancy, and all the colour sequences I had seen left me dissatisfied. There always seemed to be a profusion of violent and clashing colours, each overpowering the other. So I got in touch with the directors of Technicolor and explained to them the effects I wished to create. I wanted to use only a few colours at a time, so as to provide a feeling of harmony and *ambience*. The Technicolor people understood what I was getting at and were keen to put my ideas into practice. After the night-club, I designed an extravagant interior which was to be the home of the film's hero. The drawing-room was black and white, with one wall covered by an ermine curtain; in front of this wall stood a divan, also covered with ermine, on which were heaped cushions covered in black and white fox fur. I have always loved furs as furnishings and I still do. The drawing-room opened on to a dining-room but was separated from it by a wrought-iron grille. The dining-room was done in gold mosaic, with wrought-iron furniture. The seats were covered in panther-skin. The table consisted of a fish-tank covered with a slab of glass. The hall was star-shaped, its walls, floor and ceiling were of black and white marble.

The open-air theatre consisted of a monumental stage in white stone which emerged from a lake. The curtain was a water-fall. When the water stopped, the first setting of the ' Oriental Ballet ' came into view, disclosing an emerald green curtain embroidered in black, deep red and gold, which opened in a somewhat unusual fashion. Two women, whose costumes made them look like enormous black tassels, were suspended by the tresses of their black wigs. The hair passed through a series of gold rings which were fixed to the curtain. The ends of the hair were held by a slave covered in gold paint. When the slave released the hair, the curtain began to open so that the women, who were lowered at the same time, gave the impression that they were opening the curtain by their own weight.

Six months passed and the script for *Paris* was still not ready, even though the film had already been widely publicized in the press. I was asked to extend my contract for three months. My drawings and designs had long been ready, as had M. Gallois's copies. As usual I gave the copies to MGM, keeping the originals for myself. I was beginning to tire of doing nothing, but according to my contract I was not permitted to design for anyone else. I had, however, retained the freedom to send my monthly designs to *Harper's Bazaar*.

While awaiting the *Paris* script, it was suggested that I should design costumes for various other MGM films, especially for the principal stars. Among the beautiful women who regularly played leading roles for MGM were Marion Davies, Aileen Pringle, Norma Shearer, Eleanor Boardman, Claire Windsor, Kathleen Key, Mae Murray, Mae Busch, Pauline Stark, Carmel Myers, Paulette Duval, Blanche Sweet and Alice Terry. I considered Paulette Duval the most beautiful of them all but, unfortunately, she did not have a successful career at MGM. I believe she played only one leading role, for which I designed her clothes. Very often, in those days, the Hollywood studios would import foreign artists, only to let them languish in complete idleness. When her contract expired, Paulette Duval returned to Paris and opened a beauty parlour which specialized in ' peeling '. Her models, fairly elderly women, would parade past the clients with one half of their faces treated and the other untouched. The effect was nightmarish.

Many of the most famous Hollywood actors of that period have now been utterly forgotten, because the cinema was then entering a new phase: silent films were dying out and gradually making way for the talkies.

One of the first films for which I designed costumes was *Ben Hur*. Most of the scenes had already been shot; there remained only the scenes between Ben Hur (Ramon Novarro) and Iras, the vamp (Carmel Myers). So I designed Iras's costumes. Miss Myers was tall and very beautiful with dark hair and black eyes. She carried her superb body with flowing grace.

There was one other scene in *Ben Hur* which had not yet been filmed – the famous chariot race. I was present when they shot this sensational sequence. All Hollywood turned out for the occasion. In addition to the MGM people, there were many stars from other studios including Mary Pickford, Douglas Fairbanks, Gloria Swanson, Barbara La Marr, Dolores Del Rio, John and Lionel Barrymore.

Although *Ben Hur* was the most expensive silent film of its day, it became one of the most profitable. MGM wanted to film the story on location, so a huge expedition was arranged: technicians and equipment of incalculable value were shipped over to Italy. But once in Rome it was discovered that the deteriorating condition of the Circus Maximus would not permit the filming of a chariot race. The Italian Government, asked if they would consider restoring it, replied with a brief and pertinent ' No! '

At this point a real estate agent offered MGM a vast tract of land on which it could build a replica of the Circus Maximus. MGM bought it for an enormous amount of money and the Circus was built. Then, just when shooting was about to begin, the Italian police stepped in and banned any filming on the grounds that the location was part of a military security area in which the taking of photographs was not permitted! MGM admitted defeat and returned to America with its personnel and staggering amounts of equipment, leaving behind an impressive quantity of dollars. It was then decided to build the Circus Maximus in Culver City, and I must admit that it was marvellously well done. Only the lower half of the Circus was actually constructed. The upper part was a large model which, when placed before the camera, fitted perfectly over the ' real ' half. Trick photography is an aspect of the cinema that has always fascinated me, and I used this opportunity to learn more about the techniques involved.

When I finally saw the finished film, I loved it. The acting was of a high quality, particularly that of the hero, the handsome young Ramon Novarro. It is strange how the screen creates illusions: Ramon Novarro appeared very tall in the film but actually he was of medium height, no taller than myself. The same was true of John Gilbert, another star of that era. He was even smaller than Novarro, but he always looked huge on the screen.

I came to know Novarro quite well. He was a charming man who worked hard at his craft. He had a beautiful house in which he had built a little theatre where he could indulge his private ambition to be an opera singer. He had quite a good voice and had once even given a concert in Paris.

Since the films I was to design were going to be shot in black and white, I wanted to do the costumes in shades of grey, black and white, but this idea met with considerable opposition, despite its logic. It seemed that actors became bored if they were not surrounded by colours, and their boredom would be reflected in their eyes. I therefore had to draw the costumes in colour, but this presented problems since the various colour depths do not produce corresponding shades of grey on film. Luckily, this difficulty was resolved by the use of a small blue glass. When I studied the drawings through this glass I saw exactly what the colour would be like on the screen. I always kept the glass with me after that. I now understood why the men who wandered around the studios in evening suits or smoking jackets always wore pale blue shirts. On the screen, pale blue looks whiter than white.

Whenever I went to the studios, I was struck by the frequency with which the expression ' sex appeal ' was used. I believe it originated in the Hollywood studios and it was a veritable *leitmotiv* at the time. In fact, the two words were so firmly planted in my mind that one day, when I answered my doorbell – two venerable old ladies were collecting money for a charitable cause known as the Community Chest Appeal – I inadvertently said as I handed over my cheque, ' This is for the Community Sex Appeal '. The expression on their faces can be imagined.

At about the time of *Ben Hur*, I designed Aileen Pringle's costumes for *The Mystic*. Half the clothes were to be gypsy costumes; the others were elaborate and sumptuous gowns. After seeing the first to be completed, I was extremely displeased with the studio costumiers: I felt the clothes lacked allure. This prompted Mr Mayer to set up a special workshop in which only my costumes would be sewn. He found the most marvellous woman to run it. Although her name was Madame Van Horn, she was thoroughly French; everything she touched emerged incredibly chic. The workshop was staffed by Mexicans whose work was superb. They would even tackle complicated pieces of embroidery – of which there were a number in my costumes!

Soon after *The Mystic*, I designed the costumes for *Dance Madness*, in which Aileen Pringle played the leading role opposite Lew Cody. The film included a ballet, ' The Masks '. I was given complete liberty to create the scenario, as well as the décor and the costumes. For the décor I chose an enormous wolf's mask, whose eyes contained two small stages on which the dancers performed. The principal dancer's costume consisted entirely of masks. I did another version of this ballet for George White's *Scandals* the following year.

I very much enjoyed designing for Aileen Pringle. She was a beautiful woman who knew how to wear her clothes. When I designed clothes for the screen I always worked on the basic premise that the dresses must not look old-fashioned and ridulous a few years later, for the life of a film can sometimes be very long. Almost all clothes that are fashionable at any given time are likely to cause mirth and derision a year or two later. I would except one or two couturiers from this rule – Balenciaga and Grès – for they created many clothes that have not dated.

While I was in Hollywood, a fashion show entitled ' Her Day ' was presented at the Ambassador Hotel in Los Angeles. It consisted of all the costumes I had done for MGM, together with a few special outfits I created for the occasion. Norma Shearer, Claire Windsor, Eleanor Boardman, Aileen Pringle, Paulette Duval, Carmel Myers and Pauline Stark took part in the show. The evening was considered one of the most brilliant events of the season. Some members of various women's clubs, however, complained that a number of my clothes were too re-vealing and were an affront to their modesty. But what is modesty? Is it not a form of hypocrisy? To be shocked by the beauty of a naked body seems to me the ultimate hypocrisy. Unfortunately, hypocrisy was the reigning characteristic of the American middle classes in those days.

There were always many parties at the Ambassador Hotel. Invitations to tea and dinner poured in. At the beginning of my visit I went to one or two but soon tired of them. One always met the same people, who always said the same things. Soon I declined most invitations, pleading the pressure of work – a genuine excuse. I later discovered that many of the big stars, including Greta Garbo, never went to parties. Not only were there many parties, there were also a fair number of orgies. I went only to one but I left sickened – and I'm no prude! There was a total lack of spontaneous, orgiastic beauty. Everything seemed to be done out of a sense of duty rather than in pursuit of sensual pleasure. There was also a great deal of drug-taking. People smoked marijuana, which was brought in from Mexico. Nowadays when people talk about narcotics addiction they forget that things were exactly the same in Hollywood during the 'twenties, except that, happily, children were not yet taking drugs at school.

Every weekend, half the population of Hollywood set off for the Mexican fron-tier town of Tijuana. In those days of prohibition, people went there to get drunk. The road from the border to Hollywood on a Sunday evening had to be seen to be believed: it was crowded bumper-to-bumper with cars manned by inebriated drivers. I could never understand how anything as monstrous as prohibition could exist in a country as free as America. I said as much on one occasion to some American friends and received this unexpected reply: ' But who can talk of liberty in America? The first time you came into the port of New York, didn't you notice that the Statue of Liberty turns her back on the United States? ' I was so dis-turbed – and puzzled – by the cynicism of this statement that I promptly looked into the symbolism of the Statue of Liberty. The statue does, indeed, stand with its back to the shoreline. How else could it have welcomed the millions of immigrants from foreign lands who came to America to better their lot?

Other films for which I designed costumes were: *Time the Comedian, A Little Bit of Broadway* and *La Bohème. Time the Comedian* interested me because it called for the creation of costumes for a character symbolizing Time. This role was marvellously played by Theodore Kozloff. For *A Little Bit of Broadway*, I was called on to design a few interiors. For *La Bohème*, I created costumes for the two heroines: Mimi, played by Lillian Gish, and Musette, played by Renée Adorée. For Mimi, the unhappy little seamstress, I chose woollens and cottons so as to give an impression of poverty. To my great surprise, Lillian Gish protested, saying that her skin could only tolerate the finest silk, since she played all her roles with every pore. Pretension carried to such extremes made me lose my temper and I showed her the door. Nothing revolts me so much as pretentiousness, a fault which is normally the defence of mediocre people trying to conceal their inadequacies. I was genuinely surprised to find it in Lillian Gish, who was such a talented actress. Later on, when I read Miss Gish's version of the incident, I was amused to see that she had turned it to her advantage.

Musette's costumes, for Renée Adorée, were executed to perfection. On the day they started filming she looked very good in her costume, but the following day, when I encountered her in the studio, what did I see? A bundle of balloons! She had dispensed with the corset and had got her dresser to let out the bodice. As her costumes had full skirts and puffed sleeves you can imagine the result. Her excuse was that she could not eat while wearing a corset and that she needed to eat a lot while filming.

Several Hollywood actresses had French names. Some were genuinely French, like Claudette Colbert and Paulette Duval: others were Canadian, like Renée Adorée and Lucille Leseur (who subsequently became the famous Joan Crawford). In 1971, when the BBC presented a lengthy documentary programme about me, I was agreeably surprised to see an excerpt from a studio publicity film I had made with Joan Crawford at MGM, in which I was draping a costume on her body. Miss Crawford cut quite a different figure, in those days, from the sleek and sophisticated image she later acquired. Her beautiful face was set off by long, dark hair which she wore parted in the middle; she also had a well-developed bust and significant hips. She reminded me of a luscious Italian madonna.

During this waiting period I even designed a float which was to represent MGM in the first Motion Picture Electrical Parade and Pageant at the Los Angeles Coliseum. It was symbolic: four figures represented ' tears ', ' laughter ', ' drama ' and ' comedy '. I also designed the costumes of a prologue for the premier of ' The Big Parade '. This was a live spectacular which took place at Grauman's Egyptian Theatre with characters representing the various allied nations. I designed costumes with enormous trains symbolizing France, Great Britain, Italy, Belgium and the United States.

The actress representing America was accompanied by thirteen women, each of whom symbolized one of the original colonies. All this was personally directed by Sid Grauman, a kind man, full of enthusiasm and vitality, whose sense of showmanship sometimes went awry. When the attractive young lady symbolizing Belgium came on to the stage, Sid thundered out, ' Darling, can't you give us a smile! ' Poor Belgium's costume had as its chief accessory a vast sword which entered via the head and emerged from the stomach, followed by a huge trail of blood! I have rarely laughed as much as I did at the dress rehearsal of the prologue.

A Hollywood premiere was a splendid spectacle. Particularly striking was the way the streets leading to the theatre filled up with spectators. There were so many cars carrying invited guests that they could barely inch forward. This gave the crowd plenty of opportunity to stare at the occupants, reeling off the names of the actors and actresses whom they were accustomed to seeing on the screen. They would wildly applaud their favourites.

The women at premieres vied with each other in their toilettes, which were planned well in advance. These occasions were used to try out new notions. I had just launched the idea of using coloured wigs to match dresses (forty-five years before Courrèges). The three young women who wore them were a huge success, as was the acress Kathleen Key, for whom I had designed a coiffure featuring a white streak in her black hair.

Meanwhile, the three months of my second contract were drawing to a close and the script of *Paris* was still not finished. I was urged to sign a third contract, again for three months. I agreed with some reluctance for I was beginning to tire of Hollywood. Life was really very monotonous there, despite appearances to the contrary. Also, we had moved when my first contract came to an end. The lease on the Beechwood Drive house was only for six months and I did not wish to renew it. The area, which had been so quiet at first, had become terribly noisy. New building had been going on ever since my arrival. Already there were six new houses around mine and the noise became unbearable. We moved to Nicholls Canyon Road at the other end of Hollywood. It was a pretty house situated in a quiet, leafy area, but for some strange reason it imparted an air of sadness. When I left, I learned from the owner that her husband had died there shortly before I rented it.

Actually, the meteorological atmosphere in California that year was not calculated to please people with sensitive nerves. The earth never stopped shaking. Sometimes there would be as many as two quakes in a month. In Hollywood the damage was minimal, but Santa Barbara had been almost completely destroyed. Earthquakes had a strange effect on my nervous system. I always sensed when one was coming at least two days in advance, and would be gripped by a sort of anguish. I was just like my dog and my cat who would go berserk and refuse to eat on the eve of an earthquake.

At the end of the second month of my third contract, I at last received the *Paris* script. By the time I had finished reading it my hair was standing on end. It was indescribably absurd. The hero of the story was the darling of the people of Paris and indeed of all France. He was a couturier named Morand and he lived in the only place worthy of him – the Louvre! All my designs had been incorporated as promised, but my extravagant, ultra-modern interiors had been set down in the palace of the Kings of France! My open-air theatre was trans-ferred to the Place du Carrousel. I need hardly say that I refused to have anything more to do with a film which would caricature Paris in such a manner. A few changes to the scenario were quickly proposed, but when they were made they were so insignificant that I realized it was a hopeless situation. So I cancelled my contract. This naturally caused a great deal of comment in the American press.

Although I was upset – I had dreamed of bringing so many fresh ideas to the cinema – I was happy to regain my freedom to work once more for the theatre. Yet there were many kind people I had met in Hollywood whom I was sad to leave.

Heading the list, of course, was Louis B. Mayer. My relations with him were still cordial even after my decision to leave. In our final interview he confessed that he very much regretted having selected Harry Rapf as producer for the films I was to do. (Carmel Myers once described Rapf as a ' rough diamond '.) Mayer felt that Irving Thalberg, one of the most sensitive and artistic producers in Holly-wood at that time, would have been a much wiser choice. I certainly shared his feeling, for at my very first meeting with Thalberg we both sensed a strong current of mutual sympathy. I much admired the woman who later became his wife, Norma Shearer, for whom I had designed some costumes. Her charm was quite extraordinary. Even a slight strabismus did not mar the purity of her beauty. On the screen, of course, clever make-up, skilful lighting and fastidious direction concealed this defect almost completely.

As a parting memento, Mr Mayer gave me his photograph, on which he had written a most friendly dedication.

Then there was Peggy Hamilton, fashion editor of the *Los Angeles Times*, and Adrian, the famous designer whose marvellous creations I had always admired. He was a charming, slim, elegant boy with a very long face lit up by strange eyes. When we first met, he was so excited that he gave me a photograph on which he had written these extraordinary words: ' From one who feels like squealing '.

In June 1973, my friend Eric Estorick who, with his wife Sal, owns and operates the Grosvenor Gallery in London – I shall have much more to say about them later – met Carmel Myers in New York where she has lived for several years. He reported that Miss Myers had added an amusing footnote to my Hollywood *histoire* – one which was news to me. In one of my many interviews with American journalists I had said that Carmel Myers was the ' only star in Hollywood who knows how to wear clothes '. For days after the story appeared, Miss Myers felt a distinct coolness emanating from the other female stars on the MGM lot. She was baffled by the sudden shift in their behaviour until someone showed her this clipping. I am sure that, with her customary graciousness, she soon set things right but I would like to apologize, belatedly, for any awkwardness I may have caused her at the time. My association with Miss Myers is certainly one of my most pleasant Hollywood memories and our working relationship was easy and successful. After all those years, it was heart-warming to hear, from Eric, some of her first impressions of me:

> Erté had an instinctive knowledge of what was right. . . . He had the vitality and enthusiasm which is the secret of working well with a designer or director. I found him most stimulating. . . . With Erté I felt I was in the right hands. He always turned out something that no one else could do. I was sad to see him go.

Before my departure, I managed to leave my cat and my dog in kind hands, for the vet had told me the long voyage would be too much for them. I gave my cat to Madame Van Horn; the dog, Chéri, went to Mr Greenwood, MGM's Business Manager, who had always been very pleasant to me. Some months after I left, Greenwood wrote to tell me that Chéri came to sit each day in front of the photograph that I had given his new master, and barked a few times.

Shortly before I left Hollywood, I was rash enough to tell a journalist that I had been struck by the miracles that the camera could perform, particularly in transforming ordinary or even downright ugly people into fascinating beauties. The journalist interpreted my comments in his own fashion and wrote an article stating that I found all cinema stars ugly. This sparked off a spate of similar pieces in other papers. All were far from the truth, for I had met many beautiful women among the screen stars. One minor detail, however, had struck me particularly: rarely did one see a star with beautiful hands, yet, on the screen their hands were always beautiful. I later discovered that there was a woman in Hollywood with wonderful hands who stood in for the stars during close-ups.

On the way back to Paris I spent a few days in New York. I saw George White, who was waiting impatiently to hear my ideas for his next show. He promised to come to Paris a few weeks later to begin work on it.

Nicolas and I sailed on the SS *Paris*, the latest addition to the Compagnie Transatlantique. This beautiful ship had only one fault – it pitched slightly, owing to its long, slim shape. I was happy to return to my quiet house at Sèvres, to visit my parents in Monte Carlo and to collect my cat Mischa who had been staying with them. I am always pleased to leave Paris for a trip but I am equally glad to return. I have a nomadic soul. When I was a child my governess once told me to beware of gypsies, for they kidnapped little children and took them along on their eternal travels. My reaction was ' How marvellous! That way I shall travel all my life! '

31   With Henry Sell, New York, 1925   32   Cartoon by Ralph Barton, 1925

33   In Hollywood, 1925

34   With fashion reporters and models, Hollywood, 1925

35   Leaving Hollywood

36 With Carey Wilson, Hollywood, 1925

37 Louis B. Mayer, Hollywood, 1925

38 The designer, Adrian, Hollywood, 1925

39 Carlotta Monterey, New York, 1925

40   In the studio at Sèvres, 1924

41   In the gallery room at Sèvres   42   In the studio at Hollywood, 1925

There was an enormous amount of work waiting for me in Paris, including the tableaux for the next Folies Bergère and the new George White *Scandals*. White kept his promise and arrived in Paris soon after my return. We arranged to work the first day he arrived. I should say the first night for, as usual, White and Max Weldy came to Sèvres for late dinner and stayed all night.

Soon after my return from Hollywood discussions began on the subject of an exhibition of my work at the Galerie Charpentier, one of the most important galleries in Paris. I met M. Jean Charpentier several times and found him charming and full of enthusiasm. He offered me the large room on the ground floor because the number of important works I wished to exhibit came to over three hundred.

The first-floor room was reserved for an exhibition of works by Jean-Gabriel Domergue, one of the most fashionable painters of the day. The number of elegant women he portrayed was impressive. Unfortunately, success rendered his talent facile. He had created an image of a chic woman and this prototype served as a basis for most of his portraits: he merely modified it slightly for each model. The superficiality of Domergue's talent was high-lighted for me when, in 1973, I saw a reproduction of his portrait of 'Manouche' as a young woman in Roger Peyrefitte's biography of her. There seemed to be no connection whatever between Domergue's image of Manouche as an *ingénue* and the jacket photograph of her as a middle-aged woman, gargantuan, rough and full of perverse humour.

The ladies were, of course, delighted to see themselves looking so pretty but they soon forsook Domergue for Van Dongen, who went to even greater lengths to please his clientele. He would say, 'My one essential rule is to make women longer, without making them thinner. After that, I need only enlarge their jewels. They're thrilled by it! ' I once went to one of Van Dongen's celebrated Monday evening soirées which took place at his hotel in the rue Juliette Lambert: all sorts of famous people and snobs met there. There was a sort of cabaret with dancing, but the buffet consisted of only a few bottles of Evian water and some biscuits.

At the time of my exhibition, in April 1926, there was a large courtyard in front of the Galerie Charpentier which later became an extension of the ground floor area. Alas, the whole structure has now gone, replaced by a modern edifice that is part of the new architectural facelift given to the Faubourg St Honoré.

The favourable reaction to this first Paris exhibition exceeded my wildest dreams. In addition to many glowing comments in the daily press, *Le Gaulois Artistique* devoted a long, enthusiastic, profusely illustrated essay by Maurice Feuillet to my work. This was later successfully published in a bound format.

It gave me tremendous pleasure when I learned that the French government

had bought one of the works I exhibited, ' Le Rêve et la réalité '. This represented a woman standing at the bottom of a huge staircase, the treads of which
were done in graduated colours: those at the bottom were black and those at the
top vanished into the white of the background, after passing through various shades
of blue. The woman wore an enormous head-piece covered with feathers, which
made her look like some fantastic bird about to fly upwards towards the light;
she was enveloped in a cloak made from the dusky hide of a wild beast, whose
claws dug into the ground, preventing her from rising. This gouache had appeared
on the cover of *Harper's Bazaar*.

Quite apart from artistic considerations, the exhibition was also a financial
success: nearly all the work was sold. Charpentier suggested another show in
1928-29. I had the idea of including my ' human alphabet ', something I had
been thinking about for a long time. I do not remember how the idea came to
me, but it was not inspired by medieval, decorated uncials. I did not discover
these until a few years later. Although the execution of the Alphabet was frag-
mented, the entire plan had been clearly formulated when I first conceived the
idea. As with all my work (even the least costume or accessory design) I visualized
the final, detailed result in my mind from the start.

I began composing it in 1927. With my habitual optimism I hoped it would
be finished in time for the second exhibition, but I had not realized how much
other work I would have to do at the same time. There was my contract with
Harper's Bazaar, which required a cover design and numerous fashion and decorative drawings each month, as well as an occasional article. There was also my
work for the theatre. In 1926 I did two spectaculars for the George White
Scandals, and in 1927 another George White production, *Manhattan Mary*, a
lavish musical comedy. For the latter, in addition to modern town clothes, White
wanted a vast quantity of costumes for some sequences which took place in a
music-hall. So once more I plunged deeply into work which I found fascinating.

For the Folies Bergère in Paris, I designed many tableaux and also several
theatrical costumes for opera singers such as Lucrezia Bori (Metropolitan Opera,
New York) and Maria Kouznetsoff (Paris Opera). The result was that in 1929,
when my second exhibition at the Galerie Charpentier opened, the Alphabet had
not made much headway.

From then on, I worked at it whenever there was a period of comparative
calm. As a result, the execution of my Alphabet was spread out over many years.
In 1967, when I wanted to exhibit it at the Grosvenor Gallery in London, I
realized that two letters were still not finished. I was finally able to remedy this
situation in August of that year, on my return from Montreal.

My fascination with the shapes and forms of the human body in action goes
back to the age of seven, when I was taken to my first ballet, *The Hunchback
Horse*, based on an old Russian fairy tale. I saw it from my maternal grandmother's box at the Mariinsky Theatre in St Petersburg. I was so excited by the

experience that I began to have romantic fantasies of becoming a dancer and begged my parents to let me take ballet lessons, to which they finally agreed. For a while, I studied classical ballet with Maria Mariusovna Petipa, daughter of the famous choreographer Marius Petipa. I even went through a period when I was torn between ballet and painting. But the conflict was gradually resolved because, young as I was, I realized that my chances of successfully pursuing ballet and painting simultaneously were negligible. So, dancing became my hobby and once again painting was my ruling motivation.

During the period that I worked for Paul Poiret I used to go to many parties. As the evening warmed up, I would often improvise my own choreography. One night I did an improvisation on Eric Satie's *Gymnopédies* with Satie accompanying me on the piano. I never fell out of love with the dance and I still enjoy dancing. All of which may explain why the beauty of the human body in motion became a major motif in my work.

As for the alphabet itself, once I learned to read and write I was fascinated by the varied shapes of the letters. I would make each one into a drawing, with the series taking the form of imaginary arabesques. When I started to study painting seriously, I was dazzled by the beauty of the human form. In my imagination hundreds of objects took on human contours. If I have sometimes treated the human body in a static manner and represented it in symmetrical figures, it is merely a reaction against my habit of expressing movement. I loathe monotony in my work. More often than not there is movement in the setting within which the figure is found. In the twenty-six compositions which make up my Alphabet, I have closely associated the human body, exalted by the dance, with the graphic features of the letters. I applied the same principle to a series of ten lithographs which appeared in 1968, representing the numbers from zero to nine.

1926 saw the beginning of another activity, my collaboration with *Art et Industrie*, a new magazine founded and edited by M. de la Fortelle. This publication's name was a perfect expression of one of the basic principles of Art Deco – the marriage of pure and applied art. In my more recent work for *Harper's Bazaar* I had gradually been designing fewer dresses and more accessories such as jewellery, shoes, gloves, umbrellas and fans. I had also created designs for tables, lighting fixtures, shutters, mirrors, cushions and floral arrangements: this was an area which interested me deeply. I must confess that the popular fashions of that period, especially Chanel's perennial, sack-like uniform, had left me feeling rather bored with the whole fashion field.

It was a bracing change to be able to design for *Art et Industrie* a large number and variety of objects, along with whole interiors and occasional covers. Since we are in constant contact with so many utilitarian items, why not inject a little beauty into our daily lives with good design? When *Art et Industrie* was founded, this was still a comparatively new notion. Over the years the magazine has contributed to our modern life-style hundreds of attractive, functional objects. I am both proud of and gratified by my long association with it.

I was later to have the opportunity to do some story illustrations for *Harper's*. The first were for Richard le Gallienne's novel, *There Was a Ship*, which was to appear in the magazine in monthly instalments. These illustrations were followed by others for short stories, especially those of Lord Dunsany. This new medium brought me into contact with other American magazines, including *Cosmopolitan* and *The Delineator*. I approached the problems of illustrating a story in a purely personal way. Instead of illustrating the events which occurred during the course of the story, I illustrated the thoughts that were expressed.

In that busy year, 1926, a long article, ' The Mystery of Stones ' by Albert Flament, illustrated by my drawings, appeared in the Christmas number of *L'Illustration*. In addition to *La Gazette du Bon Ton*, my drawings also appeared in *Fémina*. Another successful exhibition followed soon after the one at the Galerie Charpentier. It took place in Brussels in 1927 at the Galerie du Studio.

Considering how much dead-line work I always had to do, it is a miracle that I ever managed to entertain my friends, or to go to the theatre with Nicolas, which I often did. The theatre at that time fascinated me, especially the plays of Pirandello, who was in the process of bringing something completely new to drama. The first of his plays that I saw was *Six Characters in Search of an Author*. After that I never missed one. After the theatre, we would sometimes dine in Montmartre, which was already losing its status as Kingdom of the Night to Montparnasse. At the beginning of the century, when most artists lived in Mont-martre, night life was very lively there. But once many modern artists began to move to Montparnasse, it was there that night life began to flourish. The Dome, the Rotonde, and the Coupole were the major meeting-places for artists, writers and others connected with the arts. Gradually, however, these places were invaded by snobs and then by all sorts of night-people and adventurers.

Many other cafés and cabarets, such as the Select and the Jockey, which were chiefly meeting-places for homosexuals, were born out of this cosmopolitan *ambience*. One place which enjoyed a considerable vogue was the Bal Nègre in the rue Blomet. Another famous place was the Sphinx, which was owned by two prominent politicians, the Sarraud brothers. Although it was actually a bordello, the clientele was by no means exclusively masculine. One often saw men in even-ing clothes accompanied by their bejewelled wives or girl friends. One of its big attractions was a not very pretty woman with a bizarre talent. Completely naked – and on the flabby side – she would circulate among the tables doing her act: customers would place a gold coin flat on the table and she would pick it up with her vagina.

Two other strange ladies were landmarks on the night club scene of those years: Kiki de Montparnasse and Bijou de Montmartre. Kiki often appeared with her bare legs painted to simulate stockings which she was, obviously, out of at the moment. She would usually turn up at the Select or the Dome, and sing for drinks, food or money. Bijou, on the other hand, was a monstrous figure, who reminded me of a Goya witch. Her shapeless, flabby body was topped by a batrachian-like head: her face was covered with thick white make-up. The paint looked as though it had never been washed off but merely covered over with another layer. She always wore black, with huge hats swathed in moth-eaten feathers and long lace veils full of holes, as well as quantities of cheap jewellery – necklaces, bracelets, brooches, chains, clips and rings on every finger. Bijou, who was a lesbian, sometimes had young and beautiful girl-friends. For me, this was one of the most extraordinary things about her. According to legend, she had been beautiful in her youth and covered with genuine jewels. Her life centred around the various night clubs of Montmartre. She would regale her ' clients ' with stories of her glorious past – her beauty, the famous people who had been her ' friends ', her jewellery, her conquests. Since she had a pleasant manner, people would frequently give her money or a drink before she even asked for them.

Jean Giraudoux based the central character in *The Madwoman of Chaillot* on Bijou. This fine play was marvellously produced in Paris with extraordinary scenic décor by Christian Bérard. The set for the bedroom was, in my opinion, one of the best things he ever did.

I always admired the plays of Giraudoux, who seemed a veritable fireworks factory of ideas. Successful as the plays were on the stage, they read even better, for one usually discovered a profusion of ideas one had missed. Louis Jouvet once asked me to design costumes for *Tessa*, but I refused because the set had already been done by another designer. I do not believe that a Giraudoux play could be properly interpreted, for the same production, by two different artists.

Gradually the artists deserted the night-clubs of Montparnasse as they were invaded by other nightbirds. Only a few stalwarts remained, like Foujita, Pascin, Kisling. But Montparnasse really went into its decline with the advent of World War II. Night life moved to Saint Germain des Prés simultaneously with the birth of existentialism.

I was living through a tumultous and exciting period in the history of modern art. Although I observed it from the side-lines – the pressure of my work left me with no time to become personally involved in movements – I was by no means indifferent to what was going on around me. I rarely missed an important or interesting exhibition. I was fascinated by Cubism but repelled by the nihilism of Dadaism and, especially, by Picabia, one of its founding fathers. Although I admired Picabia as a painter, his public behaviour often infuriated me. He had a way of taking up people, then ignoring them, setting them against each other, that was exhibitionistic, mischievous and often destructive. I was also excited by the birth of Surrealism, which had a close kinship with many of my own ideas. Abstract art, too, has always been a source of wonder for me. I idolized Kandinsky.

Yet, despite the fact that my whole life has been devoted to art, I have rarely frequented artistic milieux. The attractions and satisfactions of my ivory tower have always been irresistible.

In 1928 I was to have an operation for appendicitis. My room at the clinic was reserved for a Monday, since I had to finish some urgent work over the weekend. By some miracle, I finished it sooner than I had anticipated and found myself free on Saturday evening. I decided to do some tidying-up. I began with the escritoire in my atelier. As soon as I opened the first drawer, I saw a large envelope. It was the horoscope which Mrs Cochran had done in New York in 1925. When I returned to Paris from California, my valet had unpacked for me and put everything away. I tore open the envelope and picked out a page at random.

The first line I read was: 'Do not undergo any surgical operation before you are thirty-six years old'. At that moment I was exactly thirty-five and a half. Naturally I was shaken. I dared not telephone the surgeon to tell him how I felt – I thought he would laugh at me. I told Nicolas how worried I was and without hesitation he called the surgeon and explained the whole situation. The doctor was very understanding; he asked how many more months there were to go before my birthday. He set a new date for the operation, saying that my condition was not very serious and that I could easily afford to wait a few months. He added that even if the operation had been successful, I would always have been worried about it, thinking that he had left some surgical instrument inside me.

A few months later, directly after I had had the operation, I received a telegram from my mother in Monte Carlo telling me that my father had just died. It was a great blow. Fortunately his end was quick and painless. He had been playing the piano after dinner. Suddenly he stopped and told my mother that he was not feeling well. She immediately called his doctor. He recovered sufficiently to speak to him and ask for a cigarette. The doctor, realizing that he could do nothing, gave him one. My father took one puff, savouring the sensation. Then the cigarette dropped from his hand. His heart had stopped.

Unfortunately I was unable to attend his funeral. He was buried in the cemetery at Menton, on a beautifully landscaped hill overlooking the town. It is an extraordinary place with no atmosphere of sadness and gives one the illusion of hovering over the earth.

After this, my mother no longer wished to live in the Villa Excelsior. She went to Nice with my sister who had come to stay with my parents after her husband's departure for America.

My six-year lease on the house at Sèvres was ending. I very much wanted to buy it and the owner agreed to sell for a reasonable price. A few days later, however, just before I was due to sign the contract, he telephoned to tell me that he had thought it over and the price we had agreed on was too low. He demanded one which was nearly double what he had asked for. Outraged by this behaviour, Nicolas and I began searching for another property near Paris. During our searches we stopped for lunch one day at an inn called the Pyramide de Brunoy, in the forest of Sénart. The lunch was first class and the inn-keeper, when he learned the reason for our presence, was most sympathetic. He told us there was a very fine place on the market not far away.

We drove there immediately, and I was filled with enthusiasm for the property, part of a great estate that had once belonged to the Duke d'Orléans. The château had been burned down during the revolution of 1848 and the estate divided into four lots. The largest of these contained the old stables, which had escaped the fire. These early nineteenth-century stables were very fine with beautiful colonnades. An American had built his house among the colonnades, with much skill and taste. The second lot belonged to a religious order which had built a well-known girls' boarding school on the site.

The third lot had been bought by a lawyer and the fourth, which included the old gamekeeper's house, was for sale. The gamekeeper's house had a charming tower which pleased me very much. The park adjoining it contained a small lake, delightful streams and cascades. At the end of an avenue of chestnut trees was a ruined eighteenth-century stele, providing a backdrop to a little theatre composed of greenery. The orchard and the vegetable gardens were impressive. I was enchanted by the beautiful orangery with its great palm trees, which led off from the hothouse. The house stood on the edge of the road. From the front one could see only fields and, beyond them, the forest of Sénart. I took down the name of the estate agent, went there immediately and signed the contract a few days later. At once I began working out ideas for converting the house.

My plans were somewhat ambitious. To the existing house I wanted to add a large workshop with its own terrace, as well as guest rooms and a small theatre. I also wished to build a tennis court in the park, and to fill the orangery with monkeys and exotic birds. I started on the conversion of the attic into two apartments, for Nicolas and myself. Each was to consist of a bedroom, a bathroom and a small study. My bedroom at the top of the turret was completely round, as were the downstairs living-room and an exhibition gallery on the first floor. I have always loved round rooms – they impart a strange feeling of euphoria. The bedroom was lit by 'bull's eyes', the architectural term for round windows; columns all round the room supported a false ceiling, to conceal the fact that the room had originally been a garret.

As soon as this phase was finished, we left Sèvres and installed ourselves at Brunoy. However, winter was approaching and with all the work in progress, the house was in no state for us to live in comfortably. Nicolas therefore advised me to go to the Villa Excelsior in Monte Carlo, while he stayed on at Brunoy to supervise the building.

I went, but I was worried by the letters he sent me. He told me that each time he came home in the evening, he felt his heart contract the moment he drove through the gate. It was not until much later that I realized that he had experienced a presentiment of disaster.

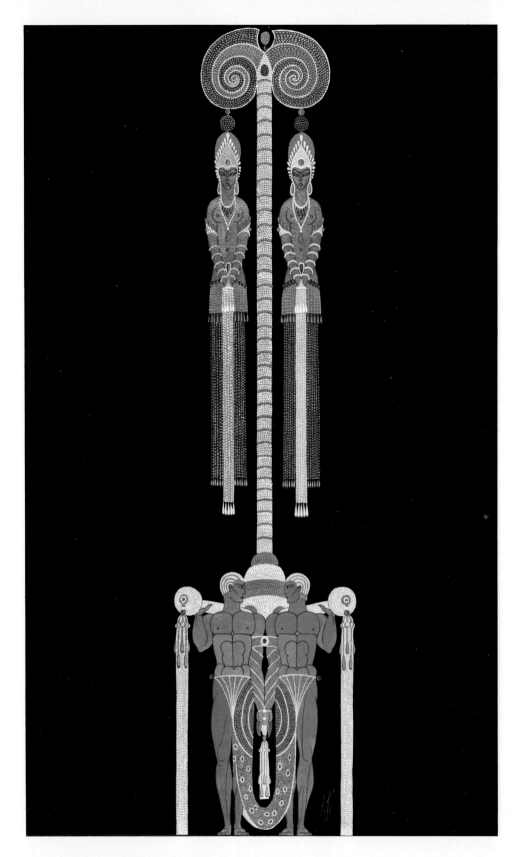

43   ' Porteurs de Pierreries ', 1927

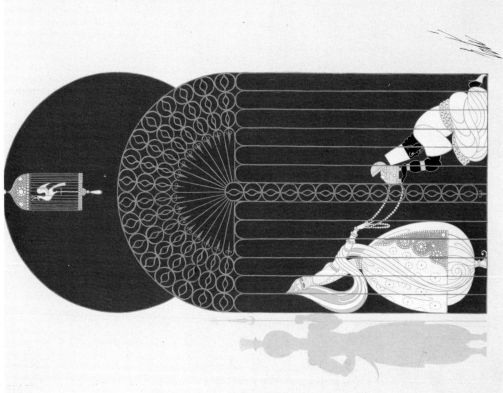

44, 45   *There Was a Ship.* Illustrations, 1929

The Thirties

Things began to go wrong in 1929, although the year began well. The opening of my exhibition at the Warren Cox Gallery in New York was a success, and the critical acclaim most gratifying. I did not go to New York for the occasion because I was too busy with my magazine and theatrical work in Paris, but shortly after the opening I received a letter from Warren Cox telling me that nearly all my works had been sold. Then the Wall Street crash occurred. As a result, at the end of the exhibition, not one of my paintings was taken by its buyer. This unfortunate event was only the first of a chain of calamities. All my capital was invested in the American stock market: for me the crash meant total financial disaster.

Obviously, work could not continue on the house at Brunoy; I had to mortgage the property. At the same time I disposed of the Villa Excelsior in Monte Carlo, and my mother moved in with me. As the Depression gathered momentum, I lost still another important source of income: George White was no longer able to stage his elaborate shows. The last revue I did for him was produced in 1929, but only because it had been completely prepared in 1928. Even *Harper's Bazaar* asked me to cut down on the amount of material I had been under contract to provide. The crash led to cut-backs in other contracts and in some cases to outright cancellations.

Nevertheless, 1929 did bring me two very great successes. The first was the production of a new version of *La Princesse Lointaine* at the Sarah Bernhardt Theatre; the other was my second exhibition at the Galerie Charpentier.

La Princesse Lointaine was a revised, unproduced version of the famous Edmond Rostand play, written originally for Sarah Bernhardt after she had undergone a

serious operation for the amputation of her leg. When the play had first been
staged in 1895 at the Théâtre de la Renaissance, Sarah Bernhardt had played
Princess Mélissinde, Lucien Guitry the role of Bertrand d'Allamon, and de Max
the part of the troubadour, Geoffrey Rudel. In the first revised version Rostand
planned to give the role of Geoffrey Rudel to Sarah Bernhardt. The character
of the troubadour, being ill throughout the play, never left his couch. Sarah could
therefore play the role from a reclining position. Unfortunately, casting difficulties, production and budgetary problems, World War I and other circumstances
had prevented this production from taking place.

In the new revised version, finally produced in 1929, the casting of *La Princesse
Lointaine* was excellent. That wonderful comedienne, Vera Sergine, took the part
of Mélissinde and Henri Rolland that of Bertrand d'Allamon; Geoffrey Rudel was
played by Paul Bernard. Paul Bernard was a fine-looking actor of great talent
who, tragically, died very young. The director was Harry Baur, for whom I had
designed one of my first theatrical costumes in 1913, when he played the leading
role in *The Minaret*. He was a sensitive artist, both as director and actor, and
it was a pleasure to work for him.

One amusing incident occurred during rehearsals. For Princess Mélissinde's
entrance in the final scene, I had made a cloak of gold and silver, completely
covered with precious stones. It must have weighed about ten kilos and Vera
Sergine complained that she could not carry so much weight. Harry Baur replied,
' That's fine, but so that it isn't completely wasted, I'll ask one of your entourage
to wear it.' Thereupon, Vera Sergine changed her mind and wore the cloak with
perfect ease.

The press was full of praise for the sets and costumes of *La Princesse Lointaine*.
The design for the galley – a black silhouette against a background of ominous
clouds – was hailed as a masterpiece; the palace of Mélissinde was said to evoke
a profound and picturesque atmosphere, that of a past filled with dreams; and the
final scene, the arrival of the Princess's ship, was described as enchanting. On
9 November, 1929, *L'Illustration* said:

> No one could surpass Erté in translating the poet's vision into material
> terms in designs which are not tied to a particular period yet manage
> to combine East and West, the Christian Middle Ages and Byzantium,
> in a composite synthesis, the taste and atmosphere of which remain,
> nevertheless, completely modern.

The exhibition at the Galerie Charpentier also drew many enthusiastic press
comments. The catalogue contained prefaces by Maurice Feuillet and Georges
Barbier. I had met Barbier, one of the great designers of the period, at the very
beginning of my career with the *Gazette du Bon Ton*, to which he was a principal
contributor. He had liked my first design for this magazine and a close friendship
had sprung up between us. He had also written several articles about my work,

two of which appeared in the *Gazette du Bon Ton*. He was a most talented costume designer and did a great deal of work for the Folies Bergère. I shall never forget the glorious costumes he designed for the film *Casanova*. Alas, he died far too young.

From this exhibition, the French government bought another of my works, ' Schéhérazade'. At the same time, the city of Paris bought ' Au sommet de la vague', which had served as the theme for a tableau in the George White *Scandals* of 1928.

I always had plenty of work to exhibit since, as I have explained, *Harper's Bazaar* used to return my originals once they had been reproduced. As for my theatrical commissions, I nearly always kept the originals. My copyists would sometimes make several copies of a design so that the costumier, the producer and sometimes even the choreographer could each have one.

In 1929 I was asked by an American textile firm, the Amalgamated Silk Corporation, to design some printed fabrics. This was something new for me. When I recalled that Raoul Dufy had designed fabrics for Paul Poiret, I felt I could contribute much in this area, and in due course I signed a contract. I found fabric design most interesting. In fact, whenever I have had the opportunity to work in a new field, I have become absorbed in it. Sometimes I hesitated before accepting a new commission, for fear that I might find it boring, but as soon as I began to think about it, I was struck by a flood of ideas and began to enjoy the work. The realm of printed materials seemed to offer numerous possibilities, but what attracted me most was the fact that I had complete liberty to create abstract forms.

I have always been attracted by the abstract. Not that I dislike representational art, but I have never been able to understand the artist who reproduces faithfully what he sees, rather than the impression that a real object has made on his mind. In my youth, one of my teachers would always tell me to paint what I saw, but I always replied, ' Why should I create something that already exists? '

The Amalgamated Silk Corporation also asked me to design clothes which could be made up in my materials. It is extremely difficult to think up interesting shapes for dresses made in printed fabrics. The printed pattern strikes one's eye in such a way that any detail in the design itself is completely obscured. So it is best to create very simple clothes, especially if the pattern of the material is elaborate. The only exception to this rule is bordered material which lends itself to a variety of interesting designs. I have devised many of this type.

Another new sphere of activity that soon presented itself was advertising. The first proposition in this area came from a large American manufacturer of stockings, Holeproof Hosiery. The offer was made by Henry Sell, who visited Paris with the firm's managing director in order to draw up a contract. Each month I was to present a design in colour; the choice of subject was left entirely to me. This design would appear in various magazines. At the same time, I would

do a black and white version of the same drawing for the daily papers. In addition,
I was to develop the same drawing into a larger display piece, which would
appear in the various windows of the numerous shops owned by Holeproof
Hosiery in various American cities.

I was delighted with this opportunity because my finances were then in a very
bad state. My collaboration with Holeproof Hosiery lasted five years. This foray
into the realms of advertising was soon followed by another, for Hermann Delman
Shoes. Once again it was Henry Sell who put me in touch with Delman, a great
friend of his. Along with the advertising, Delman asked me to do some shoe
designs. In each of his shoe collections he wanted a series of special models of
my design. Many of these are now in the Metropolitan Museum in New York. My
collaboration with Delman, which lasted until the outbreak of World War II,
was resumed after the war.

Delman and I got on very well. He was a pleasant, cheerful man who was fond
of the good life. He usually came over to Paris accompanied by his charming girl-
friend, who was descended from a line of American-Indian chiefs.

During my second exhibition at the Galerie Charpentier in 1929, I got to
know the editor of an English weekly magazine, *The Sketch*. He was impressed
by my work and asked me to submit some of it. For many years thereafter, the
Sketch ran one or more colour pages of my gouaches. Normally these drawings
were from my files, but I sometimes submitted originals such as ' Horoscopes ',
a composition consisting of twelve pieces, each representing one of the signs of
the zodiac. These Horoscopes began to appear just before 1939, but their publication ceased with the advent of war. I was able to recover the originals of the
six that had already appeared, but the other six were casualties of a bombing
raid on the headquarters of the *Sketch*. The idea of painting the signs of the
zodiac had come to me at a time when I was fired with enthusiasm for astrology.
I began to study astrology and to work out horoscopes, but this involved so many
calculations and took up so much time that I soon decided to abandon it.

Life passed busily but with rather less style than before the 1929 slump.

We had just engaged a new gardener, a young, inexperienced boy. Nicolas
was showing him how to prune the rose bushes when he gashed his finger on a
thorn. He thought no more about it, but constant movement of the finger prevented the wound from healing and it became infected.

Nicolas was taken to a clinic in Paris but, by then, septicaemia had already
set in. In those days, before the discovery of antibiotics, there was no way of
stopping the spread of such an infection. He became steadily worse and, for a
few days, lost his sight. When his condition became critical, I spent all my time
at the clinic, including the nights. I was given permission to move a bed into
his room. I summoned a Russian Orthodox priest and pretended, for Nicolas's
benefit, that he was there only to pray for his speedy recovery. Finally, after fifteen
days of great suffering, Nicolas died on 4 April, 1933.

Fabric design, 1929.

I was in despair. We had spent nearly twenty years together. Nicolas had shared my youthful dreams, my joys and my disappointments. My world seemed to crumble about me, and I felt like the sole survivor of a vanished era.

Not long before Nicolas's death, during the long days that I spent at the clinic, I had read him a novel by Germaine de Beaumont. The hero of the story, one of two children who adored each other, was to die while very young. Their favourite game was played in the library of the château where they lived. They would ask each other a question and then open a book at random: the first phrase they read gave them the answer. The young man grew up and married, but soon fell ill. Shortly before his death he promised his young wife that he would never leave her. Telling her of his favourite childhood game, he said:

' Do as we did before. Take out any book from the library, ask me a question and you will find my answer in the first sentence you read.'

The book and the circumstances made a deep impression on me. A few days after Nicolas had died, I took a book from the shelves, opened it at random and was stunned to read the words, ' Wait and see '. This was a phrase Nicolas used frequently to me, since I was impatient by nature.

I had the same experience on many subsequent occasions. Each time I received a clear reply to my question. Gradually my need for contact with him diminished, but years later I could still obtain replies to serious questions.

Somehow life went on. Now that I had to cope alone, I soon realized that life was going to be full of trials. Nicolas had looked after all my business negotiations and the day-to-day details of my work. He had managed the house and dealt with many other practical facets of our life. While he was with me, I was free to live within the world of my art, undistracted by mundane problems. I was a very inadequate businessman and I loathed negotiations, particularly financial ones. In order to curtail them I would sometimes accept ridiculous terms. What stupidities did I not commit in my business affairs after the departure of Nicolas!

When I first took things into my own hands, I discovered that my finances were in an even worse state than I had imagined. To spare me worry, Nicolas had not told me that there were some large debts outstanding. I could no longer consider keeping the property at Brunoy; besides, it had become hateful to me. Even our little companion, Mischa, was no longer there, for he had died a few days after Nicolas, and was buried in the garden under a giant elm tree.

Eventually, the house at Brunoy was sold, together with a great many objects that were left in it. These were auctioned off. I shall never forget the deep friendship that Max Weldy showed towards me at this difficult time. He did everything from arranging for Nicolas's funeral to helping me to re-establish myself. I very much appreciated all his help.

My mother was glad to leave Brunoy, since she had always found life there rather dull. She preferred to be surrounded by bustle, so she moved to Montmartre, where she was soon joined by my sister. For myself I took a seven-room furnished flat in the Avenue Hoche. On the ground floor of the building was a small theatre, where Diaghilev had once rehearsed his ballets for a season. The theatre is now a cinema club.

I dismissed my staff – chauffeur, valet, gardener and the gardener's housekeeper-laundress wife – but kept Phac, the Indo-Chinese cook, who now also became a splendid valet. Phac looked after the running of the whole apartment, including my clothes and laundry. He worked for me for nearly nine years, until 1939, when he was mobilized. After that, I never heard of him again. He was a really exceptional servant – clean, energetic, quick, quiet and honest. I never forgot what he said when we first engaged him. Nicolas jokingly asked him if, like the majority of cooks, he was a thief. He replied, ' No, sir, I only steal the bare minimum.'

Washing up the cocktail shaker one evening, Phac decided to sample the remains. This gave him a taste for alcohol which soon developed. I remember one evening when Elsa Schiaparelli was one of my dinner guests. Phac was serving as usual. With each dish he brought he seemed to grow paler and paler. Finally, after he had served the dessert, I saw Schiaparelli and two other friends burst out laughing. I turned (I was seated with my back to the door) and saw Phac crawling out on all fours.

On that same evening, Schiaparelli had painted all sorts of butterflies on my mirrors and windows, for this was the time when butterflies were the *leitmotiv* of her collection. I always liked Elsa Schiaparelli. She struck a blow against the dreary uniform created and maintained for years by Chanel. Chanel had created ' Mrs Everybody ', but Schiaparelli finally managed to resurrect individuality. At the beginning of her career in Paris, even before she had opened her couture house, she asked me to work with her. Our ideas on fashion certainly coincided but, partly because of the amount of work I had to do and partly because I enjoy my independence, I declined.

When I left Brunoy I sold my fine car, with its coach-work by Million-Guiet. It was no use to me without a chauffeur because I had never learned to drive. I was nearly always busy inventing something, with my head in the clouds, and far too absent-minded. My forgetfulness reached its peak on the day when I could not remember my own name. This occurred during World War II, when I had gone for a walk to work out an idea in my head. On my way home, a German soldier stopped me and asked to see my papers. I handed him my identity card. Not satisfied with that, he asked me to tell him my name. I could not remember it. I indicated that he could read the name on my papers which he still held. He replied that he wished to hear the name from my own mouth. I still could not remember it, but I gave him my address. Since his suspicions had been aroused, he insisted on escorting me to my house, which was nearby. On the way I finally remembered my name, but it was too late – the soldier would not believe me. When we reached my home, he asked the concierge if she knew me.

' Of course," she replied. ' M. Erté has lived here for eight years.'

Reassured, the soldier returned my papers.

My search for a small, comfortable house, which would be easy to maintain, went on for some time. Eventually I found a small town house in Boulogne-sur-Seine on the outskirts of Paris, near the Molitor swimming pool. I liked the area very much; its gardens, tennis courts and sports grounds reminded me of a spa town. Unfortunately, a few days after I moved in, I found the din of the traffic unbearable. In the evening, and especially during the night – my best working hours – there was a constant stream of large trucks bringing in provisions for Les Halles. Fortunately, I had only signed a one-year lease, but it meant that I had to look for another home.

From one of my windows I could see the upper storeys of a large block of flats which was just nearing completion. It was on a quiet road overlooking the Roland Garros stadium and fronting on the Bois de Boulogne. I went to look over it and realized that the street, rue Gutenberg, was familiar; this was where Prince Youssoupoff's old house had been.

I examined several flats and fell in love with one on the sixth floor. There were windows on two sides with magnificent views of Paris. One side looked out on the Bois de Boulogne while the other had a view of the Meudon and Saint Cloud. The apartment made me feel as if I were floating in space. I rented it on the spot and moved in a few months later. That was in 1935 and I am still living there, in spite of the decision of the owners to sell the property a few years ago. I continue to rent my flat from the new owner, and hope to do so until the end of my life.

The flat was originally decorated to my specification by an astonishing young Dane named Axel. He was introduced to me by Pavlik de Korve, secretary to the Russian opera impresario, Prince Zeritelli, and a frequent visitor at Brunoy, who had helped me considerably with my various moves. Axel had just returned from Morocco where he had been running a small furniture factory. At that time Casablanca had been a booming city and his business was very successful. Then the bubble burst and his factory went bankrupt, so Axel came back to Paris to look for work.

He was delighted at the prospect of decorating my flat. He rented a small workshop near the Bastille, among the wood merchants, where he did all the preliminary construction. He built my bar, the furniture necessary for exhibiting my pictures, all the wall cupboards and an aviary. He numbered each individual piece and, when everything was ready, brought them up to the flat and assembled them.

Shoe design, 1932 and scent bottle design, 1935.

All that now remained was to mount the straw panels that were to cover the ceilings as well as the walls. I love straw as a decorative material and had already experimented with it in my Brunoy dining-room. When the straw panels were fixed at various complementary angles, an effect like that of marquetry was created. I have never understood how Axel managed to do all this work alone. I often offered to help but he always refused – and he had a will of iron.

He also plastered the ceiling and part of one of the walls in my bedroom, decorated them entirely by hand and then gilded them. The construction of the bar was a masterpiece of precision carpentry. It is built into one of the sturdy walls and is invisible when not in use. To open it, a panel of bookshelves pivots round, disclosing the bar behind. The bottles and glasses are stored in a bright red niche built in the shape of a glass. The back of the niche consists of a large panel on which new visitors sign their names. Each may choose whatever colour or style he prefers. I have found that people usually choose a colour to correspond with their characters. Active or violent people pick red; those who are reserved but given to profound thoughts choose black; those who are undecided, green; the sentimental type, blue; the mystics, violet; the cerebral, white.

The first to sign was my cat, Micmac. I dipped her paw into a pot of ink and pressed it against the panel, leaving a footprint. There are now more than two thousand signatures on the panel, including many famous names, many forgotten ones and, above all, many from the theatre. Their signatures have the irridescent effect of a multicoloured tapestry. One day, when I had requested a signature from someone with whom I had just spent a very pleasant evening, I was asked a naive and unexpected question:

'Have you been to bed with all the people who have signed their names?'
I laughed uproariously.

In the middle of the study wall which contains the bar, Axel built me a two-sided aquarium, one side of which faces into the studio and the other into the little entrance hall, making a sort of window.

The equipment needed to exhibit my designs was not easy to construct. It consists of a series of ten panels which open like the leaves of a book. Above it, set into the window frame, is a glass-enclosed aviary, housing some turtle-doves.

I furnished the apartment with antique furniture already in my possession, most of it in Directoire or Empire style. All the seats are covered either with suede or African goatskin, and the colour of these skins blends marvellously with the old wood of the furniture. The whole flat is decorated in various shades of beige, even down to the turtle-doves' feathers. The walls are covered with curtains which, when open, reveal the panels containing framed drawings. For some years now I have kept some of these curtains open to show my 'Formes Picturales', which are hung on a background of black velvet. Apart from this small detail, all is still just as Axel made it. Except, naturally, for the carpets and curtains, which I change from time to time.

My mother, who used to visit me fairly often, liked Axel very much. He was a good-looking boy, tall and athletic (he had been a champion swimmer in Denmark). He was typically Scandinavian, with large blue eyes and blonde hair, and an easy-going manner. When he finished the work on my flat, he was still without a permanent job. Since he was so energetic and resourceful, I offered him a job as my secretary, with full responsibility for my business affairs. He proved himself very efficient, representing me on several occasions and obtaining very favourable terms.

Unfortunately he had one great vice: gambling. One day, shortly before World War II, I asked him to fetch a large sum of money for me; having done so, he then went to the races and lost it to the last centime. When he told me about this catastrophe, he promised to repay me little by little, but he never did. Since I had lost my confidence in him, I was obliged to dispense with his services. I never saw him again and no one ever mentioned him. But later, at the end of the war, I had an unpleasant shock. My mother, who was perusing the newspaper, suddenly handed me the article she was reading. It was about Axel. During the war, driven by his ever-increasing need for money, he had become a Gestapo agent. After the Liberation he was imprisoned, but while being transferred from one prison to another, he jumped the convoy and disappeared. I subsequently enquired about him from numerous friends who lived in Denmark but I never found out what had become of him, even from his family.

In 1934, via Max Weldy, I received a proposition from Billy Rose in New York. He was preparing to stage a musical comedy, *The Flying Trapeze*, and wanted me to design the sets and costumes. To play the leading female role he had chosen Marika Rökk, who was already playing it in Budapest, where the show was part of a circus. Rose wanted me to go to Budapest immediately to see the production and, especially, to see Marika Rökk. The trip was urgent because the last performance of the show was imminent, and there were other problems. The only direct flight to Budapest would arrive too late for me to watch the whole show. As a result, I had to resort to a complicated route, involving three changes, in order to arrive early enough. But it was worth it. I loved the show and Marika Rökk. It must have been her first important part, for she was still very young. In addition to dancing, singing and performing acrobatics with fantastic verve and appeal, she was a skilled comedienne. Moreover, she was ravishing. Her fine, regular features were haloed by blonde tresses, and her wicked, vivacious eyes lit up her whole face. Her wide shoulders, narrow hips and flat chest were, however, more like those of an adolescent boy.

I saw Marika Rökk again in 1952, when she and her husband, the film-maker Yacobi, asked me to design *Die Maske in Blau*, in which she was starring. Her vivacity and incredible vigour were almost unchanged, but at that time her figure was harder to dress because Dior's ' New Look ' was in full swing – opulent breasts and hips, with small waists. Nevertheless, I managed to create costumes which suited her very well, and she was delighted. The following year she asked me to design her costumes for another film, *Die Geschiedene Frau*, adapted from Leo Fall's operetta. Marika Rökk was known as an extremely temperamental star but with me she was invariably charming. I never had any difficulty in working with her.

Budapest was delightful, especially Buda, the Old Town. Its prevailing atmosphere in that period was quite extraordinary – I believe it must have been the happiest and most animated city in the whole world. Music reigned supreme. Almost every restaurant and café boasted a first-class ensemble, and even the smaller cafés had two or three good musicians. At night there were gypsy camps, with their songs and dances, so full of voluptuousness. . . .

Alas, my trip was fruitless. The deal with Billy Rose came to nothing, for some reason that I no longer remember. Many of my business projects ran into dead ends, but I regretted two in particular. One was the chance of designing *The Merry Widow* for Grace Moore, an incomparable artist for whom I cherished a fervent admiration. She was coming to Europe to discuss the arrangements for the project, but en route she died tragically in a plane crash.

The other project that excited me was a production of *Macbeth* for a new American company. I worked out the plans for the production and had already finished three of the sets when the Germans occupied Paris and all contact with foreign countries was cut off.

Sets and costumes for operettas formed a considerable part of my work after 1934. Maurice Lehmann, who ran the Théâtre du Châtelet, had seen the Christmas edition of *L'Illustration*, in which there was a series of my drawings illustrating various operas. He liked the designs and asked me to work on the new musical spectacular he was about to stage at the Châtelet. I shared the various tableaux with Vertès: he was to do one half, I the other. I always admired Vertès, whose art was full of intelligence, spontaneity, originality, charm and subtlety. The show was entitled *Au Temps des Merveilleuses*, with music by Maurice Yvain, in his day the most fashionable composer of light music. The operetta was very successful. The librettist, Albert Willemetz, then asked me to design the sets and costumes for *Les Joies du Capitole*, which he was putting on at the Théâtre de la Madeleine. The music was by Moretti, another successful composer.

We read the piece through at the home of the librettist, Louis Bousquet, in the Place du Palais-Bourbon. It was on this occasion that I first met his wife, the legendary Marie-Louise Bousquet, Paris editor of *Harper's Bazaar*. Vivacious, witty, for me she epitomized Paris. At her weekly receptions, one would find in her salon an international gathering of artistic celebrities. The cast of *Les Joies du Capitole* included two exceptional artists: Arletty was to play the part of Agrippina and Michel Simon that of Emperor Claudius. At that time Arletty was seen mostly in musical comedy roles. She looked marvellous, with her long profile and body that was slim and supple as a snake. Her intelligence was purely Parisian, her voice that of a Parisian *gamin*.

Following the great success of *Au Temps des Merveilleuses*, Maurice Lehmann asked me to design the sets and costumes for his next production at the Châtelet, the operetta *Au Soleil du Mexique*. The core of this show was the set I designed for a cloister scene: a simple perspective of vaulted archways vanishing into infinity. The nuns, in their grey and white habits and large, wing-shaped coifs, looked like angels. André Baugé, who played the starring role, was one of the greatest light opera singers in France, but at that time he was approaching the end of his career.

My next assignment was to design the sets and costumes for *Yana*, a luxuriously staged operetta. This was the year of the Paris Universal Exhibition of 1937 and Lehmann wanted to dazzle the crowds of foreigners who would be on hand. When the curtain rose on the set for the Bengali feast of ' Durbar ' in the last act, the audience burst into spontaneous applause. I had taken advantage of the fine stage proportions at the Châtelet, especially its great depth, to construct an immense and most original staircase which, in fact, was a combination of several staircases. On this stairway moved bejewelled actors clothed in sumptuous robes of red, orange and violet. The whole effect was rich and oriental. The following year I designed *Le Chant du Tzigane*, which turned out to be my last show at the Châtelet. The war interrupted any further collaboration with this theatre, which was closed down because Lehmann was Jewish.

In the mid-thirties I met Lynn Jack, a charming young girl from a good family. She was an exceptional acrobatic dancer, performing at the Tabarin, a new music-hall which already had a brilliant reputation. She introduced me to her director, Pierre Sandrini, because she felt that we would get on well and that something interesting would come of our meeting. She was right, and I shall always be grateful to her for having brought us together; from the first moment we liked each other. Sandrini promptly asked me to design his next show for the Tabarin (he put on a new one each year). He was an associate of Pierre Dubout, but Dubout had nothing to do with the staging of the shows, preferring to concentrate on the management of the house, or ' the lemonade ', as he referred to it. My collaboration with Sandrini lasted for fifteen years and left me with my best memories of the music-hall. But was it really music-hall? It might be better described as a choreographic spectacle augmented by various attractions. However, these attractions were not separate from the rest of the show, as in other music-hall revues, but were incorporated into a narrative that was part of the ballet or action. The sketches, which were built around various themes, were in two parts, each of which was based on an individual idea. The subjects were very different from the sort of thing usually found in revues; these generally consisted of tableaux of flowers, furs, jewellery, feathers, or reminiscences of famous historical characters such as Catherine the Great, Cleopatra or Madame de Pompadour. For instance, one of our subjects, 'Music', was a big ballet in which dancers symbolized Harmony, Dissonance, Syncopation, Perfect Pitch and various musical forms such as the Symphony, the Concerto and the Rhapsody.

In complete contrast to this we had 'The Newspaper' with a set depicting a stylized rotary printing press and the various pages of a daily paper – the News Page, the Leisure Page, the Sports Page, the Society Page and the Woman's Page – appearing in succession. I also worked on 'Paradise Lost', which began by showing an earthly paradise inhabited by Adam, Eve and all sorts of animals living peacefully together, until the moment when the Devil and the Serpent came on for an extraordinary acrobatic dance leading to its destruction. Hell appeared next in the form of an unusual modern ballet representing a modern factory. For this I brought the dancers on stage from above by means of a large, revolving iron wheel from which they hung.

Another theme was 'House to Let', where each room served as the pretext for a new scene. One saw the Drawing-room, Bedroom, Bathroom, Kitchen and Garden. For the final scene, which took place in the Study, I designed a set made up entirely of enormous books bound in red leather and gold. Some of them formed a stairway upon which moved figures representing famous works of literature. This set was highly successful, but I think the one which struck the public most forcibly was that for 'Château de Cristal'. This showed a completely transparent castle which rose from the basement. The whole thing was built of Rhodoid, a thin plexiglass (made by the Rhone Poulenc Company, which was owned by the family of the composer, Francis Poulenc). I was the first to utilize this material, which was then a fairly new product, in theatre design. Later I often used it, not only for sets and accessories, but also for costumes and wigs.

I have always loved working with new and unusual materials. In that respect I had a marvellous ally in Sandrini, for he too loved anything new and hated the banal, facile or *déja-vu*. Whenever an unoriginal idea came up, it was rejected by one or other of us with the same phrase: 'We can't do that, it has already been done!' This was the exact opposite of what usually happened in the preparation of a music-hall show. Normally, the producers started with an idea which they had already seen in another show and rearranged it to suit themselves. The excuse for such lack of imagination was invariably the same: 'Everything has already been done. Only the trimmings change.'

The two most successful ballets at the Tabarin were probably 'Le Poème' and 'Metal'. The first was a ballet danced without music. The dancers went through their paces to the rhythm of a poem spoken by an off-stage narrator. For the ballet entitled 'Metal', I made all the costumes out of aluminium. This was more than thirty years before the work of Paco Rabanne.

All these ballets were choreographed in marvellous fashion by Sandrini's close collaborator, Marcel Berger. At the start of his career, Berger had been a brilliant classical dancer. Sandrini had also begun his artistic life in classical ballet: he had studied at the ballet school of the Opéra in Paris and made his debut as a dancer on that stage. His mother, the famous Opéra ballerina, Emma Sandrini, had been there at the same time as Zambelli, and the two dancers had shared the laurels. Emma Sandrini retired early, but Zambelli kept up her brilliant career until she was quite elderly.

Sandrini often used modern classical music for his ballets. For example, the ballet about the factory was danced to music by Sergei Prokofiev. One also heard music by Debussy and Ravel. When my collaboration with Sandrini began, I had already stopped working for the Folies Bergère because its leading light, Louis Lemarchand, gave up his various theatrical activities in order to spend more time in the south of France on his yacht. Louis Lemarchand had been identified with the Folies Bergère's more brilliant period. After he left, the Folies gradually became an institution for foreign tourists and provincials, and ended up as a Musée Grévin of the music-hall, the Paris equivalent of the famous Madame Tussaud's in London.

Working with Sandrini was always a pleasure. We usually began planning a show a year in advance, that is, as soon as we had the previous one on the stage. The basic ideas would be discussed over lunch or dinner. Once they had been established, Sandrini would say to me, ' The canvas is ready – it is up to you to embellish it.'

Not a single shadow marred our long collaboration. Sandrini was an extremely charming man. One would never have suspected from his appearance and aura of strength that he was such a gentle person. He was very tall, with prominent features and straight dark hair. His clothes were elegant down to the smallest detail. He had a great flair for discovering new talent, and travelled continuously in search of gifted young artists who were just starting out in show business. Many launched brilliant careers from the Tabarin. I well remember Jacques Tati's wonderful performance in the ' Sports Page ' scene. During his trips, Sandrini also found some astonishing show-girls. He would bring back beautiful girls from all over the world.

Show-girls fall into two categories. The first consists of girls who approach the job as if they were working on an assembly line in a factory. They are mechanical and bored, thinking only about when they can leave. Those who qualify for the second category are unfortunately rare. They are the ones whose love of the theatre and of clothes is sufficiently well developed for them to enjoy dressing up in sumptuous costumes, even if it is only for three hours a day. I have always been astonished that so few show-girls ever seem to realize that each evening they appear could be the most important of their lives. Yet I have heard many fairy stories in which the ' prince ' (of finance) ended by marrying the ' show-girl ' (from the Folies Bergère).

One of the most beautiful girls at the Tabarin was Gizy, a young Hungarian:

she was very tall, with a face of shining beauty and a splendid body. But her body had to be seen naked, for when it was clothed it looked heavy. It was rather like that of the Venus de Milo. Imagine the Venus de Milo wearing clothes! It is most unusual for a first-class fashion model to become a good music-hall show-girl. In order to succeed in the fashion world, models must be excessively thin.

To talk about dressing naked women may seem paradoxical, yet I have often grappled with this problem. There is nothing more difficult than creating costumes for so-called naked dancers. Generally speaking, I was always guided by two principles. The first was to find one detail (hair-style, jewellery or some other accessory) which was sufficiently interesting or striking to suggest the idea for a costume. The second was to build a costume by extending the lines of the naked body into decorative arabesques.

In the days of the *Ziegfeld Follies* and George White's *Scandals,* there was very little nudity on the New York stage. Excessive prudishness has always revolted me. As I recall, American blue laws forbade even the showing of the navel! Why the navel? What is so shocking about that particular part of the body? This has never been explained.

Nudes were featured in the Folies Bergère and eventually were to be seen in all music-halls. In some countries, such as England, nudes were not really part of the show proper. Naked women were not allowed to move on stage but had to stand transfixed, like statues. Actually, this had a distinct advantage: breasts of inferior quality were never seen shaking like jelly.

I remember an amusing incident in this connection. It took place at the Nouvelle Eve during one of the final dress rehearsals, which normally finished very late at night. The artists, dropping with fatigue, were already beginning to remove their make-up and were changing into street clothes before going home, when the producer decided to run through the finale once more. The artists returned in whatever state of undress they found themselves. A nude model, waiting her turn, was seated with her hand covering her genitals. She was so tired that she felt a desperate need to yawn and, not wishing to appear rude, she lifted her hand to her mouth. Everyone burst out laughing, for she had already removed her G-string.

The audiences at the Tabarin were different from those at other music-halls. In addition to foreign tourists and provincials, there were many Parisians, including a number of artists and society people. Almost every evening one could see at least one great foreign star who was passing through Paris.

One evening, when I had taken some foreign friends to the Tabarin, Sandrini introduced me to Michael Todd. Todd wanted to stage a large, elaborate revue such as had not been seen in New York since 1929. I was excited when he asked me to design the sets and costumes for it, but unfortunately, in the event, he was unable to raise the enormous amount of money required for such an enterprise. Todd had come to Paris with his wife, Joan Blondell, and he asked me to

46 *Manhattan Mary.* Décor, 1927

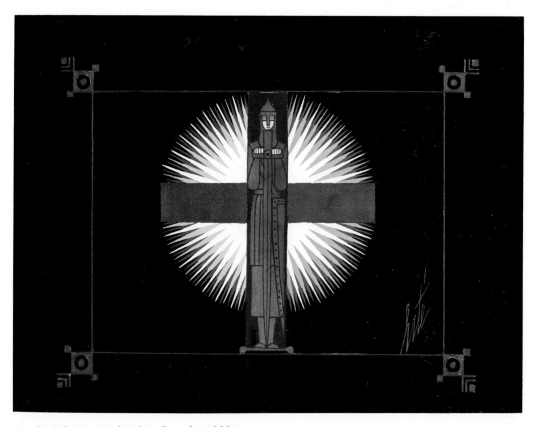

47 *La Princesse Lointaine.* Curtain, 1929

48 ‘ Lumières ’. Set, 1928

design some dresses for her. He had these made up in one of the Paris fashion houses. I must say that Joan Blondell, who was very beautiful, wore my dresses with great style.

The opening night of a new spectacular at the Tabarin was always an occasion. The whole of 'elegant Paris' would be there. Mechanically operated stage effects played an important part in each new show. Every year there would be some new invention. Finally there was no more room backstage – every inch of space was occupied by stage machinery of all kinds. Then Sandrini had the idea of reconstructing the Tabarin along more spacious lines. In order to accomplish this without interrupting the shows, he decided to buy the Bal du Moulin Rouge, which he transformed by installing splendid machinery. Alas, his plans for the Tabarin never saw the light of day.

In 1949, having nearly completed my work on a new show, I decided to go on holiday. The day before my departure, Sandrini asked me to lunch to check over final details. Since it was a fine day we were going to the Pré Catelan in the Bois de Boulogne. A splendid red and white sports car appeared before my door and Sandrini said to me, laughing, 'There's my final madness'. It was indeed his 'final madness' for it was this car which took him to his death three weeks later. The accident happened during a weekend when he was on his way to join his wife and children in Normandy. It was humid and hot; sunstroke caused him to black out and the car crashed into a ditch. I heard the tragic news a few hours after my return to Paris. I have never seen a funeral at which so many tears were shed, for he was loved by everyone.

So, sadly, the last show at the Tabarin was produced after Sandrini's death. The final details were handled by myself; Marcel Berger, the choreographer; the composer and conductor, Alfaro; the librettist, Georges Schmidt; Sandrini's widow and the son and heir of Dubout (Sandrini's partner, who had died the previous year). For Mme Sandrini, a woman of immense charm, this was her first experience with the preparation of a show. She had never before involved herself in her husband's work, being content to be a perfect hostess and mother. Nevertheless, from the first days, she was, as they say, 'in the swim', conducting rehearsals with remarkable efficiency. The final presentation was a great success, but it was the swan song of the Tabarin.

Apart from the fact that Mme Sandrini did not feel able to take on the long-term direction of such an enterprise, she did not want to work with her partner, Dubout's son. The Tabarin, like the Moulin Rouge, was subsequently sold at auction for a ludicrously low price to the Clerico brothers, who also owned the Lido. In 1952 they finally closed the Tabarin so that its world-wide reputation would be transferred to the Lido. There was nothing sadder than to pass this abandoned building which had housed some of the greatest shows in Paris during the 'thirties. The building was finally pulled down to make room for garages and offices, but a last show was put on a few days before demolition began. I did not go, as I would have found the sadness of such an occasion unbearable.

Besides my work at the Tabarin during the 'thirties, I also designed sets and costumes for various foreign productions, including many at the Scala in Berlin. In 1935 I worked on a revue at the French Casino in New York, with Jean Le Seyeux. My costumes for this show were made up by Mme Karinska, the most marvellous costumier I ever met in my theatrical career. She had a genius for working with new and unusual materials and for creating miraculous effects out of nothing. Her necklaces made from painted nuts were extraordinary. She had, and still has, amazing energy, despite her age. Throughout her life she has done physical exercises every morning and has kept her figure. Tall, with a fine and extremely expressive face, she has always known how to maintain a youthful appearance. I saw Karinska again in the early 1970s in New York, when she invited me to the Ballet Theatre to see a ballet for which she had designed and made the costumes, which were beautiful. She was the same as ever: enthusiastic, elegant, wearing strange jewels. Despite the fact that six months earlier she had fallen down the stairs of her house and broken her thigh, there was hardly a trace of a limp.

After my first encounter with Karinska, I always asked producers to have costumes made by her. Unhappily, several of them refused because she had a reputation for being expensive. But what a mistake that was. She would give an estimate before commencing the work on a show. Then she would find that this or the other material was no longer satisfactory and would replace it with another, more expensive, material, at her own cost. As a result she often lost money. She always worked out of a love for the theatre. If she didn't like a play or an actor, she would refuse the commission, however advantageous the terms. Later, Karinska relinquished her costume house in Paris to her daughter, Irene (who still runs it with great success) and set herself up in America. She is still working in New York and has a contract with the Ballet Theatre.

In 1937 I received a proposal to design a production in London. This was a revue called *It's in the Bag*, produced by Cecil Landeau at the Savile Theatre. He had greatly admired my work at the Tabarin. From our first meeting there was an atmosphere of harmonious collaboration. The costumes were made in Paris, under my supervision, by Max Weldy, who had brought us together. I have very happy memories of my collaboration with Cecil Landeau. He was a cultivated man, with a profound artistic sensibility and exquisite taste that extended to the finest detail.*

It's in the Bag was a great success. The following press comment set the tone of the others:

---

* In 1970 I designed the sets and costumes for a new musical comedy adapted by Landeau from a comedy by Jean Valmy, called *Here I Am and Here I Stay*, but the show has yet to be produced.

> This is a revue of exceptional quality . . . the real hero of the evening is a mysterious Erté, who has done all the scenery and costumes. He, or she, is a bit of a genius. Not even in Mr Cochran's great days have I seen a show more continuously beautiful to the eye. (*Evening News*, London, 5 November, 1937)

After this first London success, I had a proposal from George Black (senior) to design a series of sets for the Palladium. I designed several in 1938 for the revue *London Symphony*, and in 1939 for *Black Velvet*. The costumes for these shows were made by Alec Shanks.

It was the beginning of a long collaboration. I had met Alec Shanks several years earlier in Paris when he worked with Max Weldy. He had assisted Ciocari in building the cardboard models for my settings for *La Princesse Lointaine*. At that time he was a tall boy, pale, thin and full of complexes. After working with Weldy for a time, he returned to London, where he founded a costumier's business that became very prosperous. I met him in London during the rehearsals for *It's in the Bag*. On one occasion I had missed my return flight to Paris. There were no seats available for two days because it was just before the Paris Grand Prix. I telephoned the hotel where I had been staying, but apparently my room was already taken and nothing was available. I suddenly remembered that Alec had invited me several times to his country house, Briarfield, in Harpenden, an invitation that I had never been able to accept. So I telephoned him and spent two pleasant days with him in the country before I boarded my flight back to Paris.

In addition to all this theatrical activity, which kept me very busy throughout the 1930s, I was still working for *Harper's Bazaar*. However, in 1932, six years after I had signed a second ten-year contract, my great friend Henry Sell left the magazine, and Carmel Snow, who had been Fashion Editor of *Vogue*, became editor. Mrs Snow was a veteran of twelve years' service under Mrs Edna Woolman Chase, *Vogue's* editor and reigning arbiter of the fashion world. Although Mrs Snow had, at one point, seemed to be the obvious successor to Mrs Chase, the latter was in no hurry to retire. Eventually, Mrs Snow's capacity for waiting in the wings was undermined by the continuous blandishments of the Hearst organization. The news of her appointment to *Harper's Bazaar* shook the New York fashion world to its foundations. The reactions of most of the editorial staff of *Vogue* could have been summed up in one word, ' treason! ' And this attitude died hard. Indeed, some years later, when a *Life* magazine researcher interviewed a *Vogue* editor in connection with a story on Mrs Snow, the editor is reported to have said: ' To discuss fashion in relation to Mrs Snow is like writing the history of the United States from the viewpoint of Benedict Arnold.'

Since my work had been so closely identified with the pre-Carmel Snow image of the magazine – William Randolph Hearst had said, ' How would you know it was *Harper's Bazaar* without an Erté cover? ' – I was, naturally, one of the first targets of the new regime's big guns. Mrs Snow wanted not only to supervise my work but also to impose her own ideas. I had to submit rough sketches, from which she would make selections. As I have already said, creative freedom has always been vitally important to me. When Henry Sell left *Harper's Bazaar*, I lost that freedom.

My strained relations with Mrs Snow finally reached breaking point after an incident involving Daisy Fellowes. Mrs Fellowes, Paris editor of *Harper's Bazaar*, was a fascinating woman and the personification of elegance. Slender and beautiful, she gave an impression of great harmony in every detail of her appearance and behaviour, so that whatever she wore took on a distinctive quality. We enjoyed an easy, friendly relationship and I often visited her charming house in Neuilly. It was surrounded by a lovely garden, containing sculptures by Jean Cocteau, one of her closest friends. These sculptures were remarkable creations, consisting of metal tubes moulded into various forms.

Apparently, Daisy had had a row with Mrs Snow, the details of which I never knew. She asked me to write to Mr Hearst, telling him that my dealings with her had always been most pleasant and that we understood one another very well. Somehow, my letter fell into Mrs Snow's hands. From then on, she made my work so difficult that I finally decided to terminate my association with the magazine. What had started out as a challenging and rewarding arrangement had ended by becoming a frustrating chore. So, in 1937, a year after the expiration of my second long-term contract and a twenty-two year tenure, my *Harper's Bazaar* period came to an end.

Mrs Snow could not help gloating that she had succeeded in getting Mr Hearst to accept Cassandre to replace me as cover artist. It was, however, a somewhat empty victory, as by this time I had become totally disenchanted with the job. Mr Hearst, in a communication to Mrs Snow in December 1936, paid me all the compliments I needed when he said:

> I think the Cassandre covers are showy — let us say striking, as a more amiable word. I do not know exactly what they mean. I do not suppose it is necessary that I should know. I imagine modernistic art is not good if anybody does know what it means. The idea seems to be to draw something that everyone can put his own interpretation on.
>
> This, then, is good modernistic art and will make a striking cover; and the twelve covers for the year will be furnished by the same artist in the same definitely incomprehensible style. Thus we will have continuity.
>
> And most important of all, you like them. Therefore, I do not see why we should not go ahead on this basis.
>
> Finally, I do not know of anybody who could do worse, unless it be Picasso; what I really mean is that I do not know anybody who could do better from a modernistic standpoint. However, please do not ask me to express an opinion as to whether I like Cassandre

better than Erté; because I like Erté better, and I would hate to have
you know how wrong I am.

Mr Hearst showed his genius as a publisher by giving Mrs Snow, his editor,
the right to choose her staff and make basic policy in the publications she edited.
For his comments about me I shall be ever thankful to Mr Hearst, who concluded
his message with characteristic wit: 'However, I am definitely a back number.
I do not like Picasso or any of that kind or crew. I guess a lot of people do; and
if they do, they may be overwhelmingly right. I did not like Roosevelt.'

1937 was a particularly brilliant year in Paris. It was the year of the International
Exhibition, the first to be held there since the World's Fair of 1900.

I still remember that World's Fair vividly although I was only in my eighth
year at the time. My mother had brought my sister and me to Paris for the
occasion. Throughout my boyhood, when my father went off each summer on
naval manoeuvres, the three of us would take long trips, usually abroad. This
was always a happy time because we all loved to travel. For me, however, travel
became a life-long pleasure that I still pursue whenever possible. In 1900 we
stayed at a hotel on the rue Pierre Charron, which has long since disappeared.
As soon as I walked through the Fair entrance on the Place de la Concorde, I
was caught up in its fairyland atmosphere. I felt as if I had entered another
world.

Since the 1900 World's Fair was dedicated to the triumph of 'La Fée Elec-
tricité', electrical innovations featured prominently. I was dazzled by the brilliance
of the illuminated fountains and by Lois Fuller's Butterfly and Fire dances, which
were built around splendid electrical lighting effects. These dances subsequently
became classics of music-hall productions in the early years of this century.

The 1900 Fair was spread out over a huge area on both banks of the Seine.
The Left Bank section extended from Les Invalides to the Champs-de-Mars, the
Right Bank section from the Place de la Concorde to the Trocadero. The Grand
Palais, the Petit Palais and the Pont Alexandre III were especially built for the
occasion. I was intrigued by the *trottoir roulant,* which encircled the grounds,
and fascinated by the Palais de la Femme – my first contact with authentic
Parisian Haute Couture. In addition to all the latest fashion models, it included
a panoramic display tracing the evolution of fashion. The period costumes were
modelled by wax figures against appropriate settings. I was particularly impressed
by one of the figures – a replica of Marion de L'Orme, a beautiful seventeenth-
century courtesan. According to the legend, she lived to be 137 years old. Her
long, narrow face with its regular features, enormous dark eyes and jet black
hair was to become my ideal of feminine beauty.

For me, the impact of the 1900 World's Fair was tremendous. I have rarely
missed a major international fair since then, but, most important of all, it was

a crucial milestone in the development of my long love affair with the city of Paris.

Another high point in my boyhood travels was an extended boat trip down the Volga to the Caspian Sea when I was about ten. We then followed the 'Military Georgian Road' which crosses the Caucasus, forming a link between the Caspian Sea and the Black Sea. The Georgian landscape was overpowering and savage in comparison with Switzerland, which I had visited the previous year, and the beauty of the Georgian people was unforgettable. The men were extremely tall, with long slender legs; narrow hips and waists accentuated their broad chests and shoulders. The women were slim, supple and graceful with long, narrow faces, huge dark eyes and bluish-black hair. The Tcherkess women used to reinforce their bodices with narrow wooden splints in order to achieve a slim, flat look. I loved to watch them perform their national dance – the Lezginka – in which the girls, wearing long dresses of heavy brocade, seemed to glide over the floor. I never saw anything like it until I went to a performance of the Moisseieff Ballet years later.

During that trip, we were invited one day for lunch to the castle of a Caucasian prince. While we were being shown over the interior of the castle, my mother expressed great admiration for a particular carved silver vase. When we got back to our hotel at Kislovesdsk – where one of the principal thermal baths was located – my mother was surprised to find the silver vase in her room. This was a typical example of Georgian hospitality.

It was in the Caucasus that I developed my love of taking long solitary walks in the woods. Solitary walks are still a source of great relaxation and pleasure for me, and I experience a strong feeling of being in close touch with nature, almost to the point of becoming part of it. As woods become increasingly scarce and inaccessible, I cherish them more than ever.

On another trip that we took, this time to Sweden, I had a strange experience. During one of our excursions out of Stockholm we came upon a charming little eighteenth-century castle. Since I loved old houses, I persuaded my mother to ask the caretaker if we could look over the castle. Fortunately, the owners were away and he agreed. First he showed us the hall and the main living-room. Before he opened the door to the adjoining room, however, I said to my mother, 'The walls of this room will be yellow and on the back wall, facing the door, there will be a portrait of a beautiful lady dressed in blue.' When we entered the room, it was exactly as I had described it. Since this was an obscure castle, whose interiors had never been photographed, it was rather an uncanny coincidence. My mother was so disturbed that, shortly after we got home, she took me to a doctor. But although he gave me a thorough examination, he could find nothing wrong.

We also visited Vienna during the height of the Hapsburg era, around 1901. It had an atmosphere of gaiety and elegance that reminded me of Paris. I loved to watch the dashing open carriages, drawn by beautiful horses, and the smart ladies who rode in them. They all sported little parasols and veils to protect the whiteness of their skins. Parasols and veils, along with muffs, lorgnettes, little bouquets of flowers and fans, without which no elegant lady would ever appear in evening dress, have disappeared as smart accessories. I wonder if they will ever come back. Probably they will, since everything seems to come back into fashion sooner or later. The recent fad for feather boas was a good example of such a revival.

That same year, in Karlsbad and Marienbad, I saw King Edward VII, who was still the Prince of Wales. I was intrigued by the turnups on his trousers – something new at that time. I then discovered that the fashion had begun when the Prince had taken a walk in the country, been caught in heavy rain and turned up his trousers to keep them from getting wet. Everything the Prince did in the matter of clothes immediately affected men's fashions. He once forgot to fasten the lower button of his waistcoat. The next day, every man who either saw it or heard about it did the same.

Between 1900 and 1937 there were two other important exhibitions in Paris – the International Exhibition of Decorative Arts in 1925 and the Colonial Exhibition in 1931. The former took place during the year I spent in America. Missing this apotheosis of the style that is now known as Art Deco has been the regret of my life, especially since I made a considerable contribution to its development. Art Deco has influenced the greater part of the twentieth century. It is an evolution from Art Nouveau in combination with the geometric forms of Cubism. The revolutionary aspect of Art Deco stemmed from the fact that it fused pure with applied art, which had previously been considered faintly contemptible. Art Deco penetrated not only the homes of privileged people, but, in one form or another, those of people of more modest means. When, in 1966, I visited the ' Exhibition of 1925 ' at the Pavillon de Marsan, I was struck by the fact that almost everything we now think of as modern was created in that period. This was particularly true of the office furniture, which might have come from the House of Knoll. I was also struck by a misleading anachronism in the design of the wooden mannequins wearing the dresses of the great couturiers of the mid-'twenties. The shape of all these figures was that of the typical nineteenth- and early twentieth-century silhouette: the bust was slanted forward, the bottom backward. As a result, the dresses in the exhibition looked quite different from the way dresses actually looked in 1925.

The Colonial Exhibition was huge and varied. I often spent whole days there. Among the many fascinating exhibits was a fine reproduction of a temple at Ankor Wat. It was my inspiration for the sets and costumes of a ballet, *The Treasures of Indochina,* which later made its début at the Alcazar in Marseilles and subsequently went on what was virtually a world tour, appearing in many cities and towns in Europe and America. It was at the Colonial Exhibition, also, that I acquired a taste for exotic food. I dined frequently at the various ethnic restaurants.

I have always been fascinated by international exhibitions. They open the way to unknown lands by providing a voyage around the world in a few days. The great advantage of such a voyage is that all the characteristic features of a country are immediately visible in a single pavilion. One discovers at once the essence of soul of a country. In a real voyage, such discovery is gradual and one does not gain a sense of the whole until the end of the journey, when there has been time to sort out one's impressions. However, there is one element missing in these artificial journeys – the physical climate and intangible *ambience* of the country.

Another aspect of international exhibitions that has always appealed to me is their festive atmosphere. I have always loved the air of spontaneous and relaxed gaiety that is usually found at fairs. I particularly remember one famous fair in Paris at the beginning of the century – the Fair of Neuilly – where all classes of society rubbed shoulders and enjoyed themselves.

It is odd that I should have clearer memories of the 1900 Exhibition than of the one in 1937. Probably my childhood imagination was more responsive. I do remember, however, being struck by the beauty of the architecture of the 1937 Russian pavilion. It looked like a giant ship about to be launched into space. There are usually a few monuments left behind after every exhibition: in 1900 the Alexandre III Bridge, the Grand and the Petit Palais; in 1937 the Palais de Chaillot and the Palais de Tokyo (now the Museum of Modern Art). The architecture of the latter was heavily criticized, some finding it too classical, others too modern. For my part, I have always liked it.

1938 and 1939 passed for me with uninterrupted work in the theatre – for the Tabarin, the Palladium, the Hippodromes in London and Blackpool; for a revue with George White for the International Exhibition in San Francisco and, finally, a play by Paul Nivoix with Cécile Sorel which was never produced because of the war.

World War II and the Forties

Although I could see the catastrophe approaching, I hoped, right up to the last moment, that it would be avoided. My feelings about World War II can be compared with those of my parents about all they suffered during World War I and the Russian Revolution: 'The nightmare is over . . . let us do our best to forget it.' For me, however, this is easier said than done.

War is an inexplicable monstrosity. How is it possible, in our present state of civilization, for people to allow themselves to be manoeuvred into such madness? It makes one disgusted with the human race. How can the so-called democracies of the world presume to talk about the liberty of the individual when they send their young men to be massacred like cattle in a slaughter-house?

Hatred of war is so ingrained in my nature that I never go to see war films or read war novels. Yet, since the end of World War II, such films and books have proliferated with distressing rapidity. One would think we had not yet had enough of this plague. My sympathies are entirely with the young, who believe in – and work for – non-violence and peace.

When it became clear that Paris would inevitably be occupied, the exodus began. When, on 14 June, 1940, it was declared an open city, the flow gained momentum. I was prepared to leave with my mother and my faithful friend, Constantin Tscherkas, but at the last moment my mother felt that she would not be strong enough to undertake a journey whose ultimate destination was so uncertain. Her health was already poor and she had been living in a nursing home in nearby Boulogne-sur-Seine. We therefore decided to remain in Paris.

For those who did not live through it, it is difficult to imagine what Paris was like under the Occupation. The only cars in the streets – and they were very few – were German. One of the ironic by-products of this situation was that Paris never looked more beautiful. Parisians got around on the Metro or by bicycle-taxis (side-cars attached to bicycles). They also learned how to walk again. As the city became more isolated, long queues of Parisians waited patiently outside food shops, clutching their coupons, to buy meagre quantities of the items that made up our limited daily diet. Drab-looking, working-class women rubbed shoulders with elegant ladies perched on wooden platform shoes. One of the most evocative street sounds in silent, war-time Paris was the click of these wooden shoes on the pavements. Platform sandals, which looked like the footwear of actors in classical Greek drama, were later to be revived by Yves Saint-Laurent.

Elegance and fashion, however, never lost their place in Parisian life. With the exception of Chanel, who closed down her fashion house for the duration, it was business as usual for all the top couturiers. Skirts were short. Although it was difficult to obtain fabrics, women wore huge, cloth-draped hats which, when perched on their lofty, teased coiffures, looked like large cushions.

Naturally, in the early days of the Occupation, all artistic activity stopped dead, but little by little it revived. Many people who had fled began drifting back. One of Hitler's first gestures after Paris had fallen was his proclamation: 'Let Paris be the Reich's Luna Park!' This policy was aimed not only at currying favourable world opinion but also at keeping up the morale of his troops. Serge Lifar in his memoir, *Ma Vie*, shrewdly sums up the atmosphere of Paris at that time: 'In those first days of the Occupation the Germans were like men who have just bought a property. They were amused with and proud of their purchase, impatient to visit it and to show it off while the old owners were still on the premises.' The Germans wanted a 'Gay Paree' and many of them got it.

One of the first theatres to re-open was the Théâtre des Bouffes Parisiens. The proprietor, Albert Willmetz, revived his successful operetta of World War I, *Phi Phi*. It was a charming, typically French work, based on the character of the Greek sculptor Phidias, and was just as fresh as when it was originally created. The music was by Christiné and the libretto by Willemetz. This was Weldy's last show in Paris. I designed all the sets and costumes in blue, white and pink – a pastel version of the French tricolour, which had been removed from the Parisian scene by the German occupation authorities. The Germans, however, who flocked to the show in great numbers, never did get the joke. *Phi Phi* enjoyed a renaissance which lasted for several subsequent years, with successful productions in many different Parisian theatres.

Two familiar personalities who disappeared from the Paris theatrical scene during this period were Max Weldy and Mitty Goldin. Goldin, the founder and proprietor of the enormously successful ABC Theatre, was an interesting character. I had first met him in Max Weldy's studio when, at the start of his career, he was a minor impresario. He was plump even in those days. And whenever I saw him he was always wearing an old, moth-eaten fur cloak.

Weldy, foreseeing France's drift toward war, had at one point started negotia-tions with Goldin for the sale of his business; however, Weldy left Paris at the end of 1940, arriving in the United States in January of 1941, and Goldin, being Jewish, fled to Cannes in the south of France to escape the German occupation. The war years took their toll, nevertheless, and Goldin died in the early 1950s. I have always had a warm feeling for this able and intelligent man.*

When the war broke out, Sandrini closed the Tabarin and put on a show at the Lido, which was then owned by Leon Volterra. The Lido was equipped with a large swimming pool in which Volterra used to present nautical spectacles. For Sandrini's show, Volterra built a stage and added dressing-rooms. The show was so successful that Volterra wanted more music-hall revues for the Lido and he asked me to design sets and costumes for them. The Tabarin, meanwhile, had become an artists' canteen. Two years later, however, it opened with a very fine show, *Dans Notre Miroir*. So, while I was designing for the Tabarin, I was also working at the Lido where, eventually, there was a new production every year. Altogether I designed six shows for the Lido, most of which were put on during the war years. They were largely ballets, since a Russian choreographer called Boris Skibine, father of the famous dancer, George Skibine, was in charge of production. When Skibine's wife escaped from Russia, they had formed an acrobatic act. They made a splendid couple: she slim, dark and supple; he a fine, fair-haired athlete with typically Slav features. Later she worked with him at the Lido.

I became extremely fond of Volterra, a man of great intelligence, kindness and rough charm. His was a fantastic career. He had started out as a boy selling programmes at the Casino de Paris and ended up owning the place. In addition to the Lido, he also owned the Théâtre de Paris, the Théâtre Marigny and Luna Park, the famous pleasure garden. All were highly successful. What a shame that the pleasure gardens of Paris – there was another called Magic City – have disappeared. In the early 1900s there were similar amusement parks in all the capitals of the world. The only other survivals that I know of are the Tivoli in Copenhagen and the Tibidabo in Barcelona.

Volterra had a passion for horses and built up one of the most famous racing stables in France. He shared this passion with his second wife, Suzy, who even-

---

* After Goldin's death, his widow sold his large collection of my work, which included all the working copies and sketches – among which a number of originals had crept in – from Weldy's files, plus many originals that he had bought. The collection also contained the drawings for the sets and costumes I had designed for *Amour Royal*, starring Cécile Sorel, which had been produced at Goldin's ABC Theatre in 1935. Unfortunately, Goldin's widow, who had no sense of the value of things, let them all go for a pitifully small sum. As a result, for some time afterwards my designs could be found on many a stall along the Paris quays or in the flea market.

tually inherited the stable. Under her direction it later achieved world renown. We had a great rapport, Suzy and I. She was a very charming woman – beautiful and extremely elegant. Before meeting Volterra, she had been a dancer at the Opéra de Paris and was a great friend of Constantin Tscherkas – Cotick as he was nicknamed. Cotick often joined me at the Lido for an evening with the Volterras.

Shortly before his death, Volterra sold both the Lido and Luna Park to the Clerico brothers, who installed Pierre Guérin as manager. I designed his first production. Pierre's good friend and associate, René Fraday, had just returned from America where he had been scouting attractions and ideas for the next show. Since Guérin wanted me to collaborate on this production, he submitted his plans to me. Among them was a scene which represented an aquarium. I had just successfully staged a ballet at the Tabarin with an aquarium, so I told Guérin that it was impossible to include this scene: it would be bad for both the Lido and the Tabarin, as well as embarrassing for me. Fraday tried to persuade me to go back on my word and advise Guérin to stage the aquarium. I never could understand why he was so insistent. Naturally, I refused. After that, our relationship deteriorated rapidly and my association with the Lido ceased abruptly.

During the war years I also designed sets and costumes for the operettas that Volterra put on at the Théâtre Marigny. They included *Là-haut*, Moretti's *Trois Jeunes Filles Nues*, Messager's *Coup de Roulis* and Christiné's *Dédé*. I also worked on many operettas for Sandrini, simultaneously designing for his shows at the Tabarin. He put on operettas in various Paris theatres: *Toi, C'est Moi*, a charming work by Misraki, at the Apollo, *Les Cent Vierges* by Lecocq in the same theatre the following year, and *Une Femme Par Jour* by Van Parys, at the Théâtre des Capucines. I also designed sets and costumes for *Belamour*, an operetta by Guy Lafarge, at the Théâtre des Nouveautés. My old friend, Mme Rasimi made up the costumes for this show. I was pleased to see her again after several years, but it made me realize how easily one can lose contact with one's friends in Paris.

In 1941, while I was working on *Toi, C'est Moi*, I had an accident which prevented me from finishing the final sets. One evening, after I had dined with a young man who was a dancer at the Opéra-Comique, he took me to the Metro on his bicycle since the station was a long way from the restaurant. In the dark his bicycle hit the curb and we fell off. I knew at once that I had hurt my right arm and, once in the Metro, I saw that my coat sleeve was soaked with blood. When I reached home I washed the wound and put on some disinfectant. It healed rapidly, so I forgot the whole incident.

Suddenly, a month later, I felt pains in my arm, which had swelled up and turned blue. I was told by my doctor that I had a tubercular infection which would require surgery. Unfortunately the first operation was unsuccessful and I had to have a second. For eight months my arm was in a sling and I could not use my right hand. I was desperate – being unable to work was a tragedy for me. I tried drawing with my left hand with no success. I am sure it would take years of training to be able to draw left-handed, especially with the technique my drawings require. After this experience I was convinced that it would be a good idea to teach very young children to use both their hands with equal facility.

I saw a lot of my old friend, Cotick Tscherkas during the war. He often came to my house for dinner with his friend, the comedian, Georges Fels. Fels was a very kind boy, with a lively mind, and we would often have amusing conversations. One day he said to me, ' Philosophy? That's only a form of mental masturbation.' We would spend many enjoyable evenings in long discussions, which helped to make these difficult times more bearable. Cotick, who was usually a shy and retiring character, came to life in intimate gatherings.

Sometimes we would go to dinner with Prince and Princess Youssoupoff. On other occasions they would come to dine at my house. To call it ' dining ' is a misnomer; it would be more accurate to say ' eating ', for our meals were meagre. In the first year of the Occupation I remember eating a great many swedes, which are usually fed to animals, and turnips, which I detest to this day. I still cannot stomach duck with turnips, which is considered a French delicacy. One was only entitled to a tiny piece of meat once a week. I gave mine to my cat, Micmac, who could not have lived without meat.

Even so, I found hunger much easier to endure than cold. Naturally, there was no central heating, so I was obliged to keep warm by my own devices. Trying to achieve a temperature in which one could bear to work, in a room of which two sides were great glass bays, was no easy task. The weekly fuel ration was so small that I had a stove installed in the central room in which I burnt anything I could lay my hands on. I shall never forget the hours I spent during my working nights, trying to keep the fire going. One thing sustained me through those hours of hard work – coffee. Since real coffee was unobtainable in the shops, I always asked theatre directors, who were in a privileged position, to supply me with a certain quantity of coffee per job, as one of the conditions of my contract. It made them all laugh but, thanks to my insistence, I never went without this precious aid to work.

The only place where I ate really well was the home of Germaine Bruel, who had a fashion house called Germaine and Germaine. Cotick, who was one of her favourites, took me there several times. I shall never know how she managed to produce those excellent dinners. Powerful connections? Resourcefulness? Ingenuity? I would have considered it the height of indiscretion to have asked. In those days, however, there were many who not only asked questions but remembered the answers – real or imaginary, first-hand or otherwise – against the day of reckoning: Liberation. These were confusing times and peace-time standards of morality were often stretched to breaking point. But Germaine's evenings were oases in a dreary existence, and I always looked forward to them.

Her guests were usually theatrical people: Jean Weber, Roger Gaillard, Robert Favard, Serge Peretti – star dancer at the Opéra – and others. At Germaine's home I also met a charming lady, Hélène Poupar, widow of a prominent magistrate. We are still good friends.

Thanks to the emergence of the black market, little by little the situation improved. When Paris was no longer sealed off from the rest of the occupied zone, I managed to obtain meat from my chemist, whose parents lived in the country. Although food remained a major preoccupation, intellectual and cultural life flourished. Exhibitions, the opera, the ballet, concerts, theatres and scientific conferences drew capacity crowds. The Nazi propaganda machine worked diligently – and, for a while, successfully – at fostering a variety of Franco-German cultural activities and exchanges.

During this period, visits from my mother became more and more rare. She who had always seemed so remarkably youthful began to decline and, towards the end of the war, could no longer leave her nursing home. I would go to see her, but my visits tended to be much too short because my commitments kept me so fully occupied. My mother impatiently awaited these occasions. She still thought of me as her ' little one ', despite the fact that I was approaching fifty.

During one of my visits there was a report that Pushkin's house had been completely destroyed during a major battle between the Germans and Russians fought in the vicinity of Veliki Louki. This was sad news for us because it meant that what had been our family estate, which adjoined the Pushkin residence, must also have been hit. As a very young boy I had spent my summers on this estate, which my father, as the eldest son, had inherited. Now, one more tenuous link with our pre-Revolutionary past in Russia had been wiped out. But the beauty of our house, Fedotkovo, which had been built in the late eighteenth century, will always remain fresh in my memory. It was yellow with white columns, and overlooked a large pond complete with swans. A beautiful garden gave way to fields where sheep grazed, and in the distance was a large wooded area. The interior of the house was also beautiful. I particularly loved the handsome Empire furniture in the library, which was made of Karelian Birch rather than of the usual mahogany. The reason for this was that much of the furniture on the big estates had been made by peasant slaves who copied pieces imported from France and Italy. Since, in addition to being superb craftsmen, these peasants were genuine artists, they invariably added their own personal touches. There was a good example of this typically Russian interpretation in one of the bedrooms at Fedotkovo. The metal ornamentation on Empire furniture, which is usually made of brass or bronze, had been done in silver. In the late 1960s, I saw a revival of Tchaikovsky's *Eugène Onegin* at the Paris Opéra-Comique, with settings by Wakhewitch. I was surprised to see, in the first act, the facade of a house that was exactly like Fedotkovo. I suspect that Wakhewitch was inspired by Pushkin's house in Selo Michailovskoe, which was similar to ours.

Although my mother had never had a day's illness, her strength gradually ebbed away and, soon after the end of the war, she died at the age of eighty-four. The doctor told me that her whole system was worn out. Those terrible years in Russia after the Revolution had taken their toll. It was a bitter blow for me. Even when one knows that death is imminent, one still clings to the hope that it can, somehow, be avoided. The fact that I did not give her more time in her final days is one of my deepest regrets.

Those were dark days for me, but my sister was a great comfort. She was kind, sympathetic and thoughtful. Toward the end of my mother's life, Natalia had given up her apartment in Montmartre and moved into the nursing home; she had been with my mother when she died. By that time, I was no longer contributing to my sister's support, a fact which seems to have had a salutary effect on our subsequent relations. The tensions and conflicts of our youth were gradually dissipated and we became good friends once again. Such are the paradoxes of human behaviour. We remained on good terms until she died in August 1969, at the age of eighty-five.

A few years after my mother's death, an extraordinary thing happened. One of my friends introduced me to a strange woman, a confirmed spiritualist. She was convinced that I was a remarkable medium and persuaded me to participate in a seance. She came to my house with three friends and we installed ourselves around the big Empire table in my drawing-room. Soon there were taps on the table in response to our questions, but the woman who was recording the taps and transposing them into letters could make nothing of them. Suddenly I had the idea of using the letters of the Russian alphabet to see if they made up Russian words. My intuition was right and we obtained precise responses to all our questions. My mother's spirit was communicating with us.

The current between us became so strong that the table moved from the drawing-room into the adjoining studio, where it came to rest beside my drawing board. I found this particularly touching and significant because my mother knew how much my work meant to me. In answer to my questions she assured me that she was happy and that I was not to worry. After that seance I never tried to communicate with her again because I found the psychical and emotional strain much too exhausting. It took me several days to recover from that session.

During the final days of the war I was busy decorating all the windows of the large Printemps shops. This was absorbing and demanding work because the motifs were changed each month. At this period it was very difficult to find suitable materials. I remember, one month, dressing all the windows with paper cut and rolled up into different shapes.

Meanwhile the war entered its last violent phase. Although Paris was under fire from both sides, I never sought refuge in the cellar. I had a morbid fear that the building would collapse and bury me in the rubble. I watched it all from my apartment with my cat, Micmac. When the end finally came, after that first, glorious moment of exhilaration and relief, I started calling all my friends on the telephone. Those that I was unable to reach called me. During the next few days we were all caught up in a delirium of telephonic euphoria. By way of celebration, Cotick and I, with our mutual friend, Mme Poupar, took a three-week holiday in Blencau. We stayed at an inn and went cycling into the surrounding countryside. The purpose of the trip was to make up for the years of wartime frugality and – as far as was possible – we certainly indulged our appetites during those three weeks.

In 1944 Cotick had introduced me to another of his friends, Max de Rieux, producer at the Opéra-Comique, where Cotick was ballet-master and star dancer. Max de Rieux liked the things I designed and wanted to work with me. An opportunity soon presented itself.

Celebrations were being held for the Donizetti centenary, and it was decided to put on, in the Palais de Chaillot, one of his most famous works, *Don Pasquale*. Max de Rieux was to be the producer. He had seen on my studio wall the sketches for a production of *Don Pasquale* which I had devised in 1932 for the Riga Opera House (owned by Krüger, the famous match manufacturer who committed suicide by throwing himself from an aeroplane). That same year, as well as *Don Pasquale*, I had designed sets for Gounod's *Faust* for the same house. These were my first opera sets. Previously I had designed only costumes for the Metropolitan Opera, the Chicago Opera, the Opéra de Paris and the Opéra-Comique.

My idea for the Riga production of *Don Pasquale* was to match the four singing characters with four dancers who would mime the action during the overture and interludes. I treated the mimes and singers as four characters from the Commedia dell'arte. Don Pasquale was Pantaloon; Norina, Columbine; Ernesto, Leander; and Doctor Malatesta, Harlequin. The dancers' and singers' costumes were similar but not identical, those of the dancers being inspired by the Commedia dell'arte of the eighteenth century, while the costumes of the singers were of the early romantic period when *Don Pasquale* was composed. The set consisted of a small central scene framed on both sides by folding screens with four doors, through which the mime characters entered. Painted on the doors were the figures of Pantaloon, Columbine, Leander and Harlequin. It was only in the central scene that the décor was changed for each set, chiefly by shifting colours.

It was this innovation that de Rieux wanted me to use for the Palais de Chaillot production, which turned out to be a launching pad for a virtual *Don Pasquale* renaissance. After the Palais de Chaillot run, the opera enjoyed a full

49   'Venus de Paris'. Cover, 1935

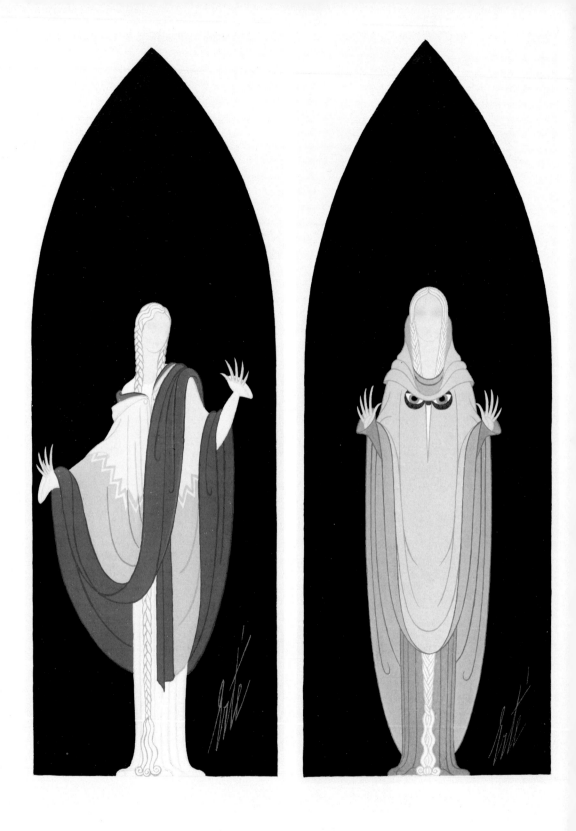

50, 51   *Pelléas et Mélisande.* Costumes, 1931

season of performances at the Théâtre des Variétés. In 1946 it was revived at the Sarah Bernhardt, and in 1959 at the Opéra-Comique.

At the Sarah Bernhardt, the role of Ernesto was sung by Tito Schipa. At the Palais de Chaillot and at the Variétés, the part was taken by a young singer who was to become known as Luis Mariano. In the early part of his career he wanted to devote himself to the opera, but the fantastic success which came to him so easily in the music-hall distracted him from pursuing these early ambitions. He had a superb but insufficiently trained voice. With his vocal gifts and his fine physique, he could have become one of the finest operatic tenors of our time. He did, indeed, make a splendid picture with his slim, elegant figure, typically Spanish face and radiant smile.

After *Don Pasquale*, set and costume designs for operas became an important part of my work. A new company called Opéra Bouffe had put on the opera at the Palais de Chaillot. Shortly after that production, the founder of the Opéra Bouffe decided to go to Brazil where she owned vast plantations. I designed the sets and costumes for Messager's opera *Fortunio*, Offenbach's *La Duchesse de Gerolstein* and Reynaldo Hahn's *Ciboulette*, which she planned to produce in São Paulo.

The success of *Don Pasquale* was the basis for my long and fruitful collaboration with Max de Rieux in opera. The following year I designed *The Barber of Seville* for French television with him, and the sets for Cimarosa's *The Secret Marriage* at the Sarah Bernhardt Theatre. But my greatest success was an opera by Francis Poulenc, *Les Mamelles de Tirésias*, based on a play by Guillaume Apollinaire. This superb work was presented at the Opéra-Comique in 1947. The composer did not want to see the opera produced in the same style as when it had first appeared in 1917. In an article in the journal *Opéra* he wrote:

> Since Apollinaire's play, with the exception of the prologue and the final scene, was written in 1903, I feel completely justified in shifting the action to a period which is for me typical of Apollinaire, the years 1910-1914. Apollinaire's *Alcools, poems 1898-1913* was published on 20 April, 1913. I also think that since the specific exoticism of the original is irrelevant, I can freely place Apollinaire's Zanzibar between Nice and Monte Carlo, where the poet grew up – Monte Carlo that I love – which also has always seemed to me the epitome of the exotic. Therefore I have asked for costume and set designs from Erté, the prestigious magician of the Tabarin, for whom 1912 was not merely a memory but a significant date, for at that time Erté was a dress designer with a great Paris fashion house. *Les Mamelles* having its ' faerie ' side, I needed a man of the theatre who had surmounted the snares of the backstage machinery. Erté exceeded my expectations in giving nobility and style to a period which is usually ridiculed by the younger generation.

Oddly enough, Poulenc and I had never met at the Tabarin. It was Max de

Rieux who first brought us together. From the moment we met, there was a bond of sympathy and understanding between us. I have always admired Poulenc's music in all its forms – opera, ballet, instrumental works, songs and religious music. After his death, several critics condemned his work for being too facile. If they had examined his religious music more closely, they would have found great depth. After all, if Poulenc's music is sometimes light and humorous, isn't this also true of a number of Mozart's works?

I gave my imagination free rein in the final scene of *Les Mamelles*. At the start of the second act the stage was filled with cradles and babies. For the final scene, these pink silk cradles rose up on poles from the floor of the stage to become standing lamps which lit up. During this sequence the buildings of the little fishing port from the beginning of the act – with its tobacconist's shop ' Zanzi-bar ' and its paper stall made entirely from newspapers – were lowered beneath the stage through trap-doors. At the dress rehearsal, which took place before an extremely elegant audience of VIPs and press representatives, the opera was a tremendous success. But at the public opening there was a scandal. The middle-class audience, which constituted the chief clientele of the Opéra-Comique, was shocked by the outspoken language of Apollinaire's text. A fight broke out in the theatre and a number of seats were broken. The press, however, was enthusiastic, particularly about my costumes and sets. These comments appeared in *L'Aube* on 4 June, 1947:

> And the sets by this fine artist Erté – an exquisite fantasy completely in keeping with the play; light, amusing, spiritual constructions, bathed in a fleeting delicate blue light under the sun and in the luminous night; towards the middle of the second act, there is a fantasy born of the machinery; the dream buildings disappear and Mr Payen's cradles are transformed into standard lamps on poles, which light up some public park beside the sea. It is as funny as it is fairylike.

After the dress rehearsal Poulenc gave a dinner at the Grand Véfour. The atmosphere was exhilarating. I sat beside Jean Cocteau, whose brilliant conversation had always cast a spell on me. I liked and admired this man of many talents. Some people tried, after his death, to minimize the importance of his talent and to stress the worldly aspects of his career. In the brilliant conversationalist who enlivened the artistic life of Paris for years, they lost sight of the more profound aspects of Cocteau's work.

I shall never forget one incident of that memorable evening. I had designed the cover for the score of *Les Mamelles de Tirésias*. On the first page of my copy, the principal guests had written a few words for me. When Christian Bérard started to write, he made a large ink blot on the page. Then, using his fingers, he turned it into a beautiful drawing of one of my lamp-cradles.

Needless to say, his fingers were somewhat black after this. But Bérard's finger nails were always dirty; Cocteau once asked him where he had bought such marvellous black nail polish.

I have never enjoyed working on a production more than I did on *Les Mamelles de Tirésias*. Collaborating with Poulenc was a pleasure, for we shared much the same tastes and views. His sudden death in 1963 came as a great shock. He had talked to me about a new work which he intended to compose on a text of Cocteau's, and for which he wanted me to do the designs.

Heading the cast of *Les Mamelles de Tirésias* was Denise Duval, a promising new artist, who sang the part of Thérèse-Tirésias. She had all the star qualities – a fine voice, acting ability, beauty, a slim figure (rare among great singers) and elegance. She had previously sung at the Folies Bergère. After *Mamelles*, Poulenc had her sing in all his works. She was sensational in *La Voix Humaine*, where she was the only character on stage, and profoundly moving in the *Dialogue des Carmelites*. Poulenc had a marvellous gift – that of perfectly matching the music to the words of the text. In Bernanos's *Dialogue des Carmelites*, as in *Les Mamelles de Tirésias*, he did not change a single word of the author's original text.*

It was a great pleasure for me to have Denise Duval as the lead in another opera in which I was involved – *La Poule Noire*, by Manuel Rosenthal, which was presented at the Opéra-Comique in 1956. Alas, illness forced Denise Duval to leave the stage much too soon.

After *Les Mamelles de Tirésias* I was commissioned by the Opéra-Comique to do the sets and costumes for Maurice Ravel's ballet, *Mother Goose*. On this occasion I had the special pleasure of working with Cotick, who was the choreographer. The ballet was a great success.

With operas and ballets, I do a great deal of preliminary work before actually designing the sets and costumes. After studying the libretto, I turn to the musical score. First of all I listen to the whole score on records several times, then I repeat the more important passages over and over again. I do not begin work until I am thoroughly steeped in the atmosphere of the music, which suggests the lines, and especially the colours, of my designs.

My work in opera did not prevent me from continuing to work for the music-hall. Unfortunately, I was no longer able to work in the United States because I was not a union member. It was not until 1964 that I joined the United Scenic Artists Union in order to design *Wonderworld*, a show put on at the New York World's Fair and produced by Leon Leonidoff, director of the Radio City Music-Hall. For several years previously he had wanted to mount a spectacular at Radio City, using my sets and costumes, but each time he had been thwarted by union

---

* In a radio interview, Poulenc was once asked if there were any analogies between the two works. With a slip of the tongue he referred to ' Les Mamelles des Carmelites '.

difficulties. His plans for me included designs for Maeterlinck's *L'Oiseau Bleu*, which I would have loved to do.

Instead, I designed many shows in Paris, Rome, Barcelona and England. Immediately after World War II, Alec Shanks, with whom I had worked at the Palladium in 1938 and 1939, came over from London to suggest that I design for a new spectacular, *Piccadilly Hayride*, at the Prince of Wales Theatre, as well as a big revue at the Coliseum.

The revue at the Coliseum was *The Night and the Laughter*, produced by Robert Nesbitt, whom I had already met on the occasion of *It's in the Bag* in 1937. I enjoyed working with Nesbitt, for he had great taste and an intimate feeling for the theatre. He and his beautiful wife, famous for their sense of style, were nicknamed ' Esquire ' and ' Vogue '. At this time I also had the pleasure of seeing Joan Davies again. It was she who had done the choreography for *It's in the Bag*.

The combined work-load of the two new shows was enormous, particularly as I was making cardboard models of all the Coliseum sets. Alec Shanks, who knew I liked to work in peace and quiet, again offered me the use of his country house, Briarfield. I accepted his kind offer with pleasure. From then on, whenever I came to London I descended on Alec, either in his Portland Place flat or at Briarfield. For his part, Alec stayed with me whenever he came to Paris. Much later, when he married, he sold the country house and the London flat and bought a lovely place in Surrey. I went there several times, but I retain a particularly fond memory of Briarfield because it was right out in the country. A young calf even used to come and munch the flowers in front of my window.

After *Piccadilly Hayride* and *The Night and the Laughter* had been successfully launched, Shanks asked me to design many of his London productions as well as a big spectacular which took place every year at the Opera House in Blackpool.

What a ghastly place Blackpool is! It looks like some huge fair, but the people there seem bored: they behave as though they were being forced to enjoy themselves. The first thing they do on arrival is to buy a funny hat which they do not remove until the day they leave. People save money all year to come to Blackpool for a fortnight's holiday. If, at the end of that time, they have any left, they squander it on all sorts of trash. Since the sea is usually too cold for swimming, they sit on the beach with their backs turned to the water so that they can watch the passing crowds on the promenade. But they do enjoy the shows. I have never seen so many anywhere in the world (except in Las Vegas). Most of them are very well produced and some are sumptuous. More extraordinary is the number of sensational attractions that come from the music-hall and the circus. Impresarii from all over the world descend on Blackpool to look for star acts to stock shows all over Europe and America.

The best shows were staged at the Opera House and many of these were subsequently transferred to London. The Opera House belonged to the Black brothers, George and Alfred. They were perfectly charming men and my dealings with them were extremely amicable. I had worked with their father, George Black, who ran the Palladium before the war. After his death, Val Parnell, who took over the running of the Palladium, often asked me to work for this theatre.

All the revues at the Palladium included several scenes devoted to the Crazy Gang, whose sketches were always screamingly funny. One or another would usually play a transvestite role. During the final years of the group's existence they performed in the big revues at the Victoria Palace where, each year, I designed the sets and costumes for the principal sketches.

This theatre was directed by Jack Hylton, the famous jazz band-leader who later became a prominent producer. He was one of Alec Shanks's best clients. Hylton brought Robert Dhery, Colette Brosset and their entire troupe over to perform the famous revue *La Plume de ma Tante* at the Garrick Theatre. This delightful, spirited show, for which I designed many of the sets and costumes, was put on again in 1958 at the Royal Theatre in New York. Between these two productions of *La Plume de ma Tante*, Robert Dhery and his company presented a show in Paris at the Théâtre de Paris, called *Pommes à l'Anglaise*, on which I also collaborated.

This work in London meant that I had to make frequent trips to England. Normally I went by air but one day, for some reason, I took the night train. The following morning I had an appointment with a theatre director to discuss a new show. Since I can never sleep in a *wagon-lit*, I decided to take a sleeping pill, something I rarely do. The next morning the staff had trouble in waking me up. Once awake, I did not even have time to wash, for the train was just pulling into the station. While I was sitting in the taxi which was taking me to Alec Shanks's apartment I fell asleep again, and the driver had to shake me awake when we arrived. Alec advised me to drink some strong coffee and to take a very hot bath. I fell asleep again in the bath. Fortunately I had left the door on the latch and Alec was able to rescue me before I drowned. Needless to say, my interview was not an unqualified success.

During this period I came to know a number of provincial English towns where London shows would have their trial runs. Once Shanks took me off to a theatre in a town where there was another big revue on tour. During the interval I said to Alec:

'I have an odd sensation of having seen a lot of those sketches somewhere before.'

Alec laughed and replied, 'The costumes and the sets were copied from your models!'

Is my memory really so bad, or were the copies from my models not very accurate?

In 1948 I was asked to design the sets and costumes for *Sueños de Viena*, at the Comico Theatre of Barcelona, for the late Artur Kaps's Viennese company. Kaps and his troupe, headed by that exceptional comic, Franz Yoham, had emigrated to Spain from Vienna after the *Anschluss*. Kaps's shows, which were purely Viennese in style, were very popular in Spain. Since I did not know Spain at all, I was happy to spend a couple of months there. I stayed in Barcelona for a few days, while Kaps and I discussed the general outline of the show. I was pleased to learn that the choreography was to be handled by Boris Skibine, for I still had pleasant memories of our long collaboration at the Lido.

Kaps took me to see his current show in Barcelona. I was most surprised to see that its star was Raquel Meller, who had been one of the queens of song in Paris during the 1920s. It was she who sang the famous songs ' La Violeterra ' and ' El Relicario '. In those days she was a tiny woman with a tiny voice, but what a wonderfully individual way of singing she had! Her stage presence was quite exceptional, even when she sang on the enormous stage of Carnegie Hall in New York. Now I saw before me a hefty, elderly woman; but she still had a unique way of singing.

She had one dream: to return to Paris to sing, and she asked me to help find an engagement for her. Sadly, she died soon after our meeting. Since she was the idol of the people of Barcelona, her funeral cortège was followed by thousands of her admirers: the crowd spread out over several kilometres.

Despite the attractions of Barcelona, I realized that I would not be able to work in such a bustling atmosphere, so I asked Kaps to find a quiet place by the sea where I could prepare my sketches. He suggested an hotel in a glorious fishing village on the Costa Brava near Blanes, which in those days had not yet been taken over by the tourists. I worked there very happily. Since no one in the village spoke any French, I was obliged to learn Spanish, little by little. When I returned to Barcelona I was able to express myself in Spanish sufficiently well to communicate with the people who were making my sets and costumes.

How beautiful the Costa Brava was. Before leaving my little village I explored the coast, partly by car and partly by boat, for there are a large number of fine coves that are inaccessible by road. At that time the coast road was very primitive and one could advance only at a snail's pace. Thanks to that, I discovered a wealth of marvellous detail that many people miss nowadays. Most striking is the variation in the sea's colour between one cove and another, which depends on the type of algae in the water. Some are deep ultramarine, some a vivid emerald green and others almost turquoise in their opalescence.

When I had finished my sketches, I returned to Barcelona to supervise the making of the sets and costumes. My agent, who had been responsible for putting me in touch with Kaps, was there at the time. His name was Leon Leonidoff, but he was not the same Leon Leonidoff who managed the Radio City Music-Hall in New York. It is odd that these two men, both of whom worked in the theatre, should never have met, although they had heard about each other.

My agent for the Spanish spectaculars was a remarkable man. He had started his career with Stanislavsky. Then he had been the agent of Chaliapin, Tito Schipa and numerous other celebrities. One day during rehearsals for the Kaps show we had lunch together. He asked me to go with him to audition a young singer whom he had just discovered, as he wished to hear my reactions. I was very much impressed by the girl's beautiful voice, and persuaded Leonidoff to sign a contract with her on the spot. This girl was to become the famous singer, Victoria de los Angeles. Leonidoff later asked me to design a dress for her.

From the moment I arrived in Spain I felt wonderfully at ease, despite my lack of knowledge of either the country or its language. I enjoyed Barcelona from the start. I am always fascinated by large ports, where everything smacks of freedom, *joie de vivre* and the chance of escape to unknown lands. I found Barcelona a city of delightful surprises. The Barrio Gotico, an area which surrounds the cathedral, is most beautiful. Built on ruins dating back to Roman times, it has many ancient statues and monuments. I have rarely seen a more impressive sight than the cathedral when it is illuminated at night. The architectural features of the building, which stands above a flight of steps, are indirectly lit from outside, while the wonderful stained-glass windows are lit from within. One has the impression that the cathedral is floating in the sky.

Besides its beautiful ancient monuments, the city is blessed by the extraordinary architecture of Gaudi and his school. No other city in the world has so many buildings of that genre. For me, Gaudi is one of the greatest modern architects. Inspired by the free forms of nature – waves, plants, rocks and other elements – all blended in a wonderfully unexpected manner, he liberated architecture from the conventional and rigid structures of the past. I find it incredible that some people consider his work to be in bad taste. It is true that many architects of the Gaudi school do not reach the heights of inspiration achieved by their Master. In fact, their work is sometimes totally devoid of artistic merit, but I believe this is usually the case when artists blindly follow the paths of leaders. To my mind, Gaudi is the father of modern architecture. I do not mean the horrible, cheap blocks of apartments that are destroying beautiful landscapes all over the world, but the buildings of Le Corbusier and his disciples.

While I was in Barcelona, I watched a bullfight for the first time. Initially I was caught up in the enthusiasm of the crowd and enchanted by the entrance of the matadors in their glittering costumes. But when the poor bull, who seemed in no mood to fight, began to be tortured by the banderillas, I was sickened. My disgust grew deeper as the combat progressed. Nevertheless, several years after this first experience, I wanted to find out if my first impression still held. On the second occasion I left almost as soon as the contest began – I could no longer endure the sight of this cruel spectacle.

When defenders of bullfighting maintain that the bull has the same chance as the matador, they are not giving a true picture. The poor animal is handicapped from the outset, when he comes from the total darkness where he has been held captive into the blinding light of the arena. He is alone, surrounded by a human mob bent on maiming him.

While Kaps was on tour with his troupe, I was often called to confer with him in the various towns of Spain. As a result, I saw large areas of this magnificent country. I was fascinated by the arid beauty of the countryside, the marvels of its architecture, its art treasures and its spellbinding music, but, above all, by a kind of mystery that seemed to belong to it. I like the Spanish people, too. They are warm and hospitable. The humblest peasant behaves with the natural dignity of a lord.

I remember one brief stay in Valencia. Having spent two days in uninterrupted conversation with Kaps, I was left with only the morning of my departure to see the town. I got up very early and went out into the empty street. In Spain, people rise very late, and never take lunch before two o'clock or dinner before ten o'clock. I saw a newspaper stall which was just opening its shutters, and asked the pro- prietor if she could tell me the way to the cathedral. She replied that her little son, who was with her, would take me there and would also act as my guide, to show me the most interesting things in the rest of the town. I accepted her offer with pleasure.

Imagine my surprise when I found that this lad, who was no more than ten years of age, had a broad knowledge of Spanish history and could give me interesting information about every monument that he showed me. When our tour was finished I naturally wanted to give him a tip. He refused, saying, ' My mother would never forgive me; we are only too pleased to show our treasures to foreigners '. I finally persuaded him to accept a bag of sweets. That he couldn't resist.

The part of Spain I like best is Andalusia – Seville and Granada work on me a special kind of witchcraft. I do not know Madrid at all well: each time I have visited it I have spent all my time in the Prado Museum. What a marvellous place it is – one of the finest museums in the world.

The only two things about Spain that distress me are the bullfights and the poverty. But there is a particular form of begging which is not motivated solely by poverty. There are groups of small children, not the children of the really poor, who accost one in the street to beg a few pennies for sweets.

I remember a story I heard from Olga Duisberg, a charming woman who ran a large fashion house in Barcelona which executed many of my designs for Kaps. Each day, when leaving her house in the morning, she saw a young woman begging at the street corner. One day she offered her the job of cleaning her studios each morning. The woman came the next day and worked perfectly well, but never returned. From that day Mme Duisberg no longer saw her in the street. She was, therefore, somewhat surprised, when visiting one of her friends in a different part of Barcelona, to see the same young woman sitting on the pavement. When she saw Mme Duisberg, however, she fled at once. Nowadays, happily, one no longer sees beggars in the streets of Barcelona.

At the time of my visit to Spain, I was not allowed to bring any foreign money into France, so I had to spend all the money I earned in Spain inside the country. I therefore decided to take a holiday in Majorca. I made the trip by the night boat because I wanted to see the island for the first time from a distance.

At sunrise the following morning, I could discern the outlines of huge rocks like sleeping giants, still shrouded in the deep blue of night. In the distance the silhouette of the marvellous cathedral of Palma was gradually illuminated by the golden rays of the rising sun. This beautiful sight was a perfect finale to a memorable night. Remaining on deck because my cabin was too hot, I had met someone who had also decided to spend the night under the stars. A relationship blossomed, which was to make my stay in Majorca extremely enjoyable.

By the time I finally set foot on the island, I was in the mood to fall in love with it, and I did. There is something enchanting in the atmosphere – one can arrive there utterly exhausted, on the verge of a nervous breakdown, but within a few days one recovers completely. The island is sometimes known as L'Isla de la Calma (the Island of Calm). The name was certainly apt when I first went there over twenty years ago. It is much less so nowadays.

At first I stayed at the hotel in Palma, but a few days later, during one of our excursions, I discovered a glorious beach, Camp de Mar, and decided to stay there.

I returned to Spain the following year, 1949, as *Sueños de Viena* was still enjoying a brilliant run. In fact, it ran for several years, and eventually toured all Spain. Since I received a percentage of the profits, I once again had money to spend in Spain, and decided to have another holiday in Majorca.

This time I took a plane and went straight to Camp de Mar. Unfortunately the hotel was full for the next few days, but as I was leaving, a young man, who had seen my long face and had guessed that I had not been able to find a room at the hotel, accosted me. He was an English student who had just received a telegram calling him home. As he was about to check out of his hotel and his reservation had not yet expired, he offered to show me his room.

It was a small hotel near another beach, about four kilometres from Camp de Mar. To reach it, we crossed a delightful pine forest which smelled as though incense were being burned, and which buzzed with the song of a multitude of cicadas. When we arrived at Cala Fornells, the name of both the beach and the hotel, I was enchanted. The sea formed a bay there, and looked almost like a lake, and the whole place breathed a marvellous feeling of peace. The hotel was tiny, with only eight bedrooms, but charming, and luckily the management had no objection to my taking over the young man's room. One ate on a huge terrace shaded by tall pine trees. The hotel was at the end of a long road, so there was no traffic noise. I enjoyed my holiday there enormously, and have returned year after year, whenever I want to work in peace.

Once I went to Majorca very late in the season, in October-November, to work on *Castor et Pollux*. The hotel was empty, with the exception of an elderly English lady, Mrs Diana Watts, and myself. We naturally got to know each other and I found her to be a remarkable woman. I was amazed when she told me she was ninety-two. Every morning, in spite of the weather, which was cold at this time of the year, she swam and dived like a water sprite. She had kept an astonishingly young-looking figure and her face, displaying hardly a wrinkle, was haloed by a magnificent head of snow-white hair. She attributed her youthful appearance to sea water. What impressed me most, however, was the youthfulness of her mind. She was interested in everything new, in any field, but especially in the arts. She loved modern art but hated modern music.

She had been a friend of George Bernard Shaw and was herself a brilliant conversationalist. An inveterate traveller, she had visited virtually every country in the world. She had only one severe handicap: she could hardly see. A few months after our meeting, she had an operation on her eyes which, sadly, was unsuccessful. Unfortunately I never saw her again, although from time to time she wrote me charming letters, one of which described her hundredth birthday and how some friends had arranged for a troupe of actors to perform *A Midsummer Night's Dream* in the garden of her house in England. (She was a great lover of Shakespeare and knew nearly all his works by heart.) That was the last letter she wrote me before she became completely blind, and two years ago I learned of her death at the age of 103.

Now, alas, one can no longer enjoy the peacefulness which used to reign at Cala Fornells. The hotel has grown year by year, and now has about sixty rooms. But, worst of all, an enormous hotel has been built next door. The tiny beach is now invaded by the guests of both hotels, so I go to bathe on the neighbouring beach at Camp de Mar. This allows me to take a pleasant walk through the pine trees, and it is then that my best ideas come to me.

In 1955, when I was working on a new production of *Sueños de Viena*, I went to Castel de Fels, a fine beach close to Barcelona. I stayed at a hotel with a terrace which ended in a jetty that went straight into the sea. As the season had not yet started (it was April) I was alone in the hotel. In the evenings I ate in the restaurant which was lit with wall lights encased in huge shells. Two head waiters and six waiters rushed to serve me. On might almost have been in the castle of Cocteau's film *Beauty and the Beast*.

Much of the island has now been invaded by tourists, and its natural beauty has been ruined by the construction of vast hotels and endless tall blocks of flats. The architecture is very poor on the whole, and there is little sign of any attempt to blend it with the countryside. It is astonishing that there is no preservation committee dedicated to maintaining the beauty of the island. When

I first visited Majorca, the houses in Palma and all the villas on the island were built in the style of those in Ibiza. An aura of perfect harmony surrounded the whole island.

I particularly loved the Villa S'Estaca at Cala Fornells. Built on a small rocky isle, it looked like a small boat heading out to sea. The house had been built by an Admiral of the Spanish fleet, a relative of the royal family. Rudolf Valentino had bought the property next door and his wife, Natasha Rambova, had supervised the construction of a villa. Alas, Valentino never saw it. He died before it was completed, and the house was inherited by his wife. Later the Admiral fell deeply in love with the beautiful widow and they married. When World War II started, Natasha went back to America and never returned. But the local people still remember this ravishing woman, who always dressed to perfection, wearing large hats with veils that floated in the breeze. For them, she has become a legendary heroine.

Despite the ugliness of most of the new buildings on Majorca, there are still some highly talented architects on the island, who have designed ultra-modern homes that blend well with the landscape. I recently saw a whole series of such villas on a peninsula, at the port of Andrait. I was visiting a charming friend, Mme Venture, who is the fortunate owner of one of them. But one cannot really call the property a villa, for it consists of three adjoining houses which bear the delightful name 'The Three Graces'. The view is fabulous. In the background is the island of La Dragonera, which actually looks like an enormous dragon floating on the surface of the sea; its colour varies with the constantly shifting position of the sun. Looking out from the terrace, there is not a house in sight. One has the feeling of solitude, yet one is never alone.

Mme Venture is so hospitable that her house is always full of guests, including many artists and international personalities. Two of her friends are the clavichord virtuoso, Robert Véron-Lacroix and the celebrated French opera star, Régine Crespin. Twentieth-century France has produced several outstanding dramatic sopranos, including Lucienne Bréval and Germaine Lubin, but Mme Crespin is surely one of the greatest. She is a veritable 'force de la nature'. Despite her imposing facade, she is the merriest person imaginable – the incarnation of the spirit of the south of France, where she was born. One night she had us all laughing uproariously as she danced the tango in the water of the illuminated swimming pool.

Since Alec Shanks had obtained a lot of work for me in London, I had always tried to find suitable projects for him to work on abroad. For example, after Sandrini's death in 1949, when his widow asked me if I knew anyone who could help us stage the new show at the Tabarin, I had immediately suggested Shanks. To my embarrassment, he made the mistake of announcing in a newspaper that he was taking over from Sandrini at the Tabarin. Mrs Sandrini was so shocked that she refused to discuss Alec Shanks any more.

In 1955 I obtained for Shanks the job of producing the second edition of Artur Kaps's Viennese revue, *Campanas de Viena,* in Barcelona. At my insistence, Kaps engaged Shanks as director and my great friend Joan Davies as choreographer. Everything went off splendidly and, as usual, after the première, I went off to the Balearic Islands.

Kaps subsequently suggested that I do another show the following year, and asked if Alec Shanks would once more act as producer. I relayed the request to Shanks. A week later, I was in my hotel at Barcelona when I received Alec Shanks's reply to Kaps, followed a few minutes later by a telephone call from Kaps asking to see me as soon as possible. When I arrived in his office at the Victoria Theatre, Kaps handed me a letter he had just received from Shanks. The envelope was addressed to him but the letter was meant for me. Alec Shanks's secretary had mixed up the envelopes. Unfortunately, in this letter, Shanks made some very frank comments about Kaps's impossible temper, the difficulties of getting money out of him, and so on. . . . Naturally, Kaps was furious and after this incident our relations cooled considerably.

Later, after the sad demise of the Tabarin, I started to work in a new music-hall called La Nouvelle Eve. Once again I suggested to its proprietor, M. Bardy, that Alec Shanks should direct. This collaboration was a great success and Alec Shanks produced several shows at La Nouvelle Eve, as well as at Eve, another night-club that belonged to Bardy.

The last show I did for Shanks was a revue at the Latin Quarter in New York in 1963. Since all the costumes were made up in Paris and the sets in London, there were no problems with the US unions. The production was a considerable success and the owner, Mr Loew, asked me to design a new show for the following year. This time Shanks did not participate.

After my long collaboration with Alec, I considered him a trusted and sincere friend. Imagine my surprise when, some time later, I learned that he was selling at Sotheby's some of the costume designs that I had done for various London shows. Such drawings always remain the property of the artist, and Shanks really had no right to sell them. I had frequently asked him to return them, but each time he replied that they must either have been stolen from the theatre or otherwise mislaid.

The Fifties

In 1951, the director of the Paris Opéra, Georges Hirsch, decided to put on a new production of *La Traviata* for the fiftieth anniversary of Verdi's death. The role of Violetta was to be sung by Solange Delmas, who had a magnificent voice. Hirsch asked me to design the sets and costumes. This was a happy coincidence, for I had already done a set of designs for this opera. *La Traviata* had been one of my favourite operas as a child. Many years later I had the idea of creating a production that would depart from conventional treatments of the opera, so – whenever I had a little time to myself – I would work on this project with no particular objective but my own pleasure. When I showed the designs to Georges Hirsch, he was most enthusiastic and accepted them on the spot. At that point they had been in my files for nearly twelve years!

My *Traviata* caused a lot of ink to flow. Part of the public and the press were shocked by the unusual aspects of my conception. There were several inflammatory articles attacking me. On the other hand, some critics responded to the novelty of the production and showered praise on me. None were indifferent.

My concept for *La Traviata* was surrealistic. The action took place within a round medallion. The frame of the stage, which produced the medallion effect, was white. Like a bouquet holder, it was cut out in a lacy pattern in the form of a crown of camellias. The curtain was painted to look like a romantic engraving of the tomb of Violetta (*La Dame aux Camélias*). As it rose on the first act, the curtain revealed a décor of velvet drapes in different shades of red with white trimmings. These curtains were arranged in such a way that they successively revealed different areas as the action progressed. The first act, which consists of several short scenes, ran without interruption, thanks to the operation of the red curtains during the music. At the start of the act, they opened on to a great white, carved door, standing out against a black velvet background. This was the guests' entrance. After the entry door had disappeared, another part of the curtains opened, to the strains of the Brindisi, on to one end of a supper table. For the waltz, the curtains parted to reveal a great crystalline chandelier which spread out over the dancers. The love scene took place on a typical Napoleon III circular sofa. For Violetta's great aria at the end of the act, the curtains parted to reveal a huge french window looking out on to a starry sky. All the elements of the décor were white against a background of black velvet.

The second act took place behind a white voile curtain dotted with pink camellias. Behind this veil was nothing but a white wall, with a french window revealing a blue sky. The only shadow in this act, the start of which is bathed in happiness, was that cast by Orbel's father arriving behind a translucent white screen, decorated with painted cupids. There was a minimal amount of furniture – a table with a pouffe for Violetta to write on, and a sofa.

The third act was treated in much the same way as the first except for a series of black velvet curtains. There appeared successively a games table, a perspective of lights, Venetian blackamoors – always dear to the Second Empire – and, at the end of the act, a great golden terrace draped with purple velvet. Everyone wore masks. Around the card table people were disguised as the kings and queens of a pack of cards.

The décor of the last act was simply a huge bed canopied in blue satin and white voile. The only other furniture encased in these drapes were a chaise-longue and a dressing table covered in muslin.

Violetta's costumes presented some little challenge. Although they were appropriate from a musical point of view, the singer interpreting the part was the exact opposite of an ideal Violetta, being extremely large. I made her appear slim by dressing her in a black velvet robe which would merge with the background. I then put a large white yoke on the front of the dress to enhance the slender appearance.

While working on the sets and costumes for *La Traviata*, I had the idea of designing a deck of playing cards based on the theme of the opera. Each act would be represented by one of the four suits: the first act was hearts, the second diamonds, the third clubs and the fourth spades. The figures on the cards (kings, queens and knaves) would depict the principal characters in the costumes they wore in different acts. Each of the low cards had a separate illustration representing one of the scenes of each act, and on each one was a bar of music indicating the musical phrase relating to the scene. Eventually these cards were exhibited in London in 1967 at the Grosvenor Gallery and were immediately bought by a collector.

Also in 1951 I designed the décor and costumes for *Parfums!*, a comic opera with music by Germaine Taillefer, which was put on at the Monte Carlo Opera with great success. The following year I designed sets and costumes for three operas: Claude Debussy's *Pelléas et Mélisande*, Albert Roussel's *Padmâvati* and Mozart's *Così fan Tutte*. The first two were performed at the San Carlo Opera House in Naples and the third at the Opéra-Comique in Paris.

What a fine theatre the San Carlo is! Bombed during World War II, it had been restored only a short time before our production opened. The enormous proscenium is two metres wider than that of the Opéra in Paris, but the stage is not so deep. It had the best dressing rooms that I have seen in any theatre. They were done entirely in marble with fine bathrooms and individual showers.

I went to Italy to supervise the execution of my designs. The sets were built in the theatre workshops in Naples under the brilliant Christiné, while the costumes were made up in Florence. When I visited Florence on these occasions, I always managed to find a few hours to explore this wonderful city. I had been to Italy once before with my mother, when I was four or five years of age, and, naturally, I had only a very vague memory of the place. In spite of that, I felt at home from the moment I arrived, and found my way around without consulting the map. I felt almost as if I had lived there all my life.

Florence is a city of dreams. I have never seen such an opalescent, pale blue sky. Incredible art treasures are not only to be found in its fabulous museums; there is scarcely a part of the city where the eye is not arrested by some beautiful architectural detail or statue.

I have only one bad memory of Florence – the day I went to visit the cathedral and climbed up to the famous Brunelleschi cupola. It was midday and there were no other tourists about when the guard opened the gate to the stairs. I went up alone. The floor of the balcony that runs around the cupola was made of ancient, slippery stone, its edge protected only by an iron bar supported on thin rods about two metres apart. I felt myself drawn towards the abyss. Utterly terrified, I crawled back towards the door on all fours. I rarely feel fear, but I gave in to it completely on that occasion.

The costumes for the San Carlo Opera production of *Padmâvati* were not delivered to the theatre until a few hours before the first performance. Nearly all the women's costumes were based on Hindu saris, but to the cast they looked like simple pieces of cloth. Since they had no idea of how to drape them around themselves, I had to work right up to the moment when the curtain rose. As there was no time to go to the hotel to change into evening clothes, one of the dressers fetched my clothes and I changed in one of the dressing rooms. There is nothing grander than an important premiere in an Italian opera house. All the men turn up in evening clothes and the women, dripping with fabulous jewels, wear gorgeously elaborate gowns. On such an occasion, Italians really know how to look elegant.

I attend the premieres of shows for which I have worked as a spectator rather than as a participant. People often ask if I suffer from first-night nerves. The answer is no. Once the curtain is up and there is absolutely nothing I can do to change anything, I deliver myself up to my fate.

The success of both *Pelléas et Mélisande* and *Padmâvati* at the San Carlo Opera House was considerable, and my contribution to the visual part of the proceedings was much appreciated.

Both operas had in their leading roles soloists from the Paris Opéra-Comique, but the chorus, the corps de ballet and the extras were drawn from the regular San Carlo Opera House company. Max de Rieux directed and the orchestra was conducted by André Cluytens. This short season of French opera was organized by the Opéra de Paris in response to the visit the San Carlo Opera had paid to Paris the previous year, when they performed on the stage of the Palais Garnier.

The divine Tebaldi was the prima donna of the San Carlo troupe. I heard her for the first time on this occasion and was absolutely dazzled by the beauty of her voice. I saw her in a very strange role, that of Joan of Arc in Verdi's opera of the same name. The libretto of this opera is somewhat bizarre. The heroine, Joan, appears as the mistress of King Charles VII, in luxurious clothes and covered with jewellery. I could not believe my eyes! But perhaps Verdi's librettist was right after all, for in recent times there have been many conflicting interpretations of the character of Joan of Arc, none of which have anything in common with the legend.

I stayed in Naples for almost two months, working on these two productions. In that time I met many charming people, including the Baroness Boracco, who lived in a delightful house at Pausillipo. This eighteenth-century house, which had once belonged to the notorious Lady Hamilton, and whose windows looked out on the panoramic Gulf of Naples, reminded me of the sets I had designed for *Così fan Tutte*, just before I came to Naples.

Besides the satisfaction of my work, I experienced the added joys of an affair of the heart which almost amounted to love. It happened one evening at a formal dinner. The moment our eyes met, all was said. The following morning I awoke in a magnificent four-poster bed in a room panelled with mirrors which was part of a glorious seventeenth-century palazzo. When the butler arrived with breakfast, he was accompanied by a magnificent cheetah who ate pieces of buttered toast from my hand like a great, greedy cat.

From that day, we did not leave each other until my departure about a month later. The object of my love was beautiful, intelligent and kind, with a degree of sensuality that I have rarely encountered. Together we visited all Naples and its environs. Naturally, we went to Pompeii and Herculaneum, and spent hours in the wonderful Neapolitan museum. I was very sad when it was time for me to leave. Once back in Paris, however, I became so overwhelmed with work that I gradually stopped thinking about this brief, enchanted interlude. For a few months, I received some delightful letters, but with time the correspondence dwindled. Being so engrossed in my work, I failed to reply to some of the letters

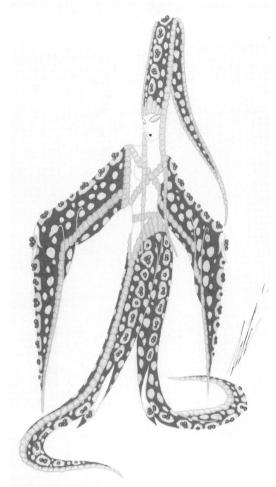

52   ' Jessie '. Costume, 1936   53   ' Starfish '. Costume, 1946

54 ' Ace of Clubs '. Lithograph, 1974

and by the time a year had passed, we were no longer writing to each other. I had completely forgotten this affair, when we met again in 1970, on the occasion of one of my exhibitions in Milan. I never dreamed that our relationship, abandoned eighteen years previously, would continue as before. Normally, such a lovers' reunion is a great disappointment, for one of the partners, if not for both. By a miracle, ours was not. Unfortunately, however, the relationship could have no further future, because of other pressures and responsibilities.

As I said, some important work awaited me in Paris on my return from Naples: the sets and costumes for Mozart's *Così fan Tutte*. The opera was to be given in a new version by Georges Hirsch, who had replaced all the recitative with spoken lines. Hirsch had directed a charming production of this work for the Paris Opéra but Maurice Lehmann, who succeeded Hirsch as head of the Opéra, decided to put it on at the Opéra-Comique. Since I had designed the sets specifically for the stage of the Paris Opéra, when the production was shifted to the Opéra-Comique, many details had to be dropped. Despite this, my *Così fan Tutte* sets and costumes brought me great personal acclaim.

On 18 April, 1952, Antoine Goléa wrote in *Témoignage Chrétien*:

> I would not like to finish this all too brief account without a mention of Mr Erté's suavely splendid sets and costumes. His lines, his colours, his blacks, his whites, and in particular his greys – all harmonize intimately with the cruel melancholy of a work in which Mozart, under cover of a bewildering farce, breathes forth that terrible pessimism which he felt in the face of human nature.

In 1953, Remigio Paone proposed that I should design his production of *Caccia al Tesoro* at the Quattro Fontane Theatre of Rome. Paone, like Kaps, asked me to work on my sketches for the sets and costumes on the spot, so I spent nearly two months in Rome, a unique and enchanting city. There is something special in its atmosphere which makes it impossible to be in a bad mood there. Thus, although certain difficulties attended the production – time was limited and there were problems with the sets – these seemed to slip away like water off a duck's back. This euphoric state comes over me every time I visit Rome. There are times when I have wished that I could live there for good. Although Rome does not have the unity of appearance of, say, Florence or Venice, the diverse styles – antique, medieval, Renaissance and Baroque – create its unique appeal, while combining to form a whole that is perfectly harmonious.

The opening night of *Caccia al Tesoro* was a brilliant occasion; almost all the great Italian film acresses were there. I found myself sitting between the late Anna Magnani and Gina Lollobrigida. Compliments came from all sides, but the most amusing comment was made by an Italian scene-painter, who asked me if I was the son of the famous Erté whom his father had known in Hollywood!

The show was a great success and the next year Paone asked me to work for him again on a production called *Rosso e Nero*, which was to have its début in San Remo. All the sets and costumes were, however, to be made in Rome. I did my preliminary work in Paris and the rest in Rome. On the way to Rome I was accompanied by someone whom I thought would become the object of a great love affair. However, each time I have been on a lengthy trip with someone, something has gone wrong, and it was so on this occasion. After several disappointments of this kind, I decided to travel alone in the future. I have never regretted this decision because, in the course of a journey, I usually enjoy some brief amorous adventure.

I have an assortment of memorabilia, received as gifts after these passing affairs. Although many are terribly ugly, I cannot bring myself to throw them away. All my life I have felt that objects have genuine sensibility and that they suffer if one treats them as unwanted. This conviction goes back to my earliest childhood feelings about my toys.

In 1956, following the success of *Così fan Tutte*, I designed (also for the Opéra-Comique) costumes and sets for *La Poule Noire* by Manuel Rosenthal, and in 1957, those for Richard Strauss's *Capriccio*, directed by Hartmann, of the Munich Opera House. Elizabeth Schwartzkopf sang the leading role in *Capriccio* on several occasions, some months after it had first appeared at the Opéra-Comique. She wanted to wear her own costumes, even though they blended neither with the other costumes nor with the set. I protested, for, according to the rules, a designer has the right to veto costumes other than his own. Nevertheless, Miss Schwartzkopf insisted – what could I do but forgive an error of taste in such a great artist?

The director of *La Poule Noire* was Max de Rieux with whom, a few months earlier, I had worked on a musical comedy, *La Leçon d'Amour dans un Parc*. This charming work was staged at the Théâtre des Bouffes Parisiens, through the efforts of André Certes, whose productions were enjoying tremendous success at that time. Certes used to put on a large number of new pieces in various Parisian theatres, as well as in the provinces. Our meeting marked the beginning of a long friendship.

The delightful music for *La Leçon d'Amour dans un Parc* was written by Guy Lafarge; Jean Valmy's libretto was based on the novel by André de Boislève. The leading role was taken by the ravishing Gisèle Pascal. At that time she was the constant companion of Prince Rainier of Monaco and it was rumoured that they would marry. As the first night of this show took place towards the end of December Max de Rieux gave a New Year dinner party at his house in Auteuil, attended by Prince Rainier with Gisèle Pascal. It was a very happy evening.

In 1959, Max de Rieux and I did a second version of *Don Pasquale*, this time at the Opèra-Comique. Unfortunately, however, this production brought to an end our long and pleasant association. During a radio interview, de Rieux passed off the production of *Don Pasquale* as his own. Since I myself had thought it out in full detail, I protested in a letter to the press, setting the record straight. De Rieux felt he had been publicly humiliated and we never saw each other again. I very much regretted the end of this friendship, which had been most sincere on both sides, and I was stunned when, a few years later, I heard of his tragic death in a car accident.

In addition to works staged in Paris, I also designed sets and costumes for operas in provincial theatres; these included Ibert's *Gonzague* in 1956 at the Opera House in Rouen, directed by Max de Rieux; Massenet's *Don César de Bazan*, performed on the same stage in 1957 in a most amusing production by Michel de Ré; and Rameau's *Castor et Pollux*, at the Lyons Festival in 1961, directed by Louis Erlo.

Georges Hirsch had once wanted to direct *Armide* (an opera by the seventeenth-century composer, Lully) at the Lyons Festival. He had asked me to design the sets and costumes and to handle the scenic effects. This I did with great pleasure, but soon after the first rehearsals, Hirsch had to abandon his plans because he had just been appointed director of the Paris Opera House and his duties did not permit him to work elsewhere. A few years later, the director of the Lyons Opera House, M. Camerlo, asked me if I could adapt my ideas for *Armide* to *Castor et Pollux*. It was an amusing idea. *Armide* was written in the seventeenth century, *Castor et Pollux* in the eighteenth. Furthermore, the subject matter of the two operas is completely different. I pointed out these problems but said that I would be prepared to design new models especially for *Castor et Pollux*. This was agreeable to M. Camerlo and I set to work with enthusiasm. The project gave my imagination immense scope.

The opera-ballets of the seventeenth and eighteenth centuries, with their ostentatious costumes and décor and their use of impressive mechanical scenic effects, were in some respects similar to contemporary music-hall revues. But there is a huge difference in the spirit of the two entertainments: the opera-ballet is aristocratic, the spectacular is for a popular audience. In the former, all is noble, majestic, slow, and the music forms a major element; in the latter, everything happens very fast and the music is, essentially, only an accompaniment. It would be a great mistake to stage an eighteenth-century opera-ballet in modern music-hall style.

I very much enjoyed preparing *Castor et Pollux*. The costumes were made in Paris and the sets in Lyons. I had to make two versions of each set, for the work was to appear first in the ancient Roman amphitheatre at Fourvières during the 1961 Lyons Festival, and then at the Lyons Opera House during the winter. Most of the sets for the open-air Roman theatre could be scaled down for the Opera House. The only full-scale set to be used on both stages was that for the last act, ' La Fête de l'Univers ', which consisted of a semi-circular colonnade draped in blue velvet and mounted on a vast dais. The men who built the set were afraid that the gale-force wind which often blows on the hills of Fourvières would sweep the whole thing away. Fortunately, each time *Castor et Pollux* was put on, the weather was good and only a light breeze ruffled the drapes, just as I had planned.

The Roman amphitheatre of Fourvières is a glorious structure. It is architecturally beautiful, and has extraordinary acoustics. One can sit in the last tier of seats and hear a whisper on any one of the three stages. I took advantage of these triple stages by setting each act on a different one. In the final scene, I used a staircase at the rear of the centre stage, leading up to a raised garden, to create a vast, celestial effect. I used smoke in such a way that the dancers representing the constellations and the signs of the zodiac looked as if they were emerging from the clouds. Since the audience were seated on ascending levels, their eyes were drawn to the base of the stage. I concentrated my effects in this area by using carpets decorated in the spirit of each act. This production of *Castor et Pollux* greatly increased my reputation as a designer of operas.

Among the revues and cabarets for which I designed in the early 'fifties was M. Bardy's new music-hall cabaret in Montmartre, La Nouvelle Eve, already mentioned in the previous chapter. The place was decorated with much taste but no practical sense; for example, the stage was almost non-existent and the artists had difficulty in getting on because the entrances were so narrow. However, for the opening show, the sets and costumes had been made perfectly, no cost having been spared. Many of my designs were carried out by high fashion houses such as Pierre Balmain and Maggy Rouff. The whole production exuded luxury and elegance.

As a result of the show's success, the Nouvelle Eve became the most fashionable music-hall cabaret in Paris. I designed a new revue there annually for several years. M. Bardy also asked me on a number of occasions to design costumes for his other establishment, Eve, which was very popular and had made his fortune. It was not always pleasant to work with Bardy, for he had a violent temper and his lack of culture was compounded by a lack of breeding. Yet he had an instinctive sense of what was beautiful. Personally, my dealings with him were always smooth until the day I began to work with M. and Mme Martini.

M. Martini owned several cabarets in Montmartre and the Champs-Elysées, as well as the famous Russian restaurant, Schéhérazade. He had just bought the Moulin Rouge and asked me to decorate it and to design all the sets and costumes for the first production which was to be put on there under the title *Champagne Cocktail*. In those first days M. and Mme Martini worked very closely with one another. Soon afterwards when they bought two new establishments, the Narcissus and the cabaret theatre Les Folies Pigalle, they again asked me to design the sets and costumes. For some reason Bardy took umbrage at my collaboration with the Martinis and my work for him ceased completely.

I subsequently designed an enormous number of décors and costumes for the Martinis, but I think the most interesting of all was *Twist Appeal* at the Folies Pigalle. Nicolas Bataille was the director and its star was an American singer, Vince Taylor, who had a brilliant but brief career. I had made most of the costumes from leather or animal skins, and the unusual combination of these materials with bodies in various degrees of nakedness created an effect of violent sexuality.

It was a pleasure to work with Nicolas Bataille and we became great friends. He was full of ideas, loved whatever was new and unusual and hated the banal and commonplace. He was the first man in Paris to put on Ionesco's *The Bald Prima Donna*, at the Théâtre de la Huchette. It had an extraordinarily successful career, travelling the entire world, including Japan, while it was still running triumphantly in Paris. I liked ' the theatre of the absurd ' initially, before it was reduced to a mere formula by a great number of writers with little talent or individuality. I loathe all forms of art when they become calcified ' artistic movements '.

I did two other shows with Nicolas Bataille, for Madame Martini. The first, which was presented at the Pigalle, was called *La Java* and the other, at the Drap d'Or, was *La Chasse Aux Folles*. Guillaume Hancteau was responsible for the libretto of the former. For *La Chasse Aux Folles*, he worked in collaboration with Robert Thomas, whose detective plays were very popular.

During the same period, I did a spectacular for the Moulin Rouge and two shows for the Casino du Liban in Beirut, in 1959 and 1960. I then worked on the décors for two ballet-films: *Le Coiffeur Miracle* and *Edition Spéciale*. These were produced by Louis Cuny with choreography by Jean Guelis.

M. Martini died suddenly in 1960. His death caused me deep pain. I had a great affection for this man, who knew how to appreciate the good things of life. His generosity was boundless: whenever he heard that one of his employees was in difficulties he would help him out before he had even been asked. His position in the theatrical world had been extremely powerful. He directed eight cabarets and two theatres (Les Bouffes Parisiens and the Comédie de Paris); shortly before his death he was negotiating for either the Châtelet or the Olympia.

Many people thought that this ' empire of the night ' would collapse after his death. They were greatly surprised when Mme Martini took over all her husband's affairs. It required fantastic courage and strength of character to defend her interests against the gangsters who dominate the cabaret world. She is the most astonishing business woman I have ever met. She appears to be the perfect society lady, yet sometimes seems like a shy young girl. Beautiful and elegant, she is the epitome of Slavic charm, with a tall, slim figure and a typically Slav face, having been born on the Russo-Polish border. I have never seen such clear blue eyes as hers. Today, after working together continuously since 1955, when she and her husband acquired the Moulin Rouge, we are still great friends. I find the combination of her sharp eye for detail and her demanding standards quite admirable. Today she is known as ' The Queen of the Night '.

After her husband's death she did not want to remain in the flat where she had lived with him, so I built one for her above two of her cabarets in Place Pigalle. This was no easy matter since a series of fussy little rooms had to be converted into a bedroom and a bathroom. However, it was great fun to overcome the difficulties that constantly arose as the conversion took place. I also designed a new décor for Mme Martini's Russian restaurant, Rasputin, for which I had done the original scheme some years ago when the restaurant opened.

Recently I have been putting the finishing touches to the décor of her château on the outskirts of Paris. It is surrounded by a hundred acres of land, through which winds a lovely little river. I think of the place as ' intimate ' because it was built originally for one or, at most, two people (there are, of course, guest rooms). The ground floor is composed of a huge living-room, a hall and a circular dining-room. This forms part of a three-storeyed tower at one side of the house. I have furnished the living-room with horn furniture covered in sealskin. Other large pieces of furniture in black leather are decorated with patterns of bronze nails and horns, following the style of two matching seventeenth-century marriage chests. They contain projectors, innumerable cameras and an imposing collection of records. One houses a refrigerator. A huge horn chandelier and bracket lamps of the same material illuminate the room, an entire wall of which is given to a great stone Renaissance fireplace. There is another splendid seventeenth-century fireplace in the circular dining-room. I made the ceiling and shutters in the dining-room entirely of mirrors. In the middle of the ceiling is a crystal chandelier of the Louis XVI period, from which loops of crystal extend all over the ceiling, creating a strange crystal composition that reflects in the mirrors. The walls of the hall are decorated entirely with shells; the furniture is Italian Grotto.

On the first floor of the tower is Mme Martini's bedroom, hung with sky-blue satin. Some of the furniture and woodwork is quilted, but instead of buttons there are little bunches of satin flowers. The furniture is Napoleon III – ebony, with painted decorations and inlays of mother-of-pearl and metal. A huge tent of white lace, suspended from a Venetian crystal chandelier, forms the ceiling and drapes over a large part of the satin walls. At the side is a little boudoir whose walls and ceiling are covered in almond green crushed velvet; the accessories are porcelain. This leads to the bathroom which is all mirrors and flowery tiles, with a round, sunken bath. The first floor also houses a library, the walls of which are covered in old gold velvet, with woodwork in white and gold. The library, besides its eighteenth-century English furniture, contains many souvenirs of distant journeys.

Above this floor are the guest rooms, one decorated in yellow, the other in pink. I think the room I most enjoyed tackling was the circular one at the top of the tower. When I first saw it, it was in a very dilapidated state, having been used as a storage room for lumber; it also contained a water tank. The ceiling was very low, but through a hole I could see some intriguing wooden beams supporting the pointed roof. I immediately suggested making something amusing and unusual out of the room. Mme Martini was reluctant at first, but she finally let me have my way. One half of the room now contains the sauna, shower, dressing room and gymnastic equipment that she requested. The other half is a rest room with a platform above the sauna section. It is this part that has for its ceiling the marvellous tangle of beams. The décor conveys something of the spirit of an attic, and includes several weird and unusual objects.

I believe that when the work at the château is finished, the effect will be distinctive, and I hope that it will give the owner as much pleasure as it has already given its designer.

The Sixties

In 1960 I received an offer to do the décor and costumes for Racine's *Phèdre* at the Festival of Liège. The idea was suggested by an old friend of mine, the film-maker Jean-Paul Le Chanois. He directed and Sylvia Montfort played the role of Phèdre. Her interpretation of the character was highly personal and completely different from those of the other great actresses I had seen in this famous role. It was much more human and utterly devoid of the false, declamatory style of some of her celebrated predecessors. She brought to Racine's poetry a beautifully pure and lyrical style.

She liked my conception of the production of *Phèdre* so much that, twelve years later in 1972, she spoke to me about doing a new production of Seneca's *Phaedra*. My 1960 version was certainly far from ordinary. I had respected the unity of place by setting the action within a semi-circular colonnade in etruscan red and black. In the centre stood an enormous white statue of an archaic Aphrodite, supporting a velarium on her head. Various mobile elements between the columns were used to evoke the forest, the port or Phèdre's chamber, but all the most important dramatic action took place at the feet of Aphrodite. After the Festival of Liège, the play was put on at the Théâtre du Vieux Colombier in Paris. Eventually it went on a long tour of France.

When I had finished *Phèdre* I went, as usual, on holiday to Majorca. One day, while I lay in a state of almost trance-like semi-consciousness on the warm sand of the sunny beach, I had a sudden vision of a strange shape composed of sparkling, shimmering colours. This was the birth of my ' Formes Picturales '.

I bought some cardboard and built my shapes out of this material. Then I went to a blacksmith and got him to reproduce them in metal. Finally I painted them in oils, using the paint very thickly so as to bring out the relief, thus extending the sculptural quality of the work. I used various materials: duraluminium, iron, copper and wood. Sometimes I used roots which I twisted into complicated shapes. I also used pieces of enamel and glass on the copper. The shapes are not completely abstract; they express a thought, an emotion, a mood or a natural element.

I found this new medium so exciting that I would have liked to devote all my time to it. When I worked on these shapes, I did so in a mental state that resembled a dream. The execution of each piece, however, was time-consuming because each layer of paint took a long while to dry, and I could not paint new areas before earlier ones were quite dry. After I had finished about twenty of these objects, I decided to exhibit them. At first I intended not to sign this work with my pseudonym, Erté. It seemed to me that my previous successes in other areas would exert undue influence on people's reactions to this new activity. It is an unfortunate fact that most critics and the public tend to ' pigeon-hole ' an artist and resent any digressions from the field to which they have relegated him. I wanted to start a new career in this medium as if I were a young artist. How marvellous that would have been at the age of seventy! But all my friends vigorously dissuaded me and I eventually allowed myself to be influenced by their arguments. I often regret it.

My first exhibition of these works took place at the Galerie Ror Volmar in Paris in 1964. For the catalogue of this Paris exhibition, Jean-Louis Bory wrote a magnificent foreword and Gérard Doscot, a highly talented young writer, contributed explanatory notes on each work. Doscot was a very good friend and it caused me much grief when the fine career which lay ahead of him was abruptly terminated by his death at the age of forty.

I now received a phone call from Jacques Charles, with whom I had often worked previously in music-halls, especially at the Paramount. He asked me to see Jacques Damase who was in the process of writing a book on the music-hall and needed some of my older models to illustrate the work. From that time on we remained good friends. I greatly admire this cultured, artistic and talented man and am grateful for the help he has given me. An art critic of deep sensitivity and a knowledgeable collector, he has written some fine books about art. After the publication of his book on the music-hall,* he asked me if I would be interested in doing a retrospective exhibition of my work for the theatre. I accepted the offer with pleasure. The exhibition was presented at the Galerie Motte in 1965 and nearly everything was sold.

The Bibliothèque de l'Arsenal, which specializes in the theatre, bought an important series of my works to add to its collection. They also arranged for the

---

* Jacques Damase, *Folies du Music Hall*, published in Great Britain by Spring Books, 1970.

Bibliothèque Nationale to photograph over three hundred of my drawings for the theatre from my personal files. A complete set of these photographs was exhibited at the Bibliothèque de l'Arsenal; two other sets are in the archives. Some are also in the archives of the Bibliothèque Nationale.

A large number of my works was bought on the occasion of the Galerie Motte exhibition by the proprietors of the Galleria de Milano. Later in the same year this gallery exhibited them in an Art Deco show which included many objects and pieces of jewellery dating from 1925, by a variety of artists.

The following year, 1966, the Galleria de Milano organized a successful new exhibition devoted entirely to my work. One of my pieces – the ' Congo ' curtain for one of George White's *Scandals* – was bought by the Museum of Modern Art of New York.

That same year the Musée des Arts Décoratifs put on an important exhibition at the Pavillon de Marsan, entitled ' Les Années 25 '. Jacques Damase insisted that I play a large part in it and a considerable number of my works was included. I found this exhibition very moving, for it aroused many memories of my youth. My feelings were compounded of nostalgia for a happy past, now vanished, and joy at seeing the style of this period emerge from the limbo where, for several years, it had been the butt of much sarcasm. Art Deco had, at last, become respectable.

The current infatuation with the style has led many people to collect cheap, worthless objects from the period, thinking that they are characteristic. How wrong they are. It was a style that was highly refined, down to the smallest detail. One need only look at Ruhlman's splendid pieces of furniture. In no other period was so much research involved, or so many different woods used – some extremely rare – in giving the whole an air of sober elegance. There were also the wrought-iron works of Brandt with designs composed of the most harmonious lines, the extraordinary pieces of jewellery by Puiforcat and, above all, the unforgettable creations of Lalique. Recently, in the Salon des Antiquaires, I saw a bathroom by Lalique. With its subdued lines, it had an astonishingly modern look.

At the time of my exhibition at the Galerie Motte, the director, Jacques Perrin, and I became good friends. The following year, he left the Galerie Motte to set up his own gallery in rue du Cherche-midi, launching it successfully with an exhibition of my works. In 1967 he mounted a second Erté exhibition in his gallery. It was then that Jacques Damase introduced me to Mr and Mrs Eric Estorick, who owned the Grosvenor Gallery in London. He had spoken to them of my work, with which they were not familiar, at the *vernissage* of their gallery's Art Nouveau exhibition, and suggested that they might like to put on an exhibition in London. They came to Paris, saw the exhibition at Jacques Perrin's gallery and also visited my studio. Excited by their new discoveries, they decided to put on two exhibitions, one at their London gallery and one at the Grosvenor Gallery in New York. We established a good relationship at our first meeting. Since then I have often referred to them as my ' new family '.

A few weeks later I had a visit from Charles Spencer, an English art critic and publicist, who was on the staff of the Grosvenor Gallery and had come to make the selections for the two exhibitions. It was a lengthy and difficult process. Luckily I had kept the originals of almost all my designs for theatrical sets and costumes, as well as those for all my illustrations for *Harper's Bazaar* and other publications. Most of these drawings were in huge trunks in my cellar. From them I was able to supply the numerous retrospective exhibitions which followed rapidly, and still leave myself with some things for future exhibitions. My relationship with Charles Spencer became very friendly. He was a great admirer of my work, about which he wrote numerous articles; most importantly, he also produced the first full-length book, *Erté,* which was published by Studio Vista of London in 1969.

While I was negotiating the two exhibitions at the Grosvenor Galleries, I made several trips to America because I was also working on a big project for the international exhibition in Montreal, ' Expo '67 '. This was a music-hall revue entitled *Flying Colours,* to be presented in a stadium seating 25,000 people. The star was Maurice Chevalier and the producer Leon Leonidoff, director of the Radio City Music-Hall in New York. I had first met Chevalier in 1918 when he had starred with Mistinguett in a show called *Colette of Paris,* for which I had designed the costumes, but I had not seen him since. However, Leonidoff and I, as already mentioned, had worked together on *Wonderworld* during the New York World's Fair in 1964. Leonidoff was a man of tremendous energy. A small, slim figure who still moved with all the vitality of youth, he had started his career as a dancer, and later became a fine choreographer. He had been head of the Radio City Music-Hall for twenty-five years. Highly-strung, he combined tremendous enthusiasm with great anxiety and insecurity. In spite of our differences of temperament, we worked well together. I have often noticed that I seem to have a calming and comforting effect on nervous people. I am, of course, often very nervous myself, but I try to conceal it. This outward control dates back to my early childhood. On one of his many long naval voyages, my father had spent some time in Japan, a country which fascinated him. He would often reminisce about its people and their customs. Once he told me that whenever a Japanese child started to cry, its parents would explain that grief is extremely personal and of no concern to other people. This made an indelible impression upon me. As a result, while I may sometimes become tense when I am under emotional or physical stress, I rarely lose my temper.

I made a preliminary visit to Montreal in 1966. It was terribly cold and the whole exhibition site was under a thick blanket of snow. I was amazed to find that the work of building the exhibition halls had scarcely begun, although the official opening was only three months away. When I returned in April I could hardly believe my eyes: everything was completed – and magnificently! From an architectural viewpoint, it was the most beautiful and original exhibition I have ever seen.

Since *Flying Colours* was to open in July '67, I had to spend nearly two months in Montreal supervising the making of the costumes and part of the sets. The production was plagued by too small a budget from the start. For example, according to the original plan, most of the costumes were to be made up in Paris. I had persuaded Leonidoff to arrange for Pierre Balmain, a good friend whom I had known since the early days of his career,* to execute all the modern dresses I had designed for the show. However, there were so many actors and extras that I could not afford to have new costumes made for all of them, and had to use ready-made costumes. I selected these from the costume rental departments of the Hollywood studios and the supplies of the chief music-halls in Las Vegas, but in each case I added my own revisions and personal touches. Those costumes that could be newly made within the budget had finally to be made up in New York instead of Paris.

Because I had known it in its heyday, I found the Hollywood of 1966 extremely depressing. It now seemed to be in a state of virtual decay. The old cinema theatres still had gaudy exteriors but they were covered with a thick layer of dust. The bungalows that had looked so smart and gay now seemed empty or neglected.

Leonidoff arranged for me to see the director of a Hollywood costume supplier. When the man heard my name, he asked, ' Is he the real Erté? ' This was the last straw.

Las Vegas made a completely different but no better impression. This great pleasure centre, which looks like a gigantic fair, is dominated by gambling. No matter what hour of the day or night you go through the lobby of your hotel, you will see all the gaming tables and slot machines surrounded by players. Gambling fever gives their faces a monstrous look. I think that if I were forced to live there for any length of time it would be like spending a season in hell. The countryside, however, is very beautiful, lit up by a burning sun with bluish mountains in the background – although you won't find a single tree on the broad avenues.

Speaking of sun, I had an unusual experience in Las Vegas. All the brochures extolling its virtues guarantee 360 days of sun. I spent five days of my stay in a steady downpour of rain! They were probably the crucial five days rounding out a full year. The only aspect of Las Vegas which filled me with admiration was its illumination at night. The effect of the myriad lights is amazing.

---

* I also knew two other great couturiers at the time of their debuts: Marcel Rochas and Jean Desses, who executed my dresses for the musical comedy, *Au Pays du Soleil* at the Théâtre du Châtelet.

In contrast, I liked Montreal. It is a booming city which has, out of respect for its past, preserved its old buildings and monuments. During the month of June '67 I flew back and forth between Montreal and New York, and each time I returned I became more enamoured of Canada. It is a country of extraordinary beauty.

The budgetary problems of *Flying Colours* did not decrease and had a drastic effect upon my costumes, with which I was most displeased. Economy also made it necessary for the floats, which were to have been built in Los Angeles by a specialist firm, to be made in New York. However, the show was interesting from the point of view of stage design. Because of the size of the hall, three large stages had been built so that everyone could see, regardless of where they sat. The action on the three stages was parallel but not identical, as were the costumes. The recorded music, with speakers in every part of the hall, formed a link between the three centres of action. The sets consisted of huge floats which were placed at the back of each of the stages. In the middle of the hall I had built an enormous rock garden on a platform, where Maurice Chevalier was to perform. Marvellous flowering plants were brought in from the Caribbean Islands, along with a number of exotic birds. During the final day of rehearsals, I worried a lot about the possibility of the parrots making noises while Chevalier sang. Fortunately, everything went off without a hitch – the parrots behaved perfectly and did not try to get into his act.

I was also concerned by the fact that Chevalier, in order to make his entrance, had to climb a flight of stairs to reach the rock garden-platform on which he was to perform. Since he was then in his eighties, I feared that this might be too much for him. I needn't have worried: he ran up those steps like a young man! Chevalier's contract stipulated that he was to perform for half an hour each night, but he usually ended up every performance having sung for at least forty-five minutes. His vitality was fantastic.

During the early part of 1967 I spent all my time travelling from Paris to Salzburg and Munich, as well as to various American cities. The reason was that, while working on *Flying Colours*, I was also designing the costumes for a ballet in a CBS television production, *The Silent Night*. Part of this film was shot in Salzburg, while the ballet sequences were filmed in the Bavaria Studios in Munich. It was a pleasure for me to return to the studios where I had worked some years before on the films of Marika Rökk. The studios hadn't changed, but I did not find a single member of the staff who had been there in 1953-4. Then I met an extraordinary woman who lived near the studios. She was Lili Dagover, the famous star of the silent films of the early 1900s, whom I had met in previous years. She had then been very beautiful and I now saw that by some miracle she had managed to keep her looks, although she was about eighty years old.

All the costumes for the *Silent Night* ballet had been executed in Paris by the admirable Marie Gromtseff. Her love for her work was demonstrated by one incident which made a great impression on me. Since a large number of the dancers represented gingerbread men, the basic material for all their costumes was the same – a soft brown crepe. Mme Gromtseff had had a large amount of this cloth dyed, but when I saw it I was very disappointed, for the colour did not match that of my sketches. I said nothing, however, because I knew that Mme Gromtseff had made a careful estimate for these costumes and that any change would cause her great financial loss. As soon as I reached my house the telephone rang. It was Mme Gromtseff calling to tell me not to worry about the colour of the material as she was going to change it. 'But I didn't say a word about it,' I said to her. 'That is true,' she replied, 'but I could see from the expression in your eyes that it would not do.'

One of my 1967 trips to New York coincided with the opening of my Grosvenor Gallery exhibition there. When I went to the gallery the day before the opening to see how the pictures were arranged, I was surprised to find a little red sticker on each of the frames. The gallery manager, Mrs Phyllis Gottlieb, a charming and very helpful woman, explained that the whole collection – 179 works – had been bought the previous day for the Metropolitan Museum in New York. It is difficult for me to express the pleasure I felt on learning this news. I was assured that this was the first time in the annals of modern art history that a complete exhibition by a living artist had been purchased by a museum. The sale had been made possible by a gift from Mr and Mrs Arnold Ginsburg who directed the Martin Foundation. The Metropolitan Museum has continued to buy my work, with the result that it must now have over two hundred pieces. It is unusual for an artist to achieve this kind of status during his lifetime – so many are recognized only after their death.

Before the opening of the Grosvenor Gallery exhibition in New York, Mrs Gottlieb invited me to lunch with John McKendry, a curator of the Metropolitan Museum, and his beautiful and fascinating fiancée, Maxime de la Falaise. John McKendry and Mrs Polaire Weissmann, head of the museum's costume department, were the instigators of the acquisition of my works. They had first been brought to the Grosvenor Gallery by Bruce Hooton, an employee of the Gallery. The Arab-Israeli war had just broken out and Mrs Gottlieb promptly announced, 'No champagne at this terrible time.' By the following Tuesday, less than a week later, however, Israel had won the war and cases of champagne were quickly re-ordered for the opening that night.

I think that the opening day was one of the most exciting of my life. The New York press was eulogistic, recalling all the successes of my long career. I was hailed as a 'living legend', a phrase that I have often heard in subsequent years. John Canaday, art critic of the *New York Times*, in writing of this show, said:

> Erté's designs are miniatures of technical brilliance: they have the precision and vivid colour of manuscript illuminations, a detailed perfection that reflects an eye like a microscope and a hand as steady

as a steel girder but as flexible as a spring. . . . He was an Aubrey
Beardsley who had mastered the fox trot and occasionally broke into
the Charleston.

Since so many people wanted to buy my works, I cabled my housekeeper,
Paulette, to ask her to take down the drawings from my studio walls and send
them air freight to New York. The Grosvenor Gallery in London also sent
additional works.

The opening of my London exhibition in September was a glittering occasion.
The attendance, press and sales exceeded all our expectations: one could hardly
move in the large room at the Grosvenor Gallery. The exhibition was much larger
than that in New York: about eight hundred works were on display, of which
more than six hundred were sold. Before the opening, my entire Alphabet,
twenty-six items, was bought by Lord and Lady Beaumont, who redecorated the
large entrance hall of their beautiful London house in order to display my work
to its best advantage. I was pleased that the twenty-six letters of the Alphabet
had not been split up, as I had feared that people would buy only the letters of
their initials. The Victoria and Albert Museum also bought several pieces.

To celebrate the opening, Mr and Mrs Estorick gave a magnificent Chinese
dinner at their splendid house, which is a veritable gallery of great twentieth-
century painting and sculpture. All the outstanding artists of the first half of
the century are represented. Yet there is no hint of a cold museum-like atmosphere. Art is an integral part of the Estoricks' lives. The delightful garden with
its swimming pool is also scattered with modern bronze sculptures.

During the evening I extended my acquaintance with the family. On entering
the house I was met by a beautiful girl whom I later saw pouring hot saki for the
guests; she was the Estoricks' daughter, Isobel. A short time later I met her
brother, Michael. I have since grown to love this new generation of Estoricks.

The next day I learned that the cinema actress, Susannah York, had bought
the whole series of set and costume designs that I had done in Hollywood.
Later, when the son of Mrs Irene Selznick (daughter of Louis B. Mayer) wanted
to buy for his mother some of the designs I had done at MGM, he had to be
content with a single example which I still had in Paris. People were literally
grabbing up my works. One morning, before the opening, Cecil Beaton came
to the Gallery to photograph me. He particularly admired two designs. After a
few minutes' conversation, however, he noticed that the pieces he wanted had
just been sold, and he had to make a fresh choice. Mr Beaton's pictures of me
were the best photographs I have ever had taken.

The British press was full of praise for the exhibition. The art critic of the
Sunday Times, John Russell, wrote: ' If Michelangelo were to come back from
the dead he could hardly have greater or more eulogious publicity than has been

accorded to Erté, whose designs for the theatre, for the cinema, and for *Harper's Bazaar* are now on show at the Grosvenor Gallery.'

Whole pages appeared in the principal London papers and numerous colour magazines devoted long articles to my work, with illustrations in colour.

During the exhibition the gallery was rarely empty. I noticed particularly that the majority of the visitors were young people, who lingered before each work, carefully examining every detail. Many art students came with sketch books and pencils to take notes. I have observed this youthful interest and euthusiasm at all my exhibitions, whether in London, New York, Paris or the various Italian cities. It gives me great pleasure to see my art appreciated by the young, with whom I have always felt a close affinity. From my childhood I have retained a certain fear of ' grown-ups ', who used to horrify me by their peremptory manner of standing in judgment upon one, a habit I have always tried to avoid.

Yet though I enjoy the company of young people and understand their enthusiasm for life, I have never had students. I have frequently been encouraged to teach but have always declined. What could I have taught my pupils? If they had a great talent based on a strong personality they would have no need of me and could only find my personality distracting. If, on the other hand, they were mediocre and lacking in individuality, happy only to copy their master, I should not have been interested in them.

At about this time, it was suggested that I should create a ' new look ' face for the famous model, Twiggy. She who had filled countless pages of magazines all over the world, with her astonishingly thin body and adorably childlike face, now wanted to look like a sophisticated vamp. I gladly accepted the commission, as I found her interesting and unique. The photograph for which I had to devise the new make-up was to appear in *Queen* at Christmas. We had to fit in a sitting one evening between my arrival in London from Paris and her departure the next morning for Japan. We began by having dinner together in the company of Justin de Villeneuve, her photographer-manager, who was also her fiancé. During the meal I was able to admire the pure beauty of her face and to appreciate her gentle simplicity. This proved to be one of *Queen's* most successful covers.

When we arrived at the photographer's studio I realized there were no accessories with which to give her a hairstyle. Fortunately, I saw some long strings of pearls around the neck of one of the photographer's assistants and a white fox fur round the shoulders of another. I commandeered those to make a strange coiffure. Twiggy's make-up was concentrated primarily about her eyes, forming a rainbow which ranged from green on her eyelids to red on her cheekbones. The extraordinary thing about her is the ease with which she can adapt to different characters, a romantic heroine, a vamp or an impish girl.

Following the success of the two Grosvenor Gallery exhibitions, Mr and Mrs

55 With Axel,
Boulogne-sur-Seine,
1935

56 In the studio,
Boulogne-sur-Seine,
1936

57 Suzy Volterra and ' Cotick ' in the 1940s

58 In Barcelona, 1948

59   With Mme Martini, early 1970s

60   At the opening of *Zizi je t'aime*, 1972

61   With Zizi Jeanmaire and Roland Petit, Paris, 1971

Estorick asked me to sign an exclusive contract with them. This I did with pleasure for I had developed a true affection for them. The Estoricks freed me not only from business affairs, but through their combined talents, accelerated the pace of my career as I turned seventy-five years of age. They initiated one-man exhibitions of my work in literally a score of cities in almost a dozen countries, and these resulted in many commissions for interesting and varied projects. They provided useful data for professional authors, academicians and students who were writing books and essays on me and my work for art courses and Ph.D theses in design. They also gave research assistance for my own books. They expanded my work into new fields of graphic work and generated interest in my earlier jewellery and textile designs. I was thus enabled, in my remaining free time, to concentrate on my theatrical design work.

A very important part of my work for the theatre is devoted to supervising the execution of my sets and costumes. In fact, I spend more time on this than on the designs themselves. I work closely with the builders and painters of my sets. For costumes, I have to select the fabrics, indicate the way in which they are to be cut, explain how the embroideries should be executed, and then assist at the fitting, supervising every detail. Although my sketches are full of detail and very clear, I still have to give a great deal of explanation. If I don't supervise everything personally, I sometimes get some unpleasant shocks when the results are seen.

I shall never forget an amusing episode which occurred when I had sent my sketches to a theatre abroad, and arrived in person only for the final rehearsal. In my costume designs I usually show the figures in action, displaying the fullness of the skirt, the folds of which are indicated by fine lines. You can imagine how horrified I was when I saw that one of the dancers' costumes had been shaped with wire to reproduce the position of the skirt on my sketch. Worse, all the lines indicating the folds in the skirt had been embroidered on the chiffon. I have never seen a costume as dreadful as this one.

When I conveyed my horror to the dressmaker, he naively replied that he could not understand my displeasure, for he had made an exact reproduction of my sketch!

Another time I had a similar experience with a setting. Before leaving on a journey, I gave my design to the builder, explaining that I wanted everything to be built in three dimensions. I often include a few human figures in my sketches, mostly to indicate the proportions of the set, and had done so on this occasion. When I returned from my trip, I went to see my setting. What was my surprise when I saw two lovely wax figures, beautifully dressed, standing in my set. The builders had carefully reproduced the two figures painted on my design!

One day Sal and Eric Estorick suggested that I think about some new lithographs. The idea excited me and I made a first set of prints on the theme of numbers. A series of ten compositions represented the numbers from 0 to 9. I treated them in the same way as the letters of my Alphabet, that is to say by giving them human or mythical characters. When this series proved a success, I produced two more: six precious stones (sapphire, ruby, diamond, emerald, amethyst and topaz) and the four seasons. Seventy-five numbered prints were made from each lithograph. The basic idea of this new form appealed to me greatly. Lithography was a means whereby many people of limited means, who could not afford originals, were able to buy one or several prints.

The year 1967 also saw two exhibitions of my work in Italy: one at the Galleria Viotti in Turin, the other at the Galleria d'Arte Cavalletto in Brescia. They were both organized by Mr and Mrs Pellegrini, owners of the Galleria de Milano. The Pellegrinis made me feel most welcome on my short trip to Italy. Since I was going to attend the opening in Turin, they organized a reception with a small exhibition of my drawings in their Milan gallery. They took me to Lake Maggiore, which I had never seen before, where Mrs Pellegrini's parents have a superb villa with a fine terraced garden. The autumn scenery was looking especially beautiful, and the lake was set off by a variety of russet and golden tones. I did not have time to go to the exhibition in Brescia, nor to another which the Pellegrinis arranged in Trieste. Somewhat later there was still another exhibition in the Paolo Barozzi Gallery in Venice.

Many of my works had been bought in Italy and elsewhere by Gunter Sachs, a dynamic man of whom I am very fond. I had lunch with him one day in his Paris apartment on Avenue Foch where I was delighted to see his Cinema Room devoted entirely to a large collection of my works. Brigitte Bardot, his wife at the time, was also an avid collector of my work.

1968 began for me with a very successful exhibition arranged by the Grosvenor Gallery at the Neues Kunst-Zentrum in Hamburg. I was pleased on this occasion to be able to revisit the city I had first known in 1910 during one of my journeys with my mother. Like all great ports, Hamburg fascinates me. I received a warm welcome from its people and on 16 January, 1968, the following notice appeared in *Die Welt*:

> Erté is the world's genius of presentation. Elegant society has honoured
> him and will honour him as its 'prophet' and at the same time as its
> 'magician'. Erté is not a star, he is an elegant bird of paradise, a
> master of pleasures for extravagant enjoyment.

Later I was invited by the Sears-Vincent Price Gallery in Chicago to the opening of a large retrospective exhibition of my work. I was warmly welcomed in Chicago and the press reviewed my work very favourably. The exhibition, which had been arranged by the Grosvenor Gallery, was sponsored by the Chicago Opera House, for which I had formerly done a great deal of work. The manage-

ment asked me to design a poster for the reopening of the Opera House which
had been closed for two years because of difficulties with the musicians' union.
The new season was to open with Richard Strauss's *Salome*, so I used the ' Dance
of the Seven Veils ' as the theme for my poster.

Chicago, a city of violent contrasts where slum areas adjoin luxurious neigh-
bourhoods, stands on a lake that looks like a sea. After dinner on my first night
in Chicago, I went for a long walk along the lake front and did not see a living
soul. When I mentioned this the next morning to Harold Patton, the director
of the Vincent Price Gallery, he looked horrified and exclaimed, ' You did that
and you are still alive! '

For me, however, the outstanding event of 1968 was the exhibition at the
Metropolitan Museum of Art in New York of the collection they had purchased
the year before. The museum set aside three rooms for this show. To reach it,
I had to pass through huge rooms devoted to the masterpieces of great painters
of all periods. I was deeply moved. The exhibition was entitled ' Erté and Some
of His Contemporaries ', for the rules of the museum did not permit one-man
shows by living artists. I would have preferred it to have been called ' Contemporary Artists ' and to have remained rather more in the land of the living.
These ' contemporaries ' included such eminent artists as Bakst, Dufy, Laurencin,
Gontcharova and Lepape. Each time I went to the exhibition I was very pleased to
see a large number of visitors and, as usual, many enthusiastic young people.

A few weeks after returning to Paris I received a letter from the young Italian
publisher, Franco Maria Ricci. He had just returned from New York where he
had seen the exhibition at the Metropolitan, and wrote that he had literally fallen
in love with my work and wanted to publish a book about me. He came to Paris
and showed me some of his publications, which impressed me by their fine type
printed on hand-made paper, illustrations in astonishingly rich colours and completely harmonious format. My book was to be the tenth in a series, ' I segni
dell uomo ' and its text was to be written by the eminent French critic, Roland
Barthes. In addition, the book would contain several first draft extracts from the
memoirs I was planning to write.

We came to an agreement on the spot. The production took a long time
because Ricci always strives for perfection. If the colour of a reproduction was
not exactly the same as that of the original, he would have it rephotographed
several times, even using different photographers, until he achieved a perfect
colour match. The Italian edition was finally published in 1971, the English
language edition a year later and the French edition at the end of 1973.

As a result of the success of my 1968 exhibition in Chicago, Harold Patton,
with the Grosvenor Gallery, organized another show there at the beginning of
February 1969. This one was confined to my ' Formes Picturales ' and lithographs. I went to Chicago again on this occasion, and, on my return journey to
Paris, stayed in New York for two days.

Early in the morning, as I was going to Kennedy Airport in a taxi, snow began to fall. It fell progressively harder during the ride and a fierce wind also made for slow driving. I was caught in a blizzard such as I have never seen – not even in my childhood in Russia. Nevertheless we arrived at the airport on time and went through all the usual formalities. But as we waited for our embarkation instructions, we learnt that the plane could not take off. Since mine was the first plane to be cancelled, all the passengers were put up in the airport hotel. This was not the case for later travellers, for the hotel soon filled up and people were obliged to remain in the airport building. The more fortunate slept on seats in the waiting rooms; others took to the floor. Food supplies were soon exhausted. The airport was completely cut off from New York, which was similarly paralysed. There were several fatal road accidents, and many people died of suffocation in their cars which were buried in the snow.

The next morning, when I awoke to brilliant sunshine, I thought the aeroplane would be able to take off, but my expectations were soon shattered. The runways were so snowed under that it was impossible to tell how long it would take to clear them. We were trapped in the hotel without luggage for two days. Fortunately, the airport was eventually provided with food by helicopter.

1969 was an important year for me. In addition to the large exhibition at the Sears-Vincent Price Gallery in Chicago, there was another large retrospective show at the Galerie René Drouet in Paris, arranged by the Estoricks. At the opening, a friend of mine bought a small ink drawing of a lady's leg clothed in a very unusual stocking. As I recall, she paid two thousand new francs (about two hundred pounds). The gentleman accompanying her quipped, ' If a drawing of a single leg is worth two thousand francs, how much would the drawing of the whole woman cost? '

Among the guests at the Galerie René Drouet opening was Paul Poiret's youngest daughter, Perrine, whom I had not seen since she was a small child. Shortly before the opening, Palmer White, an American writer living in Paris, had come to see me in connection with his book, *Poiret*. Poiret's widow had suggested that he talk to me, since the material in her possession was incomplete on a phase of his career that particularly interested White – Poiret's theatrical activities during the period when I was working for him. I was happy to be able to help and White and I had an extremely pleasant session which carried me back to the days of my 1913 Paris débuts.

I also went to London that year in connection with the publication of *Ermyntrude and Esmeralda* by Lytton Strachey, for which I had done the illustrations. This was a short, light novel – ' daring ' for 1913 – which had been discovered posthumously among Strachey's papers. I have rarely enjoyed myself so much as when I drew these illustrations. The author, in the course of a story that is more than libertine, describes the most risqué situations in an elegant manner, casting a veil of naive candour over some of the lewder moments. Anthony Blond, the publisher, with the Estoricks, organized an autographing party at the Grosvenor Gallery, where my original illustrations for the book were displayed, together with some of my other drawings.

I was also the guest of honour at the opening of an exhibition called 'The Jazz Age' at the Royal Pavilion in Brighton, which included many of my drawings. The exhibition was organized by Martin Battersby, author of the excellent books on Art Nouveau and Art Deco,* with exquisite taste and a profound sensitivity to the era of the 1920s.

The Royal Pavilion filled me with wonder: I had rarely seen such an unusual building, or one so full of unexpected baroque detail. I was enchanted by the folly of its conception. I travelled to the opening in the company of Isobel Estorick who wore for the occasion a glorious costume dating from 1925, topped with an enormous hat which prevented her from seeing anything that occurred to her left. Among the other guests were several women wearing authentic period dresses, some handed down from their mothers or even from their grandmothers.

I have only recently learned that the refurbishing of the Pavilion – using much of the original furniture which had been dispersed for years, as well as recreating some of the exquisite decorations of the Prince Regent's exotic pleasure palace – dates almost entirely from the years following World War II, and is largely the work of its energetic and imaginative former Director, Clifford Musgrave.

---

* Martin Battersby, *Art Nouveau*, Paul Hamlyn, 1969; *Decorative Twenties*, Studio Vista, 1969; *Decorative Thirties*, Studio Vista, 1971.

The Seventies

My work was still bringing me to London frequently. Two further visits were directly connected with fashion. One, in 1970, was for a fashion show by Borg, the American fake-fur company. I designed a spectacular coat, and dresses for all the models who appeared in the finale. My second visit took place in 1971 when I launched a series of three ' unisex ' shirts made up by Jasper from my designs entitled ' Adam and Eve ', ' Night and Day ', and ' The Cats '. These shirts were sold at Simpson's, who also organized a coinciding exhibition of my designs. A further exhibition was organized in June 1972 at Woburn Abbey by the Duchess of Bedford, its theme being ' The Cat in Art '. Many of my works were included and one of my designs – a portrait of my first cat, Mischa – was used as the inside cover of the catalogue, for which I also wrote an introduction.

As I have already said, I adore cats. At present I have two: Thalia, a handsome Burmese, and Caramelle, a little she-cat who shines like black onyx. Her mother was a Siamese with an impressive pedigree but this noble lady went out for a walk one evening and met up with a stray black tom cat. The result was a single kitten, Caramelle. Completely black but with a typically Siamese head, she is extraordinarily intelligent.

A great many artists love cats, but I know of none who owns quite as many, and paints them as frequently, as Leonor Fini; I believe she has about thirteen. Most are Persians and very beautiful. Leonor Fini is a most talented and fascinating woman. Like a character from the Italian Renaissance, her beauty is wild, strange and flamboyant. She is a flame in the shape of a woman.

In the late summer of 1969, Roland Petit contacted me: he wanted me to collaborate on a new spectacular he was putting on for Zizi Jeanmaire at the

Casino de Paris. The sets and costumes were to be designed by several different artists: Cesar, Soto, Yves Saint-Laurent, Vasarely and his son, Yvaral; also Matias, Clovis Trouille and Pellaert. I was delighted, for I have a deep admiration for Zizi Jeanmaire and Roland Petit, having always found their ballets outstanding.

The show was scheduled to open at Christmas. Petit wanted me to design three sets, and gave me carte blanche in the choice of themes for these. However, he particularly liked the idea of using ' Diamonds ' and ' Furs ', so that the diamond theme could be used as a setting for Zizi Jeanmaire to sing her famous song, ' La Croqueuse de Diamants '. I suggested a tableau entitled ' Hair ', in which all the costumes as well as the décor would be made of nylon hair and horsehair, and this idea was gladly accepted.

Having established a few basic ideas, I left immediately for Majorca to do some concentrated work on the models for the sets and costumes. The first models to be finished were those for ' Hair '. These were a series of costumes representing a whole range of different hair colours, from white through to black via grey, platinum blonde, golden blonde, venetian blonde, red, auburn and chestnut. Models struck decorative poses representing a pony-tail, the hair-dresser's hands, or hair flying in the wind. Petit was delighted. Alas, the costumier who was engaged to make up these clothes took an inordinately long time to find the correct fabric and when he eventually found some suitable stuff in Switzerland, it was too late, since the Swiss needed two months to deliver. Thus ' Hair ', my favourite sketch, was never staged.

' Diamonds ' and ' Furs ', however, were executed perfectly. Revillon did the work on ' Furs '. The set for this sketch, which was entirely in panther and tigerskin, consisted of a backdrop and an extension of this in the form of an immense carpet covering the entire floor of the stage. A very beautiful woman ' tigress ' and two dancers representing panthers gyrated on this carpet while girls with head-pieces and trains made out of white foxtails descended from the flies on swings of white fox fur. The fox heads were connected with gold chains.

The set for ' Diamonds ' was made entirely of plexiglass and other plastics. Since many of its components were in a state of perpetual motion, their crystalline facets projected a myriad flashes of light. A woman rose from beneath the stage and as she did so her vast coat, encrusted with diamonds, opened out to cover the floor area. This set was tremendously successful.

The only unsatisfactory thing about the scene was the fact that Zizi Jeanmaire was not in it – she simply did not have enough time to change costumes. I think she regretted the fact that she could not wear that immense, diamond-encrusted coat almost as much as I did.

I derived enormous pleasure from working with Roland Petit, so when he asked if I would collaborate on a new show the following year, I was delighted. Meanwhile, however, after the premiere of the Casino show in January 1970, I left for Barbados, where the Estoricks had invited me to spend a holiday in their house. I was very happy to take advantage of this opportunity for a change, since I had just lost my faithful housekeeper, Paulette Bourquin, after a very long and painful illness. It was a great loss, for she had looked after me for more than fifteen years and had been like a second mother to me.

The Estorick house, in St Peter, is named 'Nelson Gay' after two old Barbadian families – Nelson and Gay – who, centuries ago, built fortifications on the site to ward off marauding pirates in the Caribbean. It is a veritable Shangri-La. The large garden, with its luxuriant, tropical vegetation, extends to the beach. The house itself is furnished with exquisite taste. The drawing-room, at the centre of the structure, has only three walls: the fourth side of the room, opening on to a large terrace, consists of coral pillars; between these are combination door-shutters which are closed at night. Glorious birds fly in and out and make their nests in the delicate metal and china chandelier. When I awoke on my first morning and drew back the curtains, I was amazed to see before my eyes, framed by the window, a prospect which reminded me of a painting by the Douanier Rousseau. The first time I plunged into the Caribbean sea I felt I must be dreaming, so warm was the water. Ever since then, even Mediterranean waters have seemed glacial by comparison.

I explored the whole island of Barbados, which is most beautiful. Its two coasts are totally different, the Atlantic side being the more mountainous and picturesque, with fantastic rocks which make it dangerous to swim there, while the Caribbean side is gentle and relatively flat, with long beaches of fine sand where coconut trees grow at the edge of the water. These, of course, make ideal bathing beaches, and most of the finer houses and hotels are on this coast.

I have since spent five long holidays at 'Nelson Gay', including one Christmas and New Year. On that occasion I came straight from New York, where I had attended the opening of an exhibition of my works at the Sonnabend Gallery. The contrast between the freezing temperatures of New York and those of Barbados was hardly credible. On New Year's Eve, after the guests had departed, I swam by moonlight in the warm Caribbean sea.

There are a great many lovely homes on the island, many of which I have visited, for social life in Barbados is very busy. Several were built and decorated by Oliver Messel, whose sets and theatre costumes I have always admired. He designs equally beautiful gardens around his houses.

The house next to the Estoricks' belongs to Claudette Colbert, the film star. During my first holiday, I naturally got to know her, and in the course of our conversation she told me a most amusing story. When she was still a young girl, she wanted to be an interior designer. At art school, the first task she was given was to copy some drawings of mine which had appeared in *Harper's Bazaar*. Finding that she was unable to reproduce faithfully all the minute details, she became discouraged and finally abandoned the whole idea of a career in art. It was then that she set her sights on the cinema.

62 *Castor et Pollux.* Costume, 1961

63   ' Formes Picturales ', 1969

64   ' Formes Picturales ', 1969

65   *La Veuve Rusée*. Costume, 1972   66   *Zizi je t'aime*. Costume, 1972

68 ' Lady with Rose '. Serigraph, 1974

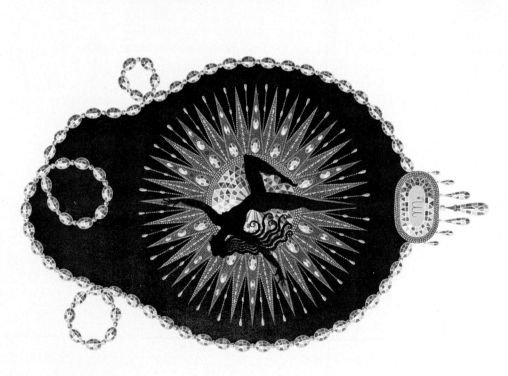

67 ' Topaz '. Lithograph, 1969

During my Barbados visit in the winter of 1972, I was presented to HRH Princess Margaret, albeit in a manner that was somewhat lacking in protocol. I was in my bathing trunks, having just emerged from the water, when I was introduced to the Princess, who had been lunching with friends near ' Nelson Gay '. On her trips to Barbados, she often stayed with Oliver Messel, an uncle by marriage. Lately, she had made Barbados a stopping-off point on the way to Mustique, a nearby island where she has a beach property, given to her as a wedding present by Colin Tennant, and a house recently completed by Oliver Messel.

I always take advantage of my trips to visit other islands, having so far been to Jamaica, Martinique and Guadeloupe. Each of these has its own special beauty, but Jamaica is, perhaps, the most spectacular, with its wonderful mountain torrents cascading in impressive waterfalls among luxuriant tropical vegetation. I have never seen such masses of flowers or such vivid colours as in Jamaica. I also visited Caracas, Venezuela, in 1974, on the occasion of my exhibition at the Galería Conkright.

After one of my visits to Barbados, I went to New York with Sal and Eric to meet Barbra Streisand, who owned a large collection of my works. She wanted me to design some decorative panels for a town house she planned to buy. Our interview took place in this house, which had been built in 1928 and whose original décor had remained intact. Throughout the entire interview, which was most cordial, I was fascinated by Barbra Streisand's hands, which are probably the most beautiful that I have ever seen. Although I completed sketches for the panels, our plans were not fulfilled, for Miss Streisand never moved into the house.

My first visit to Barbados, besides a welcome holiday, had been the initial stage of a journey to Mexico for an exhibition of my works at the Galería Arvil in Mexico City. With Sal and Eric, I left for Mexico in an aeroplane which had come from Trinidad. We were to change at Jamaica. Unfortunately, Trinidad was in the grip of political troubles at the time and these affected flight schedules. Since the plane we boarded in Barbados was more than two hours late, we missed our connection in Jamaica. The situation was very complicated and after much laborious calculation we decided there was only one way to reach Mexico within the near future: we must take a plane to Miami, spend the night there, and then catch a direct Miami-Mexico flight the following day. Although we did this, we missed the opening of another exhibition – of Feliciano Bejar's sculpture at the Mexico City Museum of Modern Art – that we had wanted to attend. I had been invited to stay with this great Mexican sculptor-painter, whose marvellous sculptures of crystal and plexiglass create quite magical effects, and who had also exhibited at the Grosvenor Gallery.

His extraordinary house is unique of its type. About fifteen years ago, he bought a very large plot just outside the city, in San Angel. On this sloping, rocky site, he has built, with his own hands, a dozen little houses, each independent of the others. They are masterpieces, built with ancient stones and the remains of old bas-reliefs from the ruins of temples or old Mexican palaces. Because of the varying levels of the site, one of these houses has five floors, each floor consisting of a single room. Many of the houses are inhabited by members of Feliciano Bejar's large family, while others are rented. The gardens in which they stand are beautiful in their tropical splendour. Numerous stone staircases link the different levels. Apart from the houses, the grounds contain a very fine open-air theatre, and Bejar is also planning to build a chapel. I saw the foundations of this building, together with some seventeenth-century statues of angels, which were to decorate the entrance.

Mexican hospitality is really marvellous. I received an extremely warm welcome and my exhibition was a great success. This retrospective exhibition of my originals had been preceded a few months earlier by another exhibition devoted solely to my lithographs. This had received enthusiastic press notices and one of Mexico's foremost art critics, Alphonse de Neuvillate, devoted a series of articles to my work.

On arriving in Mexico I was pleased to see again Charles Spencer, who was also a guest of Feliciano Bejar. We stayed in the same house and together made several excursions into the country, with Martin Foley as guide. Foley, who has a wide knowledge of all the different Mexican civilizations, drove us nearly every day to the more interesting places in and around Mexico City. I was struck by the beauty of the Pyramids and by the ruins of Tio-Ti-Jua-Clan. The photographs and postcards I had seen had given me no idea of the grandeur of these monuments, not to mention the wealth of extraordinary detail to be found on the exterior surfaces of the Pyramids.

I was equally fascinated by Mexico's baroque architecture. Mexican churches are the most astonishing in the world. Some look exactly like an enlarged version of a jewel or piece of golden filigree. Yet, despite an incredible profusion of ornamentation, they do not give an impression of heaviness, nor of surfeit. This is due to the perfect equilibrium of their proportions and to the careful relationship established between the different elements of their decoration.

The town of Pueblo is pure baroque: all the houses are painted in shades of different colours – pinks, yellows, pale greens, violets, oranges – but each one is covered in sculptured ornamentations of a dazzling white. They look rather like giant cakes decorated with whipped cream.

I should have liked to get to know Mexico better, but a detailed tour of this mysterious and beautiful country would have taken several months. So I had to content myself with the condensed version to be seen in Mexico's superb Anthropological Museum – to my mind the best in the world.

During our stay in Mexico, Charles Spencer and I talked a great deal about his book, *Erté*, which was to be published in a few months' time. Naturally I went to London for the publication, to celebrate which the Estoricks had organized a big reception at the Grosvenor Gallery. I don't think I have ever signed my name quite so often, nor written so many dedications. While everyone else drank champagne and ate all sorts of appetizing morsels, I clutched my pen without a moment's respite.

Two separate but identical editions of Spencer's book were printed, one for England and one for America. The English edition sold out within a few months, and had to be reprinted. A half-hour BBC television programme about me was scheduled to coincide with the publication of the book. I had already participated in a number of television broadcasts for the BBC, but none as long as this, which was to be broadcast live, a circumstance that always gives me stage fright. On the eve of the broadcast, I had dinner with the producer, Peter Adam, and the late James Mossman, who was to interview me. We established a general plan and agreed on the sort of questions Mossman was to ask. During the actual broadcast, however, his questions were completely different from those discussed. Nevertheless, all went off very well, and my stage fright vanished with the first few words. In addition to our conversation, the programme showed a wide variety of my works, including the short silent film I had made with Joan Crawford in Hollywood, and a parade of the costumes I had worn at various fancy dress balls. On this occasion, the costumes, which were photographed for Charles Spencer's book, were modelled by young ballet students. The costume entitled ' Clair de Lune ' figured later in Cecil Beaton's splendid exhibition of twentieth-century fashions at the Victoria and Albert Museum. I subsequently donated it to the museum.

In contrast, my relations with French television have been less trouble-free. ORTF planned a big show, to be directed by Philippe Collin. They spent three days filming at my home. Then a team of important television people set off for London to shoot in the Grosvenor Gallery and at the Victoria and Albert Museum. They also wished to film my Alphabet, which is in Lord Beaumont's collection. A great deal of money was spent on the preparation of this programme.

Meanwhile, the student riots of May 1970 upset all ORTF'S programming and the broadcast was postponed indefinitely. Shortly after that, the woman producer of ' Dim Dam Dom ' wanted to devote one of that series to me. For two days this was shot in the ORTF studios with Seligman as director. Once the filming was over, Seligman had the idea of incorporating some of the material already used in the Philippe Collin programme. He put both films on his desk and, the following day, left for the country where he was to spend a few days filming. In his absence, the films somehow fell off the desk and on to the floor, not far from a waste paper basket. The cleaning lady thought they were to be thrown away and the films ended up in the incinerator.

It was not until April 1971 that a long broadcast about me, ' Variances ', appeared on French television. It was a half-hour programme with reporting by Claude Gallot and Florence Gruère. Part of this film had been shot in my home and part at the Galerie Proscénium, which was at the time holding its first exhibition of my works, consisting of designs for operas, ballets and dramatic shows. This was the first art gallery in Paris to be devoted exclusively to the theatre and its reputation has spread with astonishing speed. This is mainly due to the efforts of its proprietors, Paul Payen and Gilles Bernard, two men of whom I am very fond. Shortly after this first exhibition, the Proscénium held a second show of my designs for the music-hall.

At the first Proscénium exhibition, an advance copy of the book published by Franco Ricci was also displayed. Roland Barthes' text surpassed my wildest hopes. He began thus:

> Before becoming well known, artists must pass through a small mythological purgatory: it must be automatically possible to associate them with an object, a school, a fashion or an era of which they are, or so it is said, the precursors, the founders, the witnesses of the symbols; in a word, it must be possible to categorize them without further effort, to subject them to a communal name.
>
> Erté's purgatory is Woman.
>
> Certainly, Erté has drawn many women; in a sense, he has drawn nothing else, as though he could never detach himself from them (soul or accessory, obsession or commodity?), as if Woman signed each of his cartoons more surely than the fine caligraphy of his name.
>
> Look at some of Erté's larger compositions (and there are some): the decorative details, the precise baroque exuberance, the abstract transcendence which carry the lines forward, all say one thing to you: Cherchez la Femme.
>
> And one always finds her: there she is, necessarily tiny, stretched out at the centre of a motif which, once it has been located, makes everything swing and converge on the altar where she is adored (if not sacrificed).

An art critic analysing the book added:

> But what sort of woman is this creature, omni-present, obsessive, unreal and yet precise? Is she something one desires, or something one would have liked to be?
>
> Erté exalts and magnifies Woman. The type he has created is, it must be said, somewhat sexless. Indifferent, sophisticatedly maleficent, inaccessible, the heroine, according to Erté, is a desirable object, fascinating, exacting and terribly frivolous. What is more, one is only half surprised to find that this woman can fascinate those who experience in her company a satisfaction which is purely aesthetic. . . .

The publication in Italy of Ricci's book had gratifying repercussions in terms of publicity for his Art Book Club and for myself. Until then, only a limited number of art lovers, who had visited the Pellegrini exhibitions, had ever heard of me in Italy. Once the book was published, followed by a number of exhibitions in various cities, my name became well known· throughout Italy.

In Parma, Gian Mario Chiavari organized an exhibition in his Galleria della Rocchetta. Soon after, a large exhibition was presented in Franco Maria Ricci's Booklovers' Club in Milan. The club, which has an art gallery, is situated in an ancient palace in the Via Bigli. It was a brilliant opening, with all the artistic and social celebrities of Milan present. I arrived a few minutes late because I had trouble forcing my way through the crowds of people in the great courtyard of the palace who were trying to enter one of the exhibition rooms.

Unfortunately I was unable to be present at all the exhibitions in Italy, but I shall always remember two that I did attend: those in Palermo and Rome. The one in Palermo took place in the spring of 1971 at the Galleria Mediterraneo. This was the first time I had visited Sicily and its magnificent countryside was a revelation to me. I loved, too, the older parts of Palermo, which had not yet been spoiled by new buildings. With each step one came across churches or palaces of extraordinary beauty. The ' Leopard ' palace struck me particularly. Since Visconti's famous film of the same name was shot in this palace, I very much wanted to visit it. Unfortunately, the owner, who was a friend of the owner of the gallery where my exhibition was being held, was not in Palermo at the time. However, friends telephoned her in Rome and she immediately gave her caretaker instructions to let me visit the palace. When I saw the film *The Leopard*, I had assumed that the palace interiors had been built in a studio, but I was mistaken: all those immense salons with their fantastic decorations are indeed part of the palace.

Palermo's most beautiful monument is perhaps the famous Monreale monastery, with its striking twelfth-century Romanesque church, full of details reminiscent of Arab ornamentation. Arabic art appears in numerous Palermo churches, some of which were converted from ancient mosques.

When I entered the cathedral, I was impressed by the grandeur and beauty of this edifice, and particularly by its marvellous mosaics. What struck me next was its theatricality. A vast stairway in golden mosiac led up to the altar; when I saw it at close range I realized that it was made of plywood, but this was well disguised. I later discovered the reason for this strange detail: Zeffirelli had been filming in the cathedral and had added this touch for technical reasons, but it had been marvellously absorbed by the architecture of the church.

My Rome exhibition took place in October of 1971 at the Galleria Marino, which was housed in one of those old palaces around the Piazza Navona. I can never get enough of the extraordinary atmosphere which pervades this beautiful place. Traffic is not allowed to enter the square and one hears only the murmur of its splendid fountains. The beautiful gallery where my exhibition took place belongs to Giuseppe Marino, a young and very enthusiastic man, who made sure that I still treasure marvellous memories of my brief but exciting stay in Rome. At the opening, my entrance, accompanied by a ravishing young lady who was ' Miss Italy ', was the subject of a short film which was later shown in the cinemas.

I have always loved Italy. Most striking is the great diversity of its cities, each of which has a character entirely its own. There are no provincial cities – every one is a capital. The reasons for this derive from the past, when each important city was in fact the capital of one of the kingdoms, principalities or duchies which formed Italy. It is certainly a country in which one can travel without monotony.

In 1972 I visited Cortina d'Ampezzo, the winter sports resort. Marino had arranged an exhibition of my graphic work in conjunction with the organizing committee of the annual Cortina Festival, which lasts a week and draws the most elegant people from all over the country. I saw in the hotel foyer a beautiful young woman who, in a single day, appeared in four different fur coats, each more exquisite than the one before. The Festival Committee asked me to present the prize for the most elegant woman in Italy as well as prizes for the best couturier, furrier, jeweller, etc.

An amusing incident occurred on my way to Cortina. I was going through Immigration Control at Orly Airport when the officer who held my passport gave me a withering look and indignantly asked, ' Madame, what makes you think you can travel on your husband's passport? ' After a moment of shocked silence, I suddenly realized that my passport photograph had been taken before I let my hair grow long. I tried to explain this to the officer but he wouldn't believe me. He insisted on calling his chief who also had difficulty in accepting my story. In desperation I brought out my identity card which included a photograph showing me with long hair. That saved the day.

My long hair has since triggered a number of amusing incidents. I once went to a party in a small, exotic country. When I was introduced to an important local personality, the first thing he asked was, ' Shall I call you Madame or Mademoiselle? ' He was totally confused when I answered, ' Just call me Monsieur.' Then there was the young, long-haired, bearded immigration officer at London airport who also called me ' Madame '. When I pointed out his error he laughed and said he had often run into the same problem, but that he had finally solved it by growing a beard.

My trip to Cortina took place just before the premiere of Roland Petit's new show at the Casino de Paris, *Zizi, je t'aime*. To my great pleasure, Zizi Jeanmaire was at last to wear my clothes in this production. Roland Petit asked me to design sets and costumes for a classical ballet, about half an hour in length, which would close the first half of the show. The ballet was based on one of Goldoni's comedies, *La Vedova Scaltra*, but the action, instead of taking place in the eighteenth century, was transposed to the early part of the twentieth, with the actors dressed in the fashions of 1913. One of the scenes was set in Maxim's –

a very stylized Maxim's. In this, *La Vedova Scaltra* (*La Veuve Rusée* or The Artful Widow) had an affinity with *The Merry Widow*.

Zizi Jeanmaire danced divinely: I thought she had never been in such good form. It was great fun to design costumes in the style of my formative period. Beautifully made by Karinska, they were superbly adorned with feathers by Mlle Parfan, whom I call the ' feather fairy '. I also designed the costumes for a strange and erotic ballet, ' Le Jardin des Délices ', for the same programme.

Many people considered this revue the height of ' kitsch ' – a fashionable term just then. But exactly what did they mean? No one has ever provided a precise definition, for each gives it his own interpretation. Some say that ' kitsch ' implies the very worst of bad taste: others use it to define excess in art, implying a certain sublime madness. For some, ' kitsch ' is synonymous with rubbish; for others it implies something unexpected, bizarre. One art critic called me ' the magician of kitsch '. I hope he meant unusual rather than rubbishy, for rubbish has always been my number one enemy.

Since then, the pace of my life has not slowed down. As *Vogue* said in September 1970, ' To be Erté in 1970 is no sinecure! ' In 1972 there were five retrospectives celebrating my eightieth birthday; these were held in Paris, London, New York, Detroit and Geneva. A new book, *Erté Fashions,* illustrated with my black and white fashion sketches, was published in London,* along with an English version of the Ricci book.

I attended all five openings and was always deeply touched by the enthusiasm of the public. At the opening of the Paris show, at the Galerie Proscénium, many celebrities from the worlds of theatre, art and fashion turned out. The following words were written in the Guest Book by Paco Rabanne:

> Monsieur Erté, que vous dire? – que ma plus grande admiration pour votre très grand talent, dont je me sens un humble continuateur.**
> Paco Rabanne

Later that evening I was the guest of honour at a big party given at the Alcazar. Jean-Marie Rivière, the owner, staged a special 1920 scene for the occasion. Then, a beautiful male dancer, wearing a rhinestone-studded costume, brought in a huge birthday cake lit with eighty candles.

Two days later I went to the London opening at the Brook Street Gallery, since the new London quarters of the Grosvenor Gallery were not intended for public exhibitions. To my astonishment – and pleasure – almost every work in the show

---

* Academy Editions, 1972.
** ' Monsieur Erté, what can I tell you? Only express my deep admiration of your great talent, of which I am a humble follower.'

was sold. Within the next few days, I left with the Estoricks for New York and my exhibition at the Rizzoli Gallery. Here I was greeted by my old friend, Carmel Myers, whom I had not seen for years, Yves Saint-Laurent, Andy Warhol, Bianca Jagger and many others. The American press has often referred to me as Bianca's fashion adviser. Although I like her very much and have often praised her beauty in interviews, I have never designed dresses for her. It is true, however, that in one of the many illustrated articles that ran in the London papers, in connection with my eightieth birthday, appeared a photograph of Bianca wearing an Erté-inspired dress that had been made up by an English dressmaker.

After the Rizzoli opening, Sal Estorick and I went to Detroit, one of the ugliest cities I have ever seen. Not far from modern sky-scrapers stand rows of small, drab, decaying houses. The only two things of beauty in the downtown area are the Detroit Art Institute and the Fisher Building, designed in the purest Art Deco style.

After Detroit, I flew back to Paris for a few days' rest. There is nothing quite so tiring as the opening of an exhibition. I am normally on my feet for about four hours during which I am either talking or signing books, posters or autograph albums. I hardly even have time for a drink.

From Paris, I went on with Eric Estorick to Geneva and an extremely warm reception. My exhibition was at the Lambert Monet Gallery, a beautiful exhibition area in the picturesque old part of the city, near the cathedral. Following the opening there was a wonderful dinner party with a fabulous birthday cake. Later, at a private club, I danced the frug until three o'clock in the morning, leaving only when Eric insisted that I would become ill if I continued. Eric, who is more than twenty years younger than I am, readily admitted to his own exhaustion.

Another exhibition had been arranged in New Orleans in conjunction with the 1973 Mardi Gras. Unfortunately, I was unable to attend the opening because I had to stay in Paris for some minor surgery. (I sometimes wonder if this would have been necessary had I stopped frug-ing sooner!) The show was held at the Downtown Gallery in a charming building, at the centre of the old city. I was sorry to have missed it because all the ladies who had been invited wore dresses copied from my *Harper's Bazaar* designs of the 1920s.

I arrived in New Orleans two weeks later. That night, the owner of the gallery, Keith Marshall, and his mother gave a big party there. I was also a guest at the Marshalls' beautiful country house, which reminds me of *Gone With the Wind*. Each year they give an opera or ballet performance in the garden. To top it all, I was made an Honorary Citizen of New Orleans. What a lively city it is – and its food, I think, must be among the best in the United States.

1973 was again a year of travel. I spent some time in the Canary Islands, since I still felt somewhat tired after my operation. I loved the Canaries, which I was visiting for the first time. I stayed in the south of Gran Canaria, which has a

69   With Isobel Estorick, 1972   70   With Leonor Fini, 1972

71   With Barbra Streisand, 1973

72   With Eric Estorick and Jack Solomon, 1974

73   Cutting my birthday cake, 1973

74   With Edith Head, 1973

75   At the David Stuart Gallery, 1973

76   On the beach at St Peter, Barbados, 1972

77   With Sal Estorick, 1972

series of enormous sandy beaches. Of the other islands, one that made a particular impression on me was Lanzarote, where one can see about a hundred volcanoes. Its landscape is somewhat unreal, and resembles a moonscape, with its fantastic colours. Some volcanoes are almost red, some green, others are purplish.

After my brief rest in the Canary Islands, I began making arrangements for a month's tour of Greece – an eightieth birthday gift from my good friend, Madame Martini. For years I had dreamed of going to Greece, but each time I made plans, some urgent work had always intervened. I was fortunate in being able to see Greece for the first time in the spring, when everything is green and all the flowers are in bloom; by summer, the vegetation is burned brown by the extremely dry climate.

As I travelled around the country, I was full of admiration for what I saw, but the place that made the deepest impression upon me was Delphi. Here, I felt that I was floating somewhere between heaven and earth, so mysterious and other-worldly is its atmosphere. I was also enchanted by my cruise of the Greek islands. Every day we landed on a new island and every day was crowded with new impressions. As so often happens when I travel, I had a charming adventure during the cruise. There is something erotic in the air of Greece: the land is full of beautiful people.

On my return to Paris, I met Roland Petit to discuss the sets and costumes for a ballet based on various compositions by Eric Satie. Petit was planning these for the Marseille Ballet Company, of which he had recently become Artistic Director. We also discussed several other future projects on which he wanted me to collaborate.

In November of 1973, I celebrated my eighty-first birthday in Beverly Hills, California, with a large, retrospective exhibition at the David Stuart Gallery. Apart from a hurried trip to Hollywood in connection with my work on *Flying Colours*, for Canada's ' Expo' 67 ', I had not returned to that part of the world since my much publicized departure from the Metro-Goldwyn-Mayer studio in 1925. This time I arrived directly from Paris in the early hours of the morning, after an eighteen-hour flight. Eric and Sal Estorick drove me to a spacious bungalow in the lovely grounds of the Beverly Hills Hotel, where they were already ensconced, and where, forty-eight years earlier, I had stayed temporarily. Although I scarcely recognized the hotel, I must say that, unlike some other film-colony landmarks, it carries its years with style and grace. By some miracle, it has managed to avoid the standardization which is rapidly taking over the world's hotels, among other things. It is a unique oasis.

The next morning I plunged into a five-day round of interviews, sessions with photographers, luncheons, dinners, receptions and parties. The high point of the first day was a gala birthday luncheon given by Eric and Sal in one of the hotel's private rooms. They had invited the West Coast editors of *Vogue* and *Harper's Bazaar*, along with several members of the press; also M. Roux, the French

Consul-General and his wife; David Stuart; Isobel Estorick, who now lives in
Santa Monica; Warren Caro, head of the Schubert theatrical organization; Michael
Blankfort, novelist and former head of the Screen Writer's Guild; and designer
Rudi Gernreich. I was delighted to see Rudi, an old fan of mine, whom I had
met in Paris several years before. Since I have always admired Rudi's unisex
creations, I was especially touched by his birthday gift – a colourful, Gernreich-
designed, unisex caftan.

Each year, on my birthday, wherever I happen to be, I usually slip into a
church for a few moments of prayer. So, towards evening, Eric drove me to the
Church of the Good Shepherd in Beverly Hills. By the time we arrived the
building was dark and the doors were locked. We were about to leave when Eric
noticed the black figure of one of the parish priests crossing the courtyard. When
Eric explained the circumstances, he promptly opened the church especially for
me. It was a perfect ending to a happy birthday.

The large crowds which jammed the opening at the David Stuart Gallery ranged
from young people in blue jeans or early 1920s costumes, through my old
friend Madame Kozloff, widow of Theodore, Rudi and his favourite model (sleek
Peggy Moffit), Alexis Smith, octogenarian Groucho Marx and assorted film-colony
personalities, to people from surrounding communities and points as far north as
San Francisco.

There was a surprise reunion with Barbra Streisand, who invited me to see how
she had hung her collection of Ertés. Miss Streisand made a striking entrance
wearing a diaphanous, red print gown made by her favourite London dressmaker.
Many photographs of us were taken against the background of her stunning grey
and red Art Deco room. All this was punctuated by a lively, blow-by-blow account
of how she had acquired many of the Art Nouveau and Art Deco treasures in
her splendid house.

The climax of the festivities, which also included a tour of the Los Angeles
County Museum, luncheon with the board members of the museum's Costume
Council, and a presentation by Edith Head of an Honorary Membership in the
Motion Picture and Television Costume Designers' Guild, was a dinner party
which Rudi gave at his house. He lives in a striking modern, Moroccan-style
house, with patio swimming pool, perched on one of Hollywood's higher hills.
The view was superb, and Rudi, looking exotic – and timeless – in caftan and
bare feet, was a charming host. Whenever I see him, I am reminded of the words
of the actress, Betty Furness, another of Rudi's admirers. She once said that
he was ' the only designer who could think of what we might be wearing in the
year 2,000 '.

Epilogue

One cannot be and have been, says the proverb. I thank God for a long, busy, rich life which gives the lie to that. If my readers feel that this statement is lacking in modesty, I can only say that I consider false modesty a kind of hypocrisy. The only form of hypocrisy that I not only accept but thoroughly approve is politeness. What would human relations be without it?

I firmly believe, too, that every human being has a duty to make himself as attractive as possible. Not many of us are born beautiful; that is why I have always attached so much importance to clothes. Clothes are a kind of alchemy: they can transform human beings into things of beauty or ugliness.

Since I was already highly fashion-conscious before I was five, I have had a rather special opportunity to watch the evolution of female fashion. From the distorted silhouette of the 1890s to the natural contours of the 1970s, its development has been dramatic. Whenever designers failed to respect individuality – with malice aforethought or otherwise – beauty became the victim of passing fads. As I wrote in *Harper's Bazaar* back in 1919, ' I do not blindly follow the current fashion. I love clothes that are luxurious and beautiful, and I believe they should enhance the good points of the woman who wears them – they should, in fact, be completely individual.' In spite of periodic aberrations, I think we have finally reached the point where most women have the good sense to select fashions which accentuate their best features and minimize their defects. In short, they have become individuals.

When I started out on my fashion career, I believed that a woman's ' Three Graces ' were beauty, charm and elegance. I have not changed my mind. Of the three, I think, elegance is paramount. Elegance is an innate quality; it cannot be acquired. A woman of humble background can be elegant by virtue of her appearance, her carriage and movements, her way of speaking and a thousand other details. Such a woman can also be chic. What is chic? For me, it is elegance within a context of what is currently fashionable. A chic woman – or man – dresses and behaves according to the taste of the day. But a person can be elegant even if he – or she – is dressed in yesterday's fashions, or in a highly personal style.

Among other rewards of my long life, I have had the pleasure of seeing an idea that I have always defended – often in the face of condescension or downright hostility – win wide acceptance. I mean greater harmony between male and female fashions. In the seventeenth and eighteenth centuries, men, like women, wore colourful, rich brocades or embroidered fabrics, along with laces, feathers and marvellous jewels. By the end of the nineteenth century all this disappeared. On formal social occasions women would light up a room with the kaleidoscopic colour of their gowns and jewels while men were encased in dinner jackets or tail-coats of stark black, looking like an army of head-waiters.

I began to preach reform in men's clothes in the early 1920s, but I have practised it for most of my life. Since I design most of my own clothes, I have never had to submit to the despotism and capriciousness of fashion. On the contrary, I have always moulded it to my taste. The charm and fantasy of current fashions, especially for men, are close to the ideas I have always cherished. But I must confess that when I wrote an article on the evolution of dress in the twentieth century, for the 1929 edition of the *Encyclopaedia Britannica*, forecasting the idea of unisex fashion, I never dreamed that I should live to see it become a reality.

I began to write this memoir in the winter of 1972, shortly after my eightieth birthday, when I was a guest at the Estoricks' house in Barbados. The five retrospective exhibitions of my work, the three books published about me and my work, and the warm and enthusiastic welcome I obtained from the public everywhere, especially from young people, had touched me deeply. These exhibitions and books created such a groundswell of interest and curiosity about my life that Eric urged me to write my own memoir. All that winter of 1972-73 I was haunted by fears that I would find it extremely difficult to write about my life. I have never lived with yesterday, but am always looking ahead to my tomorrows; one cannot change the past but one can do something about the future. Although I did not have the support of detailed personal diaries, yet with the help of photographs, clipping files and such documentary material as was available, I was surprised to find that past events came alive with such vividness and immediacy that they might almost have occurred the day before. Thanks to Eric's constant encouragement I produced a first draft. He then called in Charlotte Seitlin, an editor and old friend from New York. From both of them came a stream of questions which released many more forgotten memories.

With it, also, came the saddening realization of how many of my good friends had died; this gave me many sleepless nights, for which I do not thank them!

But the book is now completed, and I wish to express my indebtedness to Charlotte Seitlin for her guidance and help, without which I might never have finished it. I would also like to thank Beatrice Musgrave and the editorial staff of Peter Owen Ltd, London. Their efforts are deeply appreciated. Finally, affectionate thanks to Eric and Sal Estorick for their customary wise counsel and moral support, and to their staff at the Grosvenor Gallery, London, especially John Bowley.

Things I remember . . . when I began recording them I never thought there would be so many. I shall be happy if God grants me the time to write a few more.

Nelson Gay
St Peter, Barbados
1972-1975

Selected Comments

GEORGE WHITE'S SCANDALS' (1923-24)

' the costumes have combined an unequalled lavishness with the most astounding loveliness.' (*New York World*, 19 June, 1923)

' a gorgeous multi-coloured thing of shimmering drapes and curtains.' (*New York Times*, 19 June, 1923)

' a perfectly gorgeous show . . . we do not expect to find a more ravishing spectacle this side of paradise.' (*New York World*, 7 July, 1924)

' The . . . famous Erté costumes – without limit in originality and variety – caused gasps of wonderment from the first night audience.' (*New York Bulletin*, 7 July, 1924)

EXHIBITION OF WATERCOLOURS, MADISON HOTEL, NEW YORK (1925)

' Romain de Tirtoff-Erté's exhibition of watercolors at the Madison is what is known in the vernacular as a " wow ". Announced as a show of " fashion drawings ", the nearly seven hundred drawings actually comprise ballet décors, designs for ballet curtains, types from " costume " plays and a hundred and one graceful and charming fancies, that emerge in an apparently inexhaustible stream from Tirtoff-Erté's fertile imagination. . . . Charged with the spirit of the modern musical stage, these watercolors are markedly brilliant as drawings (his line is the perfection of an almost lost art), while his color is marvellous both as to range and pure beauty, the only thing comparable to it I know being that of the finest Persian miniatures. . . . I urge every art, theatre, ballet and opera lover to go and see this exhibition for the delight they will take in Tirtoff-Erté's exquisite creations.' (William B. McCormick, *New York American*, 12 March, 1925)

EXHIBITIONS, GALERIE CHARPENTIER, PARIS (1926, 1929)

'His world is a strangely refined and beautiful one, which must be explored slowly, and with a curiosity which will, little by little, give way to admiration and to love. The word miniature springs to mind when one stands before these little frames, each one of which attests a painstakingly perfect technique, as well as the patience and mastery of execution of an inspired creator, whose hand and eye are those of a miniaturist, or of a Persian illuminator, yet who knows how to maintain a sweeping line, a flight of inspiration and a harmonious power within the balance of colours. . . .

Erté is like a musician when he plays with nuances, and he is a creature for whom all the possibilities of colour exist. But he encloses them all within the taut and inflexible filigree of a carefully thought-out line; beneath their capricious gracefulness, his works display an intense power of expression. Thought is present in all his compositions. Small in format, they sometimes nonetheless evoke vast spaces.' (Camille Mauclair, from the preface for the catalogue, 1926)

'one finds with each step the delights of poetry and the surprises of a skilled user of colour.' (*Le Figaro Artistique,* 8 April, 1926)

'in their spirit and elegance, Erté's compositions have something which is very French.' (*La Liberté,* 17 April, 1926)

'I have for a long time broadcast his talent and the characteristics of his art which can be studied infinitely, without fear of weariness or boredom, so diverse and various are the facets of this delightful spirit, so full of new ideas and unexpected inventions.' (*Le Gaulois Artistique,* 28 May, 1929)

'Erté is a visionary whose imagination carries him away, keen to flee from the ugliness of everyday life; yet he is aware that the wildest creations, the most delicate arabesques are valueless except in their contact with nature, the eternal source of forms, shapes and masses.' (*Excelsior,* 30 May, 1929)

'DON PASQUALE', PARIS (1944)

'Erté has given . . . a set which has at once the grace of a toy and the stylization of a work of art. One would not know how better to preserve the atmosphere of behind-the-scene comedy of this fantasy while still enriching it with scenic elements of beautiful effectiveness.' (*L'Echo de France,* 2 January, 1944)

'LA TRAVIATA', PARIS (1951)

'I think that the work of the designer Erté was the most fortunate part of the whole enterprise. The conscious stylization of a drama of eternal love enriched it with a universality which rescued it from being a prosaic piece of documentary history, while still retaining the more spiritual aspects of its atmosphere.' (*Rivarol,* 8 March, 1951)

' CASTOR ET POLLUX ', LYONS (1961)
' Visually, everything was enchanting. . . . If anyone deserves high praise it is the designer Erté . . . and without reserve.' (*Le Progrès Soir,* 30 June, 1961)

' If the evening left one with a single unforgettable memory, the credit must go entirely to Erté, that great artist who conceived and realized a veritable fairyland of colours and lines in his costumes which were of astonishing richness and variety.' (*La Croix,* 22 July, 1961)

EXHIBITION OF ' FORMES PICTURALES ', PARIS (1964)
' I have seen Erté fashion pieces of wood and metal, and give them a shape, a life, transforming matter into ideas, something which is admirable in itself. But to paint over these shapes, to sculpt the colour as though it were another precious substance, and thus to prolong and underline his inspiration, that is the area in which he surpasses the painter and the sculptor; these pieces reveal a profound originality and can truly be called three-dimensional.' (*Art,* February, 1964)

' I imagine that to see Erté at work must be rather like coming across a miraculously accelerated version of the insidious creation of coral.' (Micheline Sendrel, *Lettres de Médecins,* May, 1965)

CASINO DE PARIS, PARIS (1970, 1972)

' the Prince of the Music Hall remains as always the great Erté, with tableaux like " Diamonds ", scintillating and transparent like a running stream.' (*Le Parisien Libéré,* 6 February, 1970)

' This miraculous old man, able to invent at the age of eighty ' Le Jardin des Délices ' and to reinvent Maxim's; Erté, in the midst of new magicians, reaffirms the enchantment of a half-century at least, in his constructions which, like the vicarage garden, have lost none of their impact.' (Louis Aragon)
' Perhaps the revue [*Zizi, je t'aime*] should have a sub-title: " Erté, je t'aime aussi ".' (*Paris Herald Tribune,* 25 February, 1972)

Chronology

1892   Born in St Petersburg, son of Piotr Ivanovitch de Tirtoff, Admiral of the Imperial Fleet, and Natalia de Tirtoff, *née* Nikolenko.

1906   Begins to study painting under the direction of Ilya Repine and his pupil, Lossevsky.

1912   Arrives in Paris, studies at the Académie Julian.
Contributes to the Russian fashion magazine, *Damsky Mir.*

1913   Signs a contract with the famous Parisian couturier, Paul Poiret. First costume designs for the theatre: his first production is *Le Minaret* by Jacques Richepin, at the Théâtre de la Renaissance, Paris.

1914   First illustrations for *La Gazette du Bon Ton,* Paris.
Costumes for the stage production of *Aphrodite* by Pierre Louys at the Théâtre de la Renaissance.
Costumes for *Le Tango* by Jacques Richepin.
Costumes for the 'Revue de Saint-Cyr' by Rip.

1915   Beginning of his long collaboration with the American review *Harper's Bazaar* (first cover for this review published 1 January, 1915).

1916   An association of six months with the American review *Vogue.*
A ten-year exclusive contract signed with *Harper's Bazaar.*
First costumes and sets designed for music-hall: work for the Théâtre Ba-ta-Clan of Madame Rasimi, Paris.
Designs and drawings for Henri Bendel, New York.

1917   Costumes and sets for *La Planète Fémina* at the Théâtre Fémina, Paris.
Costumes and sets for a production at the Ba-ta-Clan.
Designs and drawings for Henri Bendel, New York.

1918   Costumes and sets for Ba-ta-Clan revue (with Mistinguett).
Covers and illustrations for *Harper's Bazaar*.

1919   Costumes and sets for the Folies Bergère, Paris.
Costumes and sets for *La Marche à l'Etoile*, Théâtre Fémina (with Gaby Deslys).
Covers and illustrations for *Harper's Bazaar*.

1920   Costumes for Ganna Walska of the Chicago Opera Company: *Thaïs, Monna Vanna, Aphrodite, Fedora, Tosca, Manon, La Bohème, Zaza, Louise, I Pagliacci, Faust, Marta.*
Costumes for Mary Garden of the Chicago Opera Company: *L'Amore dei Tre Re.*
Costumes and sets for the film, *Restless Sex* (Cosmopolitan Productions, USA).
Covers and illustrations for *Harper's Bazaar*.

1921   Costumes and sets for the Folies Bergère.
Costumes and sets for the Alcazar, Marseilles.
Costumes and sets for the review at the Winter Garden, New York.
Covers and illustrations for *Harper's Bazaar*.

1922   Costumes and sets for George White's *Scandals*, New York.
Costumes and sets for the review at the Théâtre des Ambassadeurs, Paris.
Costumes and sets for show at the Alcazar, Marseilles.
Sets for the *Music Box Review* by Irving Berlin, New York.
Sets and costumes for the Winter Garden, New York.
Costumes for Ganna Walska (*Rigoletto*) at the Paris Opéra.
Covers and illustrations for *Harper's Bazaar*.
Illustrations for the review *Fémina*, Paris.

1923   Costumes and sets for the Folies Bergère.
Costumes and sets for the *Music Box Revue* by Irving Berlin, New York.
Costumes for Maria Kouznetsoff (*La Traviata*) at the Opéra-Comique, Paris.
Costumes and sets for the *Ziegfeld Follies*, New York.
Costumes and sets for George White's *Scandals*, New York.
Illustrations for *La Gazette du Bon Ton*.
Covers and illustrations for *Harper's Bazaar*.
Fashion drawings for the *Ladies' Home Journal*, Philadelphia.

1924   Costumes and sets for the Winter Garden, New York.
Costumes for *Le Secret du Sphinx*, by Maurice Rostand, Théâtre Sarah Bernhardt, Paris.
Costumes and sets for the Folies Bergère.

Costumes and sets for the Palladium, London.
Costumes and sets for George White's *Scandals*, New York.
Covers and illustrations for the review *Fémina*.
Illustrations for *The Sketch*, London.
Covers and illustrations for *Harper's Bazaar*.
Fashion drawings for the *Ladies' Home Journal*.

1925   Exhibition at the Hotel Madison, New York.
Costumes and sets for George White's *Scandals*, New York.
A year's stay in Hollywood,with three contracts with Metro-Goldwyn-Mayer (six months, three months, three months).
Covers and illustrations for *Harper's Bazaar*.
Fashion drawings for the *Ladies' Home Journal*.

1926   Exhibition at the Galerie Charpentier, Paris (some works bought by the French government).
Second ten-year contract with *Harper's Bazaar*.
Costumes and sets for George White's *Scandals*.
Costumes and sets for the Folies Bergère.
Covers and illustrations for the review *Art et Industrie*, Paris.
Illustrations for the review *L'Illustration*, Paris.
Covers and illustrations for *Harper's Bazaar*.

1927   Exhibition at the Studio Gallery, Brussels.
Costumes and sets for the Folies Bergère.
Costumes and sets for the musical comedy, *Manhattan Mary*, at the Majestic Theatre, New York.
Costumes for Lucrezia Bori: *Pelléas et Mélisande*, *L'Amore dei Tre Re*, *Les Contes d'Hoffmann* (Metropolitan, New York).
Covers and illustrations for *Harper's Bazaar*.
Covers and illustrations for *Art et Industrie*.
Illustrations for *The Sketch*.

1928   Sets and costumes for George White's *Scandals*.
Article and illustrations for the *Encyclopaedia Britannica* (14th Edition, 1929).
Costumes for *Lindberg*, by Sacha Guitry, Théâtre du Châtelet, Paris.
Costumes for Maria Kouznetsoff: *Tosca* and *Manon* (Opéra-Comique, Paris).
Illustrations for *International Cosmopolitan*, New York.
Covers and illustrations for *Harper's Bazaar*.

1929   Costumes and sets for the Folies Bergère.
Costumes and sets for George White's *Scandals*.
Costumes and sets for *La Princesse Lointaine* by Edmond Rostand, Théâtre Sarah Bernhardt.
Exhibition at the Galerie Charpentier, Paris (some works bought by the French Government and by the City of Paris.)
Exhibition at the William E. Fox Gallery, New York.
Covers and illustrations for *Harper's Bazaar*.

Illustrations for *International Cosmopolitan*.
Illustrations for *The Sketch*.
Collection of designs for fabrics for the Amalgamated Silk
Corporation, New York.

1930   Advertising designs for Holeproof Hosiery, New York.
Second collection of fabrics for the Amalgamated Silk
Corporation.
Covers and illustrations for *Harper's Bazaar*.
Illustrations for *Art et Industrie*.
Illustrations for *International Cosmopolitan*.
Illustrations for *The Sketch*.

1931   Advertising and shoe designs for Delman, New York.
Advertising designs for Holeproof Hosiery.
Sets and costumes for the Folies Bergère.
Covers and illustrations for *Harper's Bazaar*.
Costumes for Ganna Walska in *Pelléas et Mélisande*
(Chicago Opera Company).
Illustrations for *The Sketch*.

1932   Sets for *Faust* and *Don Pasquale* at the Riga Opera.
Advertising designs for Holeproof Hosiery.
Advertising and shoe designs for Delman.
Covers and illustrations for *Harper's Bazaar*.
Illustrations for *The Sketch*.

1933   Advertising designs for Delman.
Advertising designs for Holeproof Hosiery.
Illustrations for *The Delineator*.
Covers and illustrations for *Harper's Bazaar*.
Illustrations for *The Sketch*.

1934   Costumes for *Les Travaux d'Hercule*, operetta by Claude
Terrasse at the Théâtre des Capucines, Paris.
Costumes and sets for *Au Temps des Merveilleuses*, operetta
by Maurice Yvain at the Théâtre du Châtelet.
Advertising designs for Delman.
Advertising designs for Holeproof Hosiery.
Covers and illustrations for *Harper's Bazaar*.
Illustrations for *The Sketch*.
Exhibition at the Waldorf Astoria Hotel, New York.
Costumes and sets for the Tabarin, Paris.

1935   Costumes and sets for Cécile Sorel, in *Amour Royal*,
Théâtre de l'ABC, Paris.
Costumes and sets for *Les Joies du Capitole*, operetta by
Moretti at the Théâtre de la Madeleine, Paris.
Covers and illustrations for *Harper's Bazaar*.
Illustrations for *The Sketch*.
Costumes and sets for the Alhambra, Paris.
Advertising designs for Delman.

Costumes and sets for the French Casino, New York.
Costumes and sets for the Tabarin, Paris.

1936   Costumes and sets for *Au Soleil du Mexique,* operetta by
        Maurice Yvain at the Théâtre du Châtelet.
        Advertising designs for Delman.
        Covers and illustrations for *Harper's Bazaar.*
        Illustrations for *The Sketch.*

1937   Costumes and sets for *Yana,* operetta by Christiné and
        Tiarko Richepin, Théâtre du Châtelet.
        Costumes and sets for *Plaisir de France,* at the Tabarin.
        Costumes and sets for *It's in the Bag,* by Cecil Landeau,
        Savile Theatre, London.
        Costumes and sets for the Scala Theatre, Berlin.
        Advertising designs for Delman.
        Covers and illustrations for *Harper's Bazaar.*
        Illustrations for *The Sketch.*

1938   Costumes and sets for *Le Chant du Tzigane,* operetta at
        the Théâtre du Châtelet.
        Costumes and sets for *Les Heures sont Belles* at the Tabarin.
        Costumes and sets for *London Symphony* at the Palladium,
        London.
        Costumes and sets for *The Fleet's Lit Up* at the London
        Hippodrome.
        Costumes and sets for the Scala Theatre, Berlin.
        Advertising designs for Delman.
        Illustrations for *The Sketch.*

1939   Costumes and sets for *Un Vrai Paradis* at the Tabarin.
        Costumes and sets for the George White show at the San
        Francisco Exhibition.
        Costumes and sets for *Black Velvet* at the Palladium,
        London.
        Costumes and sets for a show at Blackpool.
        Advertising designs for Delman.
        Illustrations for *The Sketch.*
        Costumes and sets for *Cécile et le Dictateur,* by Paul Nivoix,
        at the Casino de la Baule, with Cécile Sorel.

1940   Costumes and sets for *Phi-phi,* operetta by Christiné at the
        Théâtre des Bouffes Parisiens, Paris.
        Costumes and sets for *Mes Amours,* musical comedy at the
        Théâtre Marigny, Paris.

1941   Costumes and sets for *Toi, C'est Moi,* operetta by Misraki,
        Théâtre de l'Apollo, Paris.
        Costumes and sets for *Trois Jeunes Filles Nues,* operetta by
        Moretti, Théâtre Marigny.
        Costumes and sets for the revue at the Lido, Paris.
        Costumes and sets for *Dans Notre Miroir* at the Tabarin.

1942   Costumes and sets for *Les Cent Vierges*, operetta by Lecocq
        at the Théâtre de l'Apollo.
        Revue at the Lido.
        Costumes for *Coup de Roulis*, operetta by André Messager,
        at the Théâtre Marigny.

1943   Costumes and sets for *Une Femme Par Jour*, operetta by
        Van Parys at the Théâtre des Capucines.
        Costumes and sets for the operetta *Belamour* at the Théâtre
        des Nouveautés, Paris.
        Costumes and sets for the Lido.
        Costumes and sets for the Tabarin.
        Decoration of all the windows of the Grands Magasins
        Printemps, Paris.

1944   Costumes and sets for Donizetti's *Don Pasquale*, Théâtre
        du Palais de Chaillot, Paris.
        Costumes and sets for the operetta *La-haut*, at the Théâtre
        Marigny.
        Costumes and sets for the Lido.

1945   Costumes and sets for Rossini's *Il Barbiere di Siviglia*, for
        French television.
        Costumes and sets for the Lido.
        Costumes and sets for the Tabarin.

1946   Costumes for *On Cherche un Roi*, operetta at the Théâtre
        Alhambra, Paris.
        Costumes and sets for Cimarosa's *Il Matrimonio Segreto* at
        the Théâtre Sarah Bernhardt.
        Sets for *The Night and the Laughter* at the Coliseum,
        London.
        Costumes and sets for *Piccadilly Hayride* at the Prince of
        Wales Theatre, London.
        Costumes and sets for the Tabarin.
        Costumes and sets for the Lido.

1947   Costumes and sets for *Les Mamelles de Tirésias*, opera by
        Francis Poulenc at the Opéra-Comique, Paris.
        Costumes and sets for the Tabarin.
        Costumes and sets for a revue at the Opera House, Black-
        pool.

1948   Costumes and sets for *Mother Goose*, ballet by Ravel at the
        Opéra-Comique.
        Costumes and sets for *Sueños de Viena* at the Teatro
        Comico, Barcelona.
        Costumes and sets for the Tabarin.
        Costumes and sets for the Opera House, Blackpool.

1949   Costumes and sets for *Puss in Boots* at the Palladium,
        London.
        Costumes and sets for the Tabarin.

Costumes and sets for the Opera House, Blackpool.

1950   Costumes and sets for *The Knights of Madness* at the Victoria Palace, London.
Costumes and sets for *Out of This World* at the Opera House, Blackpool.
Costumes and sets for the Palladium, London.
Costumes and sets for the opening of La Nouvelle Eve cabaret, Paris.

1951   Costumes and sets for *La Traviata* at the Paris Opéra.
Costumes and sets for *Parfums,* opera by Germaine Taille-ferre at the Monte Carlo Opera.
Costumes and sets for *Fancy Free* at the Prince of Wales Theatre, London.
Costumes and sets for *Histoires d'Eve* at La Nouvelle Eve.
Costumes and sets for *La Leçon d'Amour dans un Parc,* musical comedy by Guy Lafarge at the Théâtre des Bouffes Parisiens.
Costumes and sets for *Happy Go Lucky* at the Opera House, Blackpool.

1952   Costumes and sets for Debussy's *Pelléas et Mélisande* at the Teatro San Carlo, Naples.
Costumes and sets for *Padmâvati,* opera-ballet by Albert Roussel at the Teatro San Carlo, Naples.
Costumes and sets for Mozart's *Così fan Tutte* at the Opéra-Comique, Paris.
Costumes and sets for *Ring Out the Bells* at the Victoria Palace, London.
Costumes and sets for *Bet Your Life* at the London Hippo-drome.
Costumes and sets for *Les Filles d'Eve* at La Nouvelle Eve.
Costumes and sets for *Die Maske in Blau,* film with Marika Rökk for Bavaria Films, Munich.

1953   Costumes and sets for *Caccia al Tesoro* at the Teatro delle Quattro Fontane, Rome.
Costumes for the film *Die Geschiedene Frau,* produced by Bavaria Films, Munich.
Costumes and sets for La Nouvelle Eve.

1954   Costumes and sets for *Mother Goose* at the Palladium, London.
Costumes and sets for *Jokers Wild* at the Victoria Palace, London.
Costumes and sets for *Rosso e Nero,* San Remo.

1955   Costumes and sets for *Gonzague,* opera by Jacques Ibert at the Cannes Opera and at the Rouen Opera.
Costumes and sets for *Campanas de Viena* at the Teatro Comico, Barcelona.

Costumes and sets for *La Plume de ma Tante* at the Garrick Theatre, London.

Costumes and sets for *Champagne Cocktail* at the Moulin Rouge, Paris.

Costumes and sets for La Nouvelle Eve.

Costumes and sets for the Opera House, Blackpool.

1956   Costumes and sets for *La Poule Noire*, opera by Manuel Rosenthal at the Opéra-Comique.

Costumes and sets for *Extravagances* at La Nouvelle Eve.

Costumes and sets for the Victoria Palace, London.

Costumes and sets for the Opera House, Blackpool.

1957   Costumes and sets for *Capriccio*, opera by Richard Strauss at the Opéra-Comique.

Costumes and sets for *Pommes à l'Anglaise* at the Théâtre de Paris.

Costumes and sets for La Nouvelle Eve.

Costumes and sets for the Opera House, Blackpool.

1958   Costumes and sets for *Don César de Bazan*, opera by Massenet at the Rouen Opera.

Costumes and sets for *La Plume de ma Tante* at the Royal Theatre, York.

Costumes and sets for the revue at the Drap d'Or, Paris.

Costumes and sets for the revue at the Folies Pigalle, Paris.

Costumes and sets for La Nouvelle Eve.

1959   Costumes and sets for Donizetti's *Don Pasquale* at the Opéra-Comique.

Costumes and sets for the Casino du Liban, Beirut.

Costumes and sets for *Crown Jewels* at the Victoria Palace, London.

Costumes and sets for the Drap d'Or.

Costumes and sets for the Folies Pigalle.

Costumes and sets for the Opera House, Blackpool.

1960   Costumes and sets for Racine's *Phèdre* at the Théâtre du Vieux Colombier, Paris.

Sets for *Piège pour un Homme Seul*, by Robert Thomas, at the Théâtre des Bouffes Parisiens.

Costumes and sets for the ballet films of Louis Cuny: *Le Coiffeur Miracle* and *Edition Spéciale*.

Costumes and sets for the Casino du Liban, Beirut.

Costumes and sets for *Young in Heart* at the Victoria Palace, London.

1961   Costumes and sets for *Castor et Pollux*, opera by Rameau, at the Lyons Festival (Théâtre Antique de Fourvières).

Sets for *Olé* at the Deutschlandshalle, West Berlin.

Costumes and sets for the Moulin Rouge, Paris.

1962   Costumes and sets for *Twist Appeal*, show by Nicolas Bataille at the Folies Pigalle.

Costumes and sets for *La Java,* show by Nicolas Bataille and Guillaume Hanoteau at the Pigalle, Paris.

Costumes and sets for *La Chasse aux Folles,* by Robert Thomas and Guillaume Hanoteau at the Drap d'Or.

1963   Costumes and sets for the Latin Quarter, New York.

1964   Exhibition of ' Formes Picturales ', Galerie Ror Valmar, Paris.
Costumes and sets for *Wonderworld,* presented at the New York World's Fair.
Costumes and sets for the Latin Quarter, New York.
Costumes and sets for Terence's *The Eunuch,* presented at the Comédie de Paris.

1965   Exhibition at the Galerie Motte, Paris.
Exhibition at the Galleria de Milano, Milan.

1966   ' Les Années 25 ': exhibition at the Musée des Arts Décoratifs, Paris.
Exhibition at the Galleria de Milano, Milan.
Exhibition at the Galerie Jacques Perrin, Paris.
Exhibition: ' 100 years of *Harper's Bazaar* ', New York.

1967   Exhibition at the Grosvenor Gallery, New York. This exhibition (170 items) was purchased in its entirety by the Metropolitan Museum of New York.
Exhibition at the Grosvenor Gallery, London. Numerous works were purchased by the Victoria and Albert Museum, London.
Costumes and sets for *Flying Colours,* at the Expo '67, Montreal.
Exhibition at the Galerie Jacques Perrin, Paris.
Exhibition at the Galleria Viotti, Turin.
Exhibition at the Galleria d'Arte Cavalletto, Brescia.

1968   Exhibition at the Metropolitan Museum, New York.
Costumes for *The Silent Night,* ballet for television, New York.
Exhibition at the Vincent Price Gallery, Chicago.
Exhibition at the Galleria Paolo Barozzi, Venice.
Exhibition at the Neues Kunst-Zentrum, Hamburg.
Series of lithographs, *Les Chiffres.*

1969   Exhibition at the Galerie René Drouet, Paris.
Exhibition at the Vincent Price Gallery, Chicago.
Series of lithographs, *Les Pierres Précieuses.*
Illustrations for *Ermyntrude and Esmeralda* by Lytton Strachey.
Illustrations for the book *The Beatles.*

1970   Costumes and sets for the Zizi Jeanmaire Show produced by Roland Petit at the Casino de Paris.
Series of lithographs: *Les Quatre Saisons.*
Exhibition at the Galería Arvil, Mexico City.

1971   Exhibition at Club dei Bibliofili (Ricci publisher) of Milan,
        Bologna, Palermo.
        Exhibition at Galleria della Rocchetta, Parma.
        Exhibition at Galerie Proscénium, Paris.
        Exhibition at Sonnabend Gallery, New York.
        Exhibition at Galleria Marina, Rome.

1972   Costumes and sets for *Zizi, je t'aime,* produced by Roland
        Petit at the Casino de Paris.
        Exhibition of graphic work at Cortina d'Ampezzo.
        Exhibitions celebrating Erté's eightieth birthday at
               Galerie Proscénium, Paris.
               Brook Street Gallery, London
               Rizzoli Art Gallery, New York
               Lambert Monet Gallery, Geneva
        all in collaboration with Grosvenor Gallery, London.
        Illustrations for special number, celebrating Erté's eightieth
        birthday, of *Vogue* magazine.
        Cover design for *Studio International.*

1973   Exhibition at Downtown Gallery, New Orleans.
        Exhibition at David Stuart Gallery, Los Angeles.
        Commenced work on special letters for Guinness Beer.
        Sets and costumes for a ballet for 1974 by Erik Satie.

1974   Sets and costumes for new Zizi Jeanmaire show to be pro-
        duced by Roland Petit at Casino de Paris in 1975.
        Series of lithographs: *Four Aces* – collaboration with Berg-
        gruens et Cie., Paris.
        Retrospective exhibition at Galería Conkright, Caracas,
        Venezuela.
        Retrospective exhibition at Portland Museum, Portland,
        Oregon.
        Retrospective exhibition at Juana Mordo Gallery, Madrid.
        Exhibition of serigraphs at Circle Gallery, New York.
        Costumes and sets for Ragtime Ballet, for Ballet Theatre
        of Angers.
        Retrospective exhibition at Galerie Proscénium, Paris.
        Posters for the Alcazar night club and the Folies Bergère,
        Paris.

1975   Retrospective exhibition at Basle.
        Graphic Art Retrospective exhibition at the Circle Galleries
        in New York, Chicago, Los Angeles, San Francisco.
        Costumes for ' Schéhérazade ', with music by André Hossein
        and produced by Robert Hossein.

Illustrations

Index

Numbers in bold type refer to illustrations